Piano Syllabus

2008 Edition

The Royal Conservatory of Music Official Examination Syllabus

RCM Examinations and the National Music Certificate Program

Library and Archives Canada Cataloguing in Publication

Piano syllabus.—2008 ed.

Piano syllabus for the Royal Conservatory of Music Includes bibliographical references. ISBN 978-1-55440-196-3

1. Royal Conservatory of Music–Examinations. 2. Piano–Examinations. 3. Piano music–Bibliography–Graded lists. I. Royal Conservatory of Music

MT10.P53 2008   786.2'076   C2007-907523-1

17 16 15 14 13 12 11 10 09 08   1 2 3 4 5 6 7 8 9 10

Contents

Message from the President

The Royal Conservatory of Music was founded in 1886 with the idea that a single institution could bind the people of a nation together with the common thread of shared musical experience. More than a century later, we continue to build and expand on this vision.

Today, The Royal Conservatory of Music is recognized in communities throughout North America for outstanding service to students, teachers, and parents, as well as a strict adherence to high academic standards through a variety of activities—teaching, examining, publishing, research, and community outreach.

Our students and teachers benefit from a curriculum based on more than one hundred years of commitment to the highest pedagogical objectives. The strength of the curriculum is reinforced by the distinguished College of Examiners—a group of fine musicians and teachers carefully selected from across Canada, the United States, and abroad for their demonstrated skill and professionalism. A rigorous examiner apprenticeship program combined with regular evaluation procedures ensures consistency and an examination experience of the highest quality for candidates.

Our new home, the TELUS Centre for Performance and Learning, will make the most of the Conservatory's extraordinary potential and will allow us to share our innovative programs with teachers and students everywhere. This technologically advanced education and performance complex will reflect The Royal Conservatory of Music's broadened impact as an international leader in publishing and examinations, professional training, arts-infused public school programs, early childhood education, and concert presentation. I do hope that you will take full advantage of this great new facility, which will be an exceptional resource for students and teachers across North America and around the world.

As you pursue your studies or teach others, you become not only an important partner with The Royal Conservatory of Music in the development of creativity, discipline, and goal-setting, but also an active participant, experiencing the transcendent qualities of music itself. In a society where our day-to-day lives can become rote and routine, the human need to find self-fulfillment and to engage in creative activity has never been more necessary. The Royal Conservatory of Music will continue to be an active partner and supporter in your musical journey of self-expression and self-discovery.

Dr. Peter C. Simon
President

Getting Started

1 What's New?

- New theory examination titles (p. 11)
- Updated technical tests (p. 13)
- New Preparatory A and B examinations (p. 23)
- The Piano Pedagogy Certificate Program and the ARCT in Piano Pedagogy (p. 106)
- Teacher's Choice option (p. 130)
- Practical examination day checklist (p. 142)

2 Practical Examination Requirements

- Review "Quick Reference" on p. 10.
- Examine detailed requirements for each grade.

3 Repertoire List Format

Preparatory A and B Repertoire Lists

Celebrate Piano!®, Lesson and Musicianship 1B FHM
- Lazy Summer Day

Grades 1 to ARCT Repertoire Lists

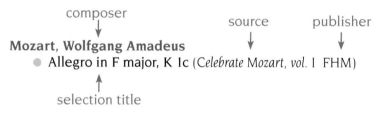

Mozart, Wolfgang Amadeus
- Allegro in F major, K 1c (*Celebrate Mozart, vol. 1* FHM)

selection title

Beethoven, Ludwig van
- Sonata in G major, op. 79 ← title of complete work
  ▲ 1st movement

part of complete work

source

Norton, Christopher
Christopher Norton Connections for Piano™, 5 FHM
  ▶ Scamp

in *Celebration Series Perspectives®: Piano Repertoire 5*

Hook, James
- Sonata in D major, op. 12, no. 1
  ▲ 1st movement

part of complete work in *Celebration Series Perspectives®: Piano Repertoire 6*

For selections where no publisher is given, candidates should use any standard edition.

4 Online Examination Registration (see p. 117 for more details)

CANADA
- Go to www.rcmexaminations.org.
- Check deadlines and examination dates.
- Click on "Register for an Examination."
- Enter the candidate's RCME Number and date of birth.
- Follow the instructions to register.
- Enter payment information (Visa and MasterCard are accepted).
- Select the date and time of the piano examination.
- Change the date and time of the examination (optional) by going to the website and clicking on "Examination Scheduling."
- Print out the "Examination Program Form."
- Verify the date and time of the examination two weeks before the first day of the examination session by clicking on "Examination Scheduling."

Contact Us
- Phone: 905-501-9553
- Fax: 905-501-1290

USA
- Go to www.nationalmusiccertificate.org.
- Check deadlines and examination dates.
- Click on "Register for an Examination."
- Enter the Candidate ID Number and date of birth.
- Follow the instructions to register.
- Enter payment information (Visa and MasterCard are accepted).
- Select the date and time of the piano examination.
- Change the date and time of the examination (optional) by going to the website and clicking on "Examination Scheduling."
- Print out the "Examination Program Form."
- Verify the date and time of the examination two weeks before the first day of the examination session by clicking on "Examination Scheduling."

Contact Us
- Phone: 866-716-2223
- Fax: 866-716-2224

The first time a candidate registers for an examination, the candidate will be assigned a permanent RCME Number. This number is eight characters long (for example, 07W12345).

The RCME Number. . .
- is a **permanent** identification number with RCM Examinations
- must be used each time the candidate applies for an examination
- enables RCM Examinations to maintain the integrity of the candidate's academic record
- can be found on the Examination Schedule

Write the RCME Number on the inside cover of repertoire books for future reference!

The first time a candidate registers for an examination, the candidate will be assigned a permanent Candidate ID Number. This number is eight characters long (for example, 07W12345).

The Candidate ID Number. . .
- is a **permanent** identification number with NMCP
- must be used each time the candidate applies for an examination
- enables NMCP to maintain the integrity of the candidate's academic record
- can be found on the Examination Schedule

Write the Candidate ID Number on the inside cover of repertoire books for future reference!

Teachers may register their students by logging into "Teacher Services" and using the "Student Registration" feature.

About Us

RCM Examinations . . . fostering human potential through music education

The Royal Conservatory of Music

The Royal Conservatory of Music is a world-class institution recognized for high standards in teaching, performance, examining, publishing, and research. It comprises six divisions:

- RCM Examinations and the National Music Certificate Program
- Glenn Gould School
- RCM Community School
- Learning Through the Arts
- The Young Artists Performance Academy
- The Frederick Harris Music Co., Limited

RCM Examinations and the National Music Certificate Program

RCM Examinations and the National Music Certificate Program set the standard for excellence in music education. These divisions of The Royal Conservatory of Music reach more than a quarter of a million candidates annually by providing:

- graded examinations that establish clear, progressive learning goals
- internationally recognized certificates, diplomas, and medals
- teacher development through workshops and communications

Meet our Examiners

Examiners are highly trained, professional musicians and theorists from across North America. All examiners complete an Examiner Apprenticeship Program before being admitted to the College of Examiners. Professional development and training continues throughout each examiner's career to ensure consistent examination standards throughout North America.

Read about our College of Examiners, including examiner biographies, at www.rcmexaminations.org or www.nationalmusiccertificate.org.

Examinations Offered

Practical Examinations

Accordion, Bassoon, Cello, Clarinet, Double Bass, Euphonium, Flute, French Horn, Guitar, Harp, Harpsichord, Oboe, Organ, Percussion, Piano, Recorder, Saxophone, Speech Arts and Drama, Trombone, Trumpet, Tuba, Viola, Violin, Voice

Theory Examinations

Rudiments, Harmony, Keyboard Harmony, History, Counterpoint, Analysis

Musicianship Examinations

Junior, Intermediate, Senior

Piano Pedagogy Examinations

Elementary, Intermediate, Advanced

Notable Alumni

Our notable alumni include:

- Isabel Bayrakdarian
- the Gryphon Trio
- Aline Chrétien
- Adrienne Clarkson
- Bruce Cockburn
- Naida Cole
- David Foster
- Glenn Gould
- Robert Goulet
- Norman Jewison
- Lois Marshall
- Oscar Peterson
- Richard Raymond
- Paul Shaffer
- Mitchell Sharp
- the St. Lawrence String Quartet
- Teresa Stratas
- Jon Vickers

Excellence Since 1886

1886 The Toronto Conservatory of Music is founded.

1887 The Conservatory has its official opening in a two-storey space above a music store. In addition to weekly lessons, courses include acoustics and piano tuning.

1896 Affiliation with the University of Toronto enables preparation for university degree examinations.

1898 Local examination centers are established outside of Toronto.

1906 The Toronto Conservatory Orchestra is founded; two years later, this group becomes the first Toronto Symphony Orchestra.

1907 Approximately 1,500 students across Canada take Toronto Conservatory examinations—more than half from outside of Toronto.

1916 The first piano repertoire book based on the Conservatory curriculum is published by The Frederick Harris Music Co., Limited and distributed throughout Canada.

1928 Composer Boris Berlin begins teaching at the Conservatory; he remains on the faculty until his death in 2001.

1935 A ten-level examination system is established.

1946 Pianist Glenn Gould receives an ARCT. In the same year, the Conservatory Opera School is established; several years later it plays a major role in the formation of the Canadian Opera Company.

1947 In recognition of its status as one of the Commonwealth's greatest music schools, the Conservatory receives a Royal Charter from King George VI, allowing it to be called The Royal Conservatory of Music.

1991 The Conservatory re-establishes independence from the University of Toronto. Plans for restoration and expansion of its Toronto facilities begin.

2002 The Conservatory launches its *Building National Dreams Campaign* to expand its Toronto facilities and build a state-of-the-art center for performance and learning.

2003 RCM Examinations expands into the United States of America.

2008 The Conservatory's TELUS Centre for Performance and Learning opens.

Quick Reference— Examination Requirements

Certificate Program Overview

A progressive assessment program for every examination candidate

Internationally recognized certificates and diplomas are awarded for successful completion of each practical level and its co-requisites. Candidates may enter the Certificate Program at any level from Preparatory A to Grade 10. Candidates must complete prerequisite examinations at least one session prior to attempting the ARCT in Piano Performance (p. 99) examination and any of Parts 1, 2, or 3 of the Intermediate Piano Pedagogy level (p. 108) and the Advanced Piano Pedagogy level (p. 110).

Certificates	Examinations Required
Preparatory A	Preparatory A
Preparatory B	Preparatory B
Grade 1 Piano	Grade 1 Piano
Grade 2 Piano	Grade 2 Piano
Grade 3 Piano	Grade 3 Piano
Grade 4 Piano	Grade 4 Piano
Grade 5 Piano	Grade 5 Piano; Basic Rudiments
Grade 6 Piano	Grade 6 Piano; Intermediate Rudiments
Grade 7 Piano	Grade 7 Piano; Advanced Rudiments
Grade 8 Piano	Grade 8 Piano; Advanced Rudiments
Grade 9 Piano	Grade 9 Piano; Advanced Rudiments; Basic Harmony *or* Basic Keyboard Harmony; History 1: An Overview
Grade 10 Piano	Grade 10 Piano; Advanced Rudiments; Intermediate Harmony *or* Intermediate Keyboard Harmony; History 1: An Overview; History 2: Middle Ages to Classical
Elementary Piano Pedagogy	Elementary Piano Pedagogy Parts 1, 2, and 3
Intermediate Piano Pedagogy	Intermediate Piano Pedagogy Parts 1, 2, and 3

Diplomas	Examinations Required
ARCT in Piano Performance	ARCT in Piano Performance; Counterpoint; Advanced Harmony *or* Advanced Keyboard Harmony; History 3: 19th Century to Present; Analysis
ARCT in Piano Pedagogy	Advanced Piano Pedagogy Parts 1, 2, and 3; Counterpoint; Advanced Harmony *or* Advanced Keyboard Harmony; History 3: 19th Century to Present; Analysis

Theory Examinations

Essential Tools for Musical Development

- Candidates are encouraged to begin theory studies as early as possible.
- Beginning in Grade 5, candidates must complete the required theory examinations in order to receive Practical Examination Certificates.

See the current RCM Examinations *Theory Syllabus* for detailed theory examination requirements.

Overview of Theoretical Subjects

In 2006, the titles of theory examinations were updated to be more descriptive and to better reflect the content of the examinations.

The following table lists all of the written theory examinations in the Certificate Program with brief details including the length of the examination, a summary of the content, and the title given to the same examination in previous syllabi.

Subject	New Theory Examination Title	Previous Title
Rudiments	Preparatory Rudiments (1 hour) Building blocks of music notation	Preparatory Theory
	Basic Rudiments (1 hour) Elements of music for the beginner	Preliminary Rudiments
	Intermediate Rudiments (2 hours) Continuation of basic rudiments	Grade 1 Rudiments
	Advanced Rudiments (2 hours) Continuation of rudiments and preparation for harmony	Grade 2 Rudiments
Harmony and Counterpoint	Introductory Harmony (2 hours) Chord symbols and non-chord tones; elementary four-part and melodic writing	Introductory Harmony
	Basic Harmony (3 hours) or Basic Keyboard Harmony (held during practical sessions) Four-part writing, melodic composition, and harmonic and structural analysis in major and minor keys	Grade 3 Harmony or Grade 3 Keyboard Harmony
	Intermediate Harmony (3 hours) or Intermediate Keyboard Harmony (held during practical sessions) Four-part writing and melodic composition in major and minor keys; modulation; harmonic and structural analysis of musical forms	Grade 4 Harmony or Grade 4 Keyboard Harmony
	Counterpoint (3 hours) Composition and anaysis of simple counterpoint in Baroque style	Grade 4 Counterpoint
	Advanced Harmony (3 hours) or Advanced Keyboard Harmony (held during practical sessions) Advanced harmonic and contrapuntal techniques	Grade 5 Harmony or Grade 5 Keyboard Harmony
Analysis	Analysis (3 hours) Advanced harmonic and structural analysis of musical forms	Grade 5 Analysis
History	History 1: An Overview (3 hours) Introduction to styles, composers, and music from 1600 to the present	Grade 3 History
	History 2: Middle Ages to Classical (3 hours) Styles, composers, and music of the Medieval, Renaissance, Baroque, Rococo, and Classical periods	Grade 4 History
	History 3: 19th Century to Present (3 hours) Styles, composers, and music of the Romantic era to the present	Grade 5 History

Preparing for a Theory Examination
- Theory examinations test music theory and knowledge of music history in a formal written setting.
- Each examination requires preparation with a qualified teacher.
- *Official Examination Papers*, available at music retailers, are published annually by The Frederick Harris Music Co., Limited to aid with examination preparation.

Co-requisites and Prerequisites

The following table summarizes all the co-requisite and prerequisite examinations required to obtain certificates for Grades 5 to 10, the ARCT in Piano Performance, and Elementary, Intermediate, and Advanced Piano Pedagogy. There are no prerequisite or co-requisite theory examinations for Preparatory A to Grade 4.

Grade	5	6	7	8	9	10	Perf. ARCT	Elem. Ped.	Int. Ped.	Adv. Ped.
Required Examinations (**C** = Co-requisite **P** = Prerequisite)										
Basic Rudiments [formerly Preliminary Rudiments]	C									
Intermediate Rudiments [formerly Grade 1 Rudiments]		C								
Advanced Rudiments [formerly Grade 2 Rudiments]			C	C	C	C	P	C	P	P
Basic Harmony [formerly Grade 3 Harmony]						C		C		
Intermediate Harmony [formerly Grade 4 Harmony]						C	P		C	P
Counterpoint [formerly Grade 4 Counterpoint]							C			C
Advanced Harmony [formerly Grade 5 Harmony and Counterpoint]							C			C
Analysis [formerly Grade 5 Analysis]							C			C
History 1: An Overview [formerly Grade 3 History]					C	C	P	C	P	P
History 2: Middle Ages to Classical [formerly Grade 4 History]						C	P		C	P
History 3: 19th Century to Present [formerly Grade 5 History]							C			C
Grade 9 Piano								C	P	
Grade 10 Piano							P		C	P
Elementary Piano Pedagogy Part 2: *Viva Voce* and Part 3: Written									P	
Intermediate Piano Pedagogy Part 2: *Viva Voce* and Part 3: Written										P
Optional Examinations										
Preparatory Rudiments [formerly Preparatory Theory]										
Introductory Harmony										
Alternative Examinations										
Basic Keyboard Harmony (can be substituted for Basic Harmony)						C			C	
Intermediate Keyboard Harmony (can be substituted for Intermediate Harmony)							C	P	C	P
Advanced Keyboard Harmony (can be substituted for Advanced Harmony)							C			C
Junior Musicianship (can be substituted for Grade 8 Ear Tests and Sight Reading)				C						
Intermediate Musicianship (can be substituted for Grade 9 Ear Tests and Sight Reading)					C				C	
Senior Musicianship (can be substituted for Grade 10 and Advanced Piano Pedagogy Ear Tests and Sight Reading)							C		C	C

Technical Tests

The following charts provide a summary of the scales, chords, and arpeggios required for all levels from Preparatory A and B to Grade 10 and Advanced Piano Pedagogy. Requirements for each grade are also provided in a chart in the Technical Tests section of the respective grade.

Technical Tests Summary: Scales

Level / Scale Type	Major Keys	Harmonic Minor Keys	Melodic Minor Keys	Natural Minor Keys	Hands	Octaves	Tempo $\quad\bullet=$	Note Values
Preparatory A								
Pentascales (end with solid root position triad)	C G D			A	HS	tonic to dominant	100	♩
Preparatory B								
Pentascales (end with solid root position triad)	A E F			E D	HS	tonic to dominant	60	♫
Scales	C G			A	HS	1	60	♫
Contrary Motion	C				HT	1	60	♫
Grade 1								
Scales	C G F	A E D		A E D	HS	2	69	♫
Staccato	C G F				HS	1	69	♫
Contrary Motion	C				HT	2	69	♫
Chromatic	beginning on C				HS	tonic to dominant	69	♫
Grade 2								
Scales	C G F B♭	A E D G	A E D G	A E D G	HS	2	80	♫
Staccato	C G F B♭				HS	1	80	♫
Parallel Motion	C G				HT	1	80	♫
Contrary Motion	G				HT	2	80	♫
Formula Pattern	C				HT	2	80	♫
Chromatic	beginning on C				HS	1	80	♫
Grade 3								
Scales	G D F B♭	E B D G	E B D G		HS	2	92	♫
Staccato	G D F B♭				HS	2	92	♫
Parallel Motion	G D F B♭	E B D G	E B D G		HT	1	80	♫
Formula Pattern	G				HT	2	80	♫
Chromatic	beginning on G				HS	1	92	♫
Grade 4								
Parallel Motion	D A B♭ E♭	B F♯ G C	B F♯ G C		HT	2	92	♫
Staccato	D B♭	B G			HS	2	104	♫
Formula Pattern		C			HT	2	92	♫
Chromatic	beginning on D				HS	1	104	♫

Technical Tests Summary: Scales (continued)

Level / Scale Type	Major Keys	Harmonic Minor Keys	Melodic Minor Keys	Natural Minor Keys	Hands	Octaves	Tempo ♩=	Note Values
Grade 5								
Parallel Motion	A E Eb Ab	F# C# C F	F# C# C F		HT	2	104	♫
Staccato	A Eb	F# C			HS	2	112	♫
Formula Pattern	Eb	C			HT	2	104	♫
Chromatic	beginning on A				HT	1	104	♫
Grade 6								
Parallel Motion	G E F Ab Db	G E F G# C#	G E F G# C#		HT	2	60	♬
Staccato	E F	E	E		HT	2	60	♬
Formula Pattern	E F	E			HT	2	60	♬
Chromatic	beginning on E, Db				HT	2	60	♬
Grade 7								
Parallel Motion	C D B F Bb Ab Db	C D B F Bb G# C#	C D B F Bb G# C#		HT	2	76	♬
Staccato	C D	C D	C D		HT	3	76	♬
Formula Pattern	C D	C D			HT	2	76	♬
Chromatic	begining on D Ab				HT	2	76	♬
Scale in 6ths (solid *staccato*) or	C (tonic as upper note)				HS	1	88	♫
Scale in Octaves (broken *legato*)	C				HS	1	100	♫
Grade 8								
Parallel Motion	C D A E B Bb Eb Gb	C D A E B Bb Eb F#	C D A E B Bb Eb F#		HT	4	88	♬
Staccato	A B Bb	B	B		HT	3	88	♬
Formula Pattern	A B Bb	B			HT	4	88	♬
Chromatic	beginning on A, Bb				HT	2	88	♬
Scales in Octaves (solid *staccato*) or	A Bb				HS	1	88	♫
Scales in Octaves (broken *legato*)	A Bb				HS	1	108	♫
Grade 9								
Parallel Motion	all keys	all keys	all keys		HT	4	104	♬
Staccato	B Ab Db	G# F Bb	G# F Bb		HT	3	104	♬
Formula Pattern	B Ab Db	G# F Bb			HT	4	96	♬
Chromatic	beginning on any note				HT	4	96	♬
Scales in Octaves (solid *staccato*) or	B Ab Db	F	F		HT	2	60	♬
Scales in Octaves (broken *legato*)	B Ab Db	F	F		HT	2	72	♬
Chromatic Scales in Octaves (solid *staccato*) or	beginning on any note				HT	2	60	♬
Chromatic Scales in Octaves (broken *legato*)	beginning on any note				HT	2	72	♬

Technical Tests Summary: Scales (continued)

Level / Scale Type	Major Keys	Harmonic Minor Keys	Melodic Minor Keys	Natural Minor Keys	Hands	Octaves	Tempo ♩ =	Note Values
Grade 10								
Parallel Motion	all keys	all keys	all keys		HT	4	120	♬♬
Staccato	Bb Ab Gb	F# C# Eb	F# C# Eb		HT	3	120	(triplet)
Separated by a 3rd	C Db D Eb				HT	4	104	♬♬
Separated by a 6th	E F Gb G				HT	4	104	♬♬
Separated by a 10th	Ab A Bb B				HT	4	104	♬♬
Formula Pattern	Bb Ab Gb	F# C# Eb			HT	4	112	♬♬
Chromatic	beginning on any note				HT	4	120	♬♬
Scales in Octaves (solid *staccato*)	Bb Ab Gb	F# C# Eb			HT	2	80	♬♬
Chromatic Scales in Octaves (solid *staccato*)	beginning on any note				HT	2	80	♬♬
Candidates must prepare one of the following exercises:								
Triplet Repeated-Note Pattern Scales (3–2–1 fingering)	D Ab Gb	D F#	D F#		HT	2	100	(triplet)
Double 3rd Scales, *legato*	C B Bb				HT	2	60	♫
Scales in Octaves with Alternating Hands (solid *staccato*)	any key				HT LH leads	2	84	♬♬
Cross-Rhythm Scales (2 against 3)	D Ab Gb	D F#			HT	LH 2 RH 3	100	LH ♪♪ RH ♬♬
Chromatic Scales Separated by a Minor 3rd (parallel *or* contrary motion)	LH beginning on any note				HT	4	100	♬♬
Advanced Piano Pedagogy								
Parallel Motion	all keys	all keys	all keys		HT	4	120	♬♬
Staccato	Bb Eb Ab Db Gb	Bb Eb G# C# F# F B	Bb Eb G# C# F# F B		HT	3	120	(triplet)
Separated by a 3rd	Ab A Bb B				HT	4	104	♬♬
Separated by a 6th	C Db D Eb				HT	4	104	♬♬
Separated by a 10th	E F Gb G				HT	4	104	♬♬
Formula Pattern	Bb Eb Ab Db Gb	Bb Eb G# C# F# F B			HT	4	120	♬♬
Chromatic	beginning on any note				HT	4	120	♬♬
Scales in Octaves (solid *staccato*)	Bb Eb Ab Db Gb	Bb Eb G# C# F# F B	Bb Eb G# C# F# F B		HT	2	84	♬♬
Chromatic Scales in Octaves (solid *staccato*)	beginning on any note				HT	2	104	♬♬
Candidates must prepare one of the following exercises:								
Modal Scales — Supertonic (Dorian), Mediant (Phrygian), Subdominant (Lydian), Dominant (Mixolydian)	beginning on different scale degrees of A Eb Db				HT	4	100	♬♬
Double 3rd Scales, *legato*	D Ab	A D			HT	2	60	♫
Tonic Arpeggios Beginning at the 6th *or* 10th	C D Ab	C D G#			HT	4	80	♬♬
Arpeggio Sequence I–i–bVI⁶–vi⁶–IV⁶₄–iv⁶₄–I	beginning and ending on C or F				HT	4	80	♬♬
Chromatic Scales in Octaves, *legato*	beginning on any note				HT	2	72	♫

Technical Tests Summary: Chords and Arpeggios

*Play diminished 7th chords and arpeggios on the leading notes of the *minor* keys only.

Level / Chord or Arpeggio Type	Major Keys	Minor Keys	Position	Hands	Octaves	Cadence/Progression	Tempo ♩=	Note Values
Preparatory A — none								
Preparatory B — Chords, Triads, broken	C G	A	root, 1st	HS	n/a		50	♩
Grade 1 — Chords, Triads, broken	C G F	A E D	root, 1st, 2nd	HS	1		50	♩
Grade 1 — Chords, Triads, solid (blocked)				HS	1		100	♪
Grade 2 — Chords, Triads, broken	C G F B♭	A E D G	root, 1st, 2nd	HS	1		60	♩
Grade 2 — Chords, Triads, solid (blocked)				HS	1		112	♪
Grade 3 — Chords, Triads, broken	G D F B♭	E B D G	root, 1st, 2nd	HS	2		69	♩
Grade 3 — Chords, Triads				HT	1	V–I	50	♩
Grade 3 — Chords, Triads, solid (blocked)				HS	2		120	♪
Grade 4 — Chords, Triads, broken	D A B♭ E♭	B F♯ G C	root, 1st, 2nd	HS	2		76	♩
Grade 4 — Chords, Triads				HT	1	V–I	60	♩
Grade 4 — Chords, Triads, solid (blocked)	A E E♭ A♭			HS	2		132	♪
Grade 4 — Chords, Triads				HT	1	V–I	120	♪
Grade 4 — Arpeggios, Tonic	D A	G C	root	HS	2		72	♩
Grade 5 — Chords, Triads, broken	A E E♭ A♭	F♯ C♯ C F	root, 1st, 2nd	HT	2	V–I	66	♩
Grade 5 — Chords, Triads, solid (blocked)	A E E♭ A♭	F♯ C♯ C F	root, 1st, 2nd	HT	2	V–I	132	♪
Grade 5 — Chords, Dominant 7th, broken	A E E♭ A♭		root, 1st, 2nd, 3rd	HS	1		72	♩
Grade 5 — Chords, Dominant 7th, solid (blocked)	A E E♭ A♭		root, 1st, 2nd, 3rd	HS	1		120	♪
Grade 5 — Chords, Diminished 7th, broken		F♯ C♯ C F	root, 1st, 2nd, 3rd	HS	1		72	♩
Grade 5 — Chords, Diminished 7th, solid (blocked)		F♯ C♯ C F	root, 1st, 2nd, 3rd	HS	1		120	♪
Grade 5 — Arpeggios, Tonic	A E E♭ A♭	F♯ C♯ C F	root	HS	2		80	♩

Technical Tests Summary: Chords and Arpeggios (continued)

Level / Chord or Arpeggio Type			Major Keys	Minor Keys	Position				Hands	Octaves	Cadence/ Progression	Tempo ♩=	Note Values
Grade 6													
Chords	Triads	broken	G E F A♭ D♭	G E F G♯ C♯	root	1st	2nd		HT	2	V–I	80	
		solid (blocked)							HT	2	V–I	80	
	Tonic Four-note	broken	G E F A♭ D♭	G E F G♯ C♯	root	1st	2nd		HS	1		88	
	Dominant 7th	broken	G E F A♭ D♭	G E F G♯ C♯	root	1st	2nd	3rd	HS	2		88	
		solid (blocked)							HS	2		72	
	Diminished 7th	broken		G E F G♯ C♯	root	1st	2nd	3rd	HS	2		88	
		solid (blocked)							HS	2		72	
Arpeggios	Tonic		G E F A♭ D♭	G E F G♯ C♯	root	1st			HS	2		92	
	Dominant 7th		G E F A♭ D♭	G E F G♯ C♯	root				HS	2		92	
	Diminished 7th			G E F G♯ C♯	root				HS	2		92	
Grade 7													
Chords	Tonic Four-note	broken	C D B F B♭ A♭ D♭	C D B F B♭ G♯ C♯	root	1st	2nd		HS	2		69	
									HT	1	V–I	60	
	Dominant 7th	broken	C D B F B♭ A♭ D♭	C D B F B♭ G♯ C♯	root	1st	2nd	3rd	HT	2		60	
		solid (blocked)							HT	2		80	
	Diminished 7th	broken		C D B F B♭ G♯ C♯	root	1st	2nd	3rd	HT	2		60	
		solid (blocked)							HT	2		80	
Arpeggios	Tonic		C D B F B♭ A♭ D♭	C D B F B♭ G♯ C♯	root	1st	2nd		HT	2		60	
	Dominant 7th		C D B F B♭ A♭ D♭	C D B F B♭ G♯ C♯	root				HT	2		60	
	Diminished 7th			C D B F B♭ G♯ C♯	root				HT	2		60	
Grade 8													
Chords	Tonic Four-note	broken	C D A E B B♭ E♭ G♭	C D A E B B♭ E♭ F♯	root	1st	2nd		HT	2	I–IV–V–I	80	
	Dominant 7th	broken	C D A E B B♭ E♭ G♭	C D A E B B♭ E♭ F♯	root	1st	2nd	3rd	HT	2		80	
		solid (blocked)							HT	2		100	
	Diminished 7th	broken		C D A E B B♭ E♭ F♯	root	1st	2nd	3rd	HT	2		80	
		solid (blocked)							HT	2		100	
Arpeggios	Tonic		C D A E B B♭ E♭ G♭	C D A E B B♭ E♭ F♯	root	1st	2nd		HT	4		69	
	Dominant 7th		C D A E B B♭ E♭ G♭	C D A E B B♭ E♭ F♯	root				HT	4		69	
	Diminished 7th			C D A E B B♭ E♭ F♯	root				HT	4		69	

Technical Tests Summary: Chords and Arpeggios (continued)

Level / Chord or Arpeggio Type		Pattern	Major Keys	Minor Keys	Position	Hands	Octaves	Cadence/Progression	Tempo ♩=	Note Values
Grade 9										
Chords	Tonic Four-note	broken	all keys	all keys	root, 1st, 2nd	HT	2	I–IV–I^6_4–V–I	104	
		solid (blocked) or broken alternate-note pattern				HT	2	I–IV–I^6_4–V–I	80	
								I–IV–I^6_4–V–I	80	
	Dominant 7th	broken	all keys	all keys	root, 1st, 2nd, 3rd	HT	2		104	
		solid (blocked)				HT	2		104	
	Diminished 7th	broken		all keys	root, 1st, 2nd, 3rd	HT	2		104	
		solid (blocked)				HT	2		104	
Arpeggios	Tonic		all keys	all keys	root, 1st, 2nd	HT	4		84	
	Dominant 7th				root, 1st, 2nd, 3rd					
	Diminished 7th				root, 1st, 2nd, 3rd					
Grade 10										
Chords	Tonic Four-note	broken	all keys	all keys	root, 1st, 2nd	HT	2	I–IV–I^6_4–V^7–I	120	
		solid (blocked)				HT	2	I–IV–I^6_4–V^7–I	120	
		broken alternate-note pattern			3rd	HT	2	I–IV–I^6_4–V^7–I	96	
	Dominant 7th	broken	all keys	all keys	root, 1st, 2nd, 3rd	HT	2		120	
		solid (blocked)				HT	2		120	
		broken alternate-note pattern				HT	2		96	
	Diminished 7th	broken		all keys	root, 1st, 2nd, 3rd	HT	2		120	
		solid (blocked)				HT	2		120	
		broken alternate-note pattern				HT	2		96	
Arpeggios	Tonic		all keys	all keys	root, 1st, 2nd	HT	4		92	
	Dominant 7th				root, 1st, 2nd, 3rd					
	Diminished 7th				root, 1st, 2nd, 3rd					
Advanced Piano Pedagogy										
Chords	Tonic Four-note	broken	all keys	all keys	root, 1st, 2nd	HT	2	I–vi–ii^6_5–I^6_4–V^7–I	120	
		solid (blocked)				HT	2		120	
		broken alternate-note pattern			3rd	HT	2		104	
	Dominant 7th	broken	all keys	all keys	root, 1st, 2nd, 3rd	HT	2		120	
		solid (blocked)				HT	2		120	
		broken alternate-note pattern				HT	2		104	
	Diminished 7th	broken		all keys	root, 1st, 2nd, 3rd	HT	2		120	
		solid (blocked)				HT	2		120	
		broken alternate-note pattern				HT	2		104	
Arpeggios	Tonic		all keys	all keys	root, 1st, 2nd	HT	4		92	
	Dominant 7th				root, 1st, 2nd, 3rd					
	Diminished 7th				root, 1st, 2nd, 3rd					

Technical Patterns

Examples of all scale, chord, arpeggio, and cadence patterns are provided in *The Royal Conservatory of Music Piano Technique Book*, 2008 Edition (The Frederick Harris Music Co., Limited).

Scales

Pentascales (Preparatory A and B)

Two-octave formula pattern in eighth notes (Grades 2 to 5)

Two-octave formula pattern in sixteenth notes (Grades 6 to 7)

Four-octave formula pattern (Grades 8 to 10 and Advanced Piano Pedagogy)

Triads, Chords, and Arpeggios

Solid (blocked) triads and broken triads
Consult the "Technical Tests" section of each grade for the required rhythm.

Dominant 7th chords
Consult the "Technical Tests" section of each grade for the required rhythm.

Diminished 7th chords *

Consult the "Technical Tests" section of each grade for the required rhythm.

* Start on the leading note of the minor key.

Major and minor arpeggios*

Consult the "Technical Tests" section of each grade for the required rhythm.

* Beginning in Grade 9, candidates may be asked to begin major and minor arpeggios on any inversion, or to play any single inversion in isolation.

Broken alternate-note pattern for major and minor chords
(Grades 9, 10, and Advanced Piano Pedagogy)

Broken alternate-note pattern for dominant 7th and diminished 7th chords
(Grades 9, 10, and Advanced Piano Pedagogy)

Cadences and Chord Progressions

Other versions of these progressions are acceptable.

V–I cadence (Grades 4 to 7)

I–IV–V–I chord progression (Grade 8)

I–IV–I$_4^6$–V–I chord progression (Grade 9)

I–IV–I$_4^6$–V^7–I chord progression (Grade 10)

I–vi–ii$_5^6$–I$_4^6$–V^7–I chord progression (Advanced Piano Pedagogy)

Grade-by-Grade Requirements

Preparatory A

Candidates at the Preparatory A level learn keyboard geography, the basic fundamentals of note-reading and rhythm, and articulation. Candidates may choose from an array of character pieces from method books and contemporary collections. This examination eases the candidate's transition from method books into the Certificate Program.

	Preparatory A Requirements	Marks
1	**Repertoire**	**60**
	two selections from the Repertoire Lists	20 (2)
		20 (2)
	one Teacher's Choice	20 (2)
	(The figures in parentheses indicate marks awarded for memory as a portion of the total mark for each selection.)	
2	**Technical Requirements**	**20**
	Technical Tests	
	Major keys: C, G, D	
	Minor keys: A	
	– pentascales	
3	**Ear Tests**	**10**
	Clapback	5
	Playback	5
4	**Sight Reading**	**10**
	Playing	7
	Clapping	3
	Theory Co-requisites	
	None	
	Total possible marks (pass = 60)	**100**

- Candidates may choose to begin this examination with either Repertoire or Technical Requirements.
- The Ear Tests and Sight Reading sections are conducted at the end of the examination.

Resources for Preparatory A Examination Preparation

See p. 125 for a complete list of piano method books suitable for Preparatory A examination preparation.

Technique: *Preparatory Technical Requirements for Piano*

Ear Training and Sight Reading: see p. 135 for ear-training and sight-reading resources.

1 Repertoire

Candidates must prepare *two* contrasting selections from the following Repertoire Lists and *one* selection of the teacher's choice that is of equal difficulty and musical quality to the required works in Preparatory A. Selections must be memorized. Please note that two marks per piece will be deducted if music is used.

Bullets used to denote selections for examination purposes:
- one selection

Repertoire

Berlin, Boris
Our Animal Friends GVT
- The Playful Pup
- Starlight the Pony

Chatman, Stephen
Amusements, 1 FHM
- Foolin' Around
- Monkey Business

Ferrell, Billie
Solos Now (primer level) MYK
- Little Monster

Kabalevsky, Dmitri
24 Pieces for Children, op. 39 SCH
- Melody (no. 1)
- March-Like (no. 3)

Niamath, Linda
In My Garden FHM
- Spider's Web

Poe, John Robert
Simon Says KJO
- Walk Like a Duck

Thompson, John
John Thompson's Easiest Piano Course, 2 WIL
- The Dancing Bear
- Turkey in the Straw

Repertoire from Method Books

The ABC of Piano Playing, 2 FHM
- The Cuckoo
- On Parade
- We Play Hockey

The ABC of Piano Playing, 3 FHM
- The Ballerina
- Cradle Song
- A Skating Waltz

Alfred's Basic Piano Library, Lesson Book 1A ALF
- Horse Sense

Alfred's Basic Piano Library, Lesson Book 1B ALF
- The Clown
- The Cuckoo
- Oom-Pa-Pa
- The Rainbow
- Waltz Time
- The Windmill

Alfred's Premier Piano Course, Lesson 1B ALF
- I Asked My Mother
- The Joke
- My Sombrero

Alfred's Premier Piano Course, Lesson 2A ALF
- Qwerty

Alfred's Premier Piano Course, Performance 1B ALF
- As Morning Dawns
- My Dog
- Pogo Stick

Bastien Piano Basics, Piano 1 KJO
- Cops and Robbers
- March
- Rock Group
- Sing, Bird, Sing
- Space Walk
- Spooks
- Swingin' Beat

Bastien Piano Basics, Performance 1 KJO
- Golden Trumpets
- On the Planet of Mars
- Seconds, Please!

Celebrate Piano!®, Lesson and Musicianship 1B FHM
- Aura Lee
- Lazy Summer Day
- The Sad Dragon

Celebrate Piano!®, Lesson and Musicianship 2A FHM
- Easy Day

Celebrate Piano!®, Solos 1 FHM
- Ladybug Waltz
- The Teeter-Totter
- Trumpet Parade

Celebrate Piano!®, Solos 2 FHM
- Clowns
- The Mouse in the Grandfather Clock

Hal Leonard Student Piano Library, Piano Lessons 2 HAL
- Bayou Blues
- Circle Dance
- First Light

Hal Leonard Student Piano Library, Piano Solos 2 HAL
- Goofy Gadget
- The Stream
- Take It Slow
- Those Creepy Crawly Things on the Cellar Floor
- Viva La Rhumba

Music for Young Children, Moonbeams 1 MYC
- Andante
- Hurrah
- Melody for Alphorn
- Music Signs
- Wake Up!

Music for Young Children, Moonbeams 2 MYC
- Frère Jacques
- Lady Bug
- Pixie Waltz

Music for Young Children, Sunbeams 2 MYC
- Go to Sleep

The Music Tree, Student's Book 1 SUM
- Drum and Bugle
- First Boogie
- Forest Echoes
- Over the Rainbow
- Pony Song
- When the Saints Go Marching In

The Music Tree, Student's Book 2A SUM
- La Bamba
- Brisk March
- The Merry-Go-Round Broke Down
- The Modern Dragon

Piano Adventures®, Lesson Book 1 FJH
- Dinosaur Stomp
- The Haunted Mouse
- The Juggler
- Song for a Scarecrow

Piano Adventures®, Lesson Book 2A FJH
- Moonlight Melody
- My Daydream
- Our Detective Agency
- Storms on Saturn

Piano Adventures®, Lesson Book 2B FJH
- Carefree Waltz

Piano Discoveries, Explorer Book 1A HMP
- Eek! Bump! Yikes! Jump!
- Giggling Goblins
- Have You Seen the Leprechaun?
- The Mirror

Piano Discoveries, Explorer Book 1B HMP
- Let's Go to the Fair
- The Phantom Returns
- Ragamuffin Rag
- Things That Go Bump in the Night
- Where Have All the Socks Gone?

Teaching Little Fingers to Play More WIL
- Go Tell Aunt Rhody
- The Pet Parade
- 'Tis A Gift To Be Simple
- Waltz without Words

2 Technical Requirements

Technical Tests

Candidates must play all Technical Tests from memory, ascending and descending, with good tone and logical fingering, at a steady tempo. The metronome marking indicates minimum speed.

See "Technical Patterns" on p. 19 for examples.

Keys for Preparatory A   Major C, G, D
                                         Minor A

Scale	Keys	Played	Tempo	Note values
Pentascales* (five-finger pattern)	C, G, D major A minor	HS tonic to dominant ending with solid (blocked) root position triad	♩=100	♩

* A pentascale comprises the first five degrees of a scale: tonic, supertonic, mediant, subdominant, and dominant.

3 Ear Tests

Clapback

Candidates will choose to either clap, tap, or sing the rhythm of a short melody after the examiner has played it *twice*. The second measure will consist of only one note.

Time signature	Note values	Approximate length
3/4 4/4	o ♩. ♩ ♩ ♫	two measures

Example only

Playback

Candidates will be asked to play back a melody based on the first three notes of the pentascale. The melody will move in only one direction (up or down) and will contain a repeated note and stepwise motion. The examiner will name the key, play the tonic triad *once*, and play the melody *twice*.

Beginning note	Approximate length	Keys
tonic or mediant	four notes	C, G, F major

Example only

4 Sight Reading

Playing

Candidates will be asked to play by sight *two* four-note melodies written on the grand staff:

- one melody in the bass clef, played with the left hand
- one melody in the treble clef, played with the right hand

The melodies will move by step in one direction only (up or down) and may contain a repeated note. Fingering will be indicated for the first note only.

Time signature	Note values	Keys
4/4	o ♩ ♩	C major

Clapping

Candidates will be asked to clap or tap a simple two-measure rhythm. A steady pace and rhythmic accentuation are expected.

Time signature	Approximate length	Note values
2/4	two measures	♩ ♩ ♫

Example only

Preparatory B

Candidates at the Preparatory B level continue their exploration of the keyboard, articulation, and tone color while moving away from the five-finger position. One-octave *legato* scales, contrary motion scales, and triads in first inversion support the technical challenges found in the repertoire. Pieces include traditional favorites from the early pedagogical repertoire, along with more contemporary styles.

	Preparatory B Requirements	Marks
1	**Repertoire**	**60**
	two selections from the Repertoire Lists	20 (2)
		20 (2)
	one Teacher's Choice	20 (2)
	(The figures in parentheses indicate marks awarded for memory as a portion of the total mark for each selection.)	
2	**Technical Requirements**	**20**
	Technical Tests	
	Major keys: C G A E F	
	Minor keys: A E D	
	– pentascales	
	– scales	
	– contrary motion scale	
	– triads	
3	**Ear Tests**	**10**
	Clapback	5
	Playback	5
4	**Sight Reading**	**10**
	Playing	7
	Clapping	3
	Theory Co-requisites	
	None	
	Total possible marks (pass = 60)	**100**

- Candidates may choose to begin this examination with either Repertoire or Technical Requirements.
- The Ear Test and Sight Reading sections are conducted at the end of the examination.

Resources for Preparatory B Examination Preparation

Repertoire: *Celebration Series Perspectives®: Preparatory Piano Repertoire*

Technique: *Preparatory Technical Requirements for Piano*

Ear Training and Sight Reading: see p. 135 for ear-training and sight-reading resources.

Visit **www.frederickharrismusic.com** for information about publications.

1 Repertoire

Candidates must prepare *two* contrasting selections from the following Repertoire Lists and *one* selection of the teacher's choice that is of equal difficulty and musical quality to the required works in Prepatory B. Repertoire selections must be memorized. Please note that two marks per selection will be deducted if music is used.

Bullets used to denote selections for examination purposes:
- one selection
▶ selection is found in *Celebration Series Perspectives®: Preparatory Piano Repertoire* FHM

Repertoire

Alexander, Dennis
Finger Paintings, 3 ALF
- A Summer Morning
- Sun Fun
Just for You, 1 ALF
- Celebration

Archer, Violet
Here and Now ALK
- The Haunted Cave

Bartók, Béla
The First Term at the Piano EMB
- Dialogue (no. 3)

Berlin, Boris
Our Animal Friends GVT
- Bunny's Cradle Song
- The Marching Pigs
- The Sleepy Kitten
- The Swiss Cuckoo

Berr, Bruce
Imaginations in Style HAL
- Fanfare

Chatman, Stephen
Amusements, 2 FHM
▶ Broken Music Box
Away! FHM
▶ Birding
Escapades, 1 FHM
- A Forgotten Promise
Sports FHM
▶ Olie the Goalie

Clementi, Muzio
▶ Arietta in C Major, op. 42, no. 5

Coulthard, Jean
▶ Birthday Morning (*Music of Our Time*, Preliminary WAT)
- The New Dolly Dances (*Music of Our Time*, Preliminary WAT)

Crosby, Anne
Freddie the Frog FHM
- ● Freddie the Frog
- ▶ Starfish at Night
- ▶ To Fly Like an Eagle
In My Dreams FHM
- ● Floating in Space

Donkin, Christine
Comics & Card Tricks FHM
- ▶ The Tired Turtle Express
- ▶ The Path of the Ping-Pong Ball

Dunhill, Thomas
First Year Pieces ABR
- ● Melody in C
- ● On the River Bank
- ● A Song of Erin

Gallant, Pierre
Clowning Around FHM
- ● March of the 2nds and 3rds
- ▶ Sakura (Japanese koto song) (arr.)
- ● The Rhythm Machine
- ● Teasing

Garścia, Janina
Winter Fun PWM
- ● The Leveret

Gedike, Alexandr
60 Simple Piano Pieces for Beginners, op. 36
- ● A Song (no. 3)

George, Jon
- ● Distant Chimes (*The Music Tree*, Students' Choice: Recreational Solos 3 SUM)
- ● Strolling in the Park (*Supplementary Solos*, 1 SUM)

Gillock, William L.
Accent on Solos, 2 WIL
- ● Stars on a Summer Night

Hansen, Joan
- ▶ Aeolian Lullaby (*Music of Our Time*, 1 WAT)

Hook, James
- ▶ Minuetto, op. 37, Lesson 2

Kabalevsky, Dmitri
Children's Adventures, op. 89 EMB
- ▶ First Waltz (no. 5)
24 Pieces for Children, op. 39 SCH
- ▶ Polka (no. 2)
- ● A Little Joke (no. 6)

Köhler, Christoph Louis Heinrich
- ● Children's Song (*Everybody's Perfect Masterpieces*, 1 ALF)

Last, Joan
Contrasts, 4 BOS [OP]
- ▶ An Argument
- ▶ By the Mill Pond
Roof Tops FOR
- ● The Dove-cot
- ● Scurrying Clouds

Markow, Andrew
- ▶ Jumping Jacks FHM

Milligan, John
- ● Tippi-Toes (*Legacy Collection*, 1 FHM)

Niamath, Linda
In My Garden FHM
- ● Swinging
Marching Mice and Other Pieces FHM
- ● Balloons
Soda Pop and Other Delights FHM
- ▶ Playful Puppy
- ● Sleepy Little Kitten

Norton, Christopher
The Microjazz Collection, 1 B&H
- ● After the Battle
- ▶ Struttin'

Parsons, Margaret (arr.)
- ● Hush-a-bye (*Legacy Collection*, 1 FHM)

Sheftel, Paul
Merry and Mellow HIN
- ▶ Chimes

Snell, Keith, and Diane Hidy
- ● School's Out (*Piano Town*, Lessons 2 KJO)

Tansman, Alexandre
On s'amuse au piano / Happy Time, 1 WAR
- ● Arabia

Türk, Daniel Gottlob
Handstücke für angehende Klavierspieler, 1 ABR
- ▶ A Carefree Fellow
- ● Children's Ballad
- ▶ Sad Feelings
- ▶ Youthful Happiness
Handstücke für angehende Klavierspieler, 2 ABR
- ● Phrase Endings

Repertoire from Method Books

The ABC of Piano Playing, 3 FHM
- ● A Canoe Trip
- ● En roulant ma boule
- ▶ Halloween Pranks
- ● Hop Scotch
- ▶ Old MacDonald Had a Farm
- ● On the Merry-Go-Round
- ● Springtime
- ● The Swiss Cuckoo

Alfred's Basic Piano Library, Lesson Book, Complete Levels 2–3 ALF
- ▶ A 16th-Century March
- ● 18th-Century Dance
- ● Calypso Carnival
- ● Lone Star Waltz
- ● Malagueña
- ● Red River Valley

Alfred's Premier Piano Course, Lesson 2A ALF
- ● Boom, Boom!
- ● Butterfly World
- ● Desert Gold
- ● King Arthur's Adventure
- ● Mystery Movie
- ● Tilt-a-Whirl

28

Alfred's Premier Piano Course, Lesson 2B ALF
- Quiet Thoughts

Bastien Piano Basics, Performance 3 KJO
- Fireworks

Bastien Piano Basics, Piano 2 KJO
- Dancing the Minuet
- Tarantella

Bastien Piano Basics, Piano 3 KJO
- German Folk Song
- Gypsy Dance
- The Minstrel's Song
- Prelude in A Minor
- Viennese Waltz

Celebrate Piano!®, Lesson and Musicianship 2A FHM
- The Boogie Bugler

Celebrate Piano!®, Lesson and Musicianship 2B FHM
- Alouette
- Donkey Riding
- Graceful Swan
- Jumping Jacks
- Last Train to Bluesville
- Popcorn Man
- Rhythm Ace
- Riding the Waves
- Russian Dance
- Sea Chanty

Celebrate Piano!®, Solos 2 FHM
- Allegro, op. 1, no. 4
- ▶ Bouncing on My Bed (*Rise and Shine* FHM)
- Minuetto, op. 1, no. 1

Celebrate Piano!®, Lesson and Musicianship 3 FHM
- Dancin'Shoes
- Erie Canal
- Jiggety-Jog
- A Moonlight Waltz
- ▶ On a Greek Island
- On the Trampoline
- ▶ Singin' the Blues
- ▶ Sparklers
- Tarantella

Celebrate Piano!®, Solos 3 & 4 FHM
- Melody
- Minuetto

Celebrate Piano!®, Lesson and Musicianship 4 FHM
- Minuet in F Major
- Takin' it Easy

Hal Leonard Student Piano Library, Piano Lessons 3 HAL
- Chorale
- The Fife'n'Horn
- Inchworm Waltz
- Romance

Hal Leonard Student Piano Library, Piano Solos 3 HAL
- Blues Prelude
- The Clockwork Ballerina
- Fiesta March
- Leap Frog
- Porcupine Pizzicato
- The Winter Wind

Music for Young Children, Sunbeams 3 MYC
- Days of the Week
- Hello to Spring
- Ketchup
- Our Friend
- Tis a Gift to Be Simple
- Waltz of the Sunbeams

Music Pathways, Piano Discoveries C FIS
- The Famous Haunted House
- On the Move

Music Pathways, Piano Solos B FIS
- ▶ Lady Moon

The Music Tree, Student's Book 2A SUM
- Knights at the Ball
- Morning Has Broken

The Music Tree, Student's Book 3 SUM
- The Ants Go Marching
- Broken Record Boogie
- Changing the Guard
- Country Fiddler
- Mountain Ballad
- Pop Goes the Weasel
- Stomp Dance

Piano Adventures®, Lesson Book 2A FJH
- Snake Charmer
- Whirling Leaves

Piano Adventures®, Lesson Book 2B FJH
- Amaryllis
- Canoeing in the Moonlight
- Carefree Waltz
- Jumpin' Jazz Cat
- Pumpkin Boogie
- Riding the Wind
- Spanish Caballero

Piano Discoveries, Adventure Book 2A HMP
- At Dawn
- Bedtime Story
- Children's Song
- Clowns Shoe Shuffle
- Day Dreaming
- Hop, Skip and a Jump Blues
- March of the Clowns
- March of the Magician
- Simple Gifts
- Twinkling Star
- The Water Is Wide

Piano Discoveries, Explorer Book 1B HMP
- Hobgoblin Hop

Suzuki Piano School, rev. ed., 1 SUM
- Allegretto 1
- Au clair de la lune
- Cuckoo
- French Children's Song
- Good-bye to Winter
- Lightly Row

Preparatory B

2 Technical Requirements

Technical Tests

Candidates must play all Technical Tests from memory, ascending and descending, with good tone and logical fingering, at a steady tempo. The metronome marking indicates minimum speed. All scales are to be played *legato*.

See "Technical Patterns" on p. 19 for examples.

Keys for Preparatory B   Major C, G, A, E, F
                          Minor A, E, D

Scale	Keys	Played	Tempo	Note values
Pentascales* (five-finger pattern)	A, E, F major E, D minor	HS tonic to dominant end with solid (blocked) root position triad	♩ = 60	♫
Scales	C, G major A minor (natural)	HS 1 octave	♩ = 60	♫
Contrary Motion	C major	HT 1 octave	♩ = 60	♫

Chords	Keys	Played	Tempo	Note Values
Triads (root position and 1st inversion) broken	C, G major A minor	HS 1 octave	♩ = 50	♪♪♪

* A pentascale comprises the first five degrees of a scale: tonic, supertonic, mediant, subdominant, and dominant.

3 Ear Tests

Clapback

Candidates will choose to either clap, tap, or sing the rhythm of a short melody after the examiner has played it *twice*.

Time signature	Note values	Approximate length
3/4 4/4	o 𝅗𝅥. 𝅗𝅥 ♩ ♫	two measures

Example only

Playback

Candidates will be asked to play back a melody based on the first three notes of the major scale. The melody may change direction and may contain repeated notes or skips of a 3rd. The examiner will name the key, play the tonic triad *once*, and play the melody *twice*.

Beginning note	Approximate length	Keys
tonic or mediant	four notes	C, G, F major

Example only

4 Sight Reading

Playing

Candidates will be asked to play a short melody based on the notes of the pentascale. The melody will be written on the grand staff and divided between the hands. Fingering will be indicated for the first note of each hand only.

Time signature	Note values	Approximate length	Keys
4/4	o 𝅗𝅥 𝅗𝅥	four measures	C or G major

Clapping

Candidates will be asked to clap or tap a simple two-measure rhythm. A steady pace and rhythmic accentuation are expected.

Time signature	Approximate length	Note values
2/4 3/4	two measures	𝅗𝅥. 𝅗𝅥 ♩ ♫

Example only

Grade 1

Candidates at the Grade 1 level are introduced to elements of Baroque and early Classical style through binary and ternary dance forms. Character pieces help candidates develop their creativity and imagination. Inventions develop hand independence, supported further with scale and triad technique.

	Grade 1 Requirements	Marks
1	**Repertoire**	**50**
	one selection from List A: Baroque and Classical Repertoire	18
	one selection from List B: Romantic, 20th-, and 21st-century Repertoire	18
	one selection from List C: Inventions	14
	Memory (2 marks per selection awarded for memory)	**6**
2	**Technical Requirements**	**24**
	Studies / Etudes: *one* study / etude from the *Syllabus* list	12
	Technical Tests	12
	Major keys: C G F	
	Minor keys: A E D	
	– scales	
	– *staccato* scales	
	– contrary motion scale	
	– chromatic scale	
	– triads	
3	**Ear Tests**	**10**
	Clapback	5
	Playback	5
4	**Sight Reading**	**10**
	Playing	7
	Clapping	3
	Theory Co-requisites	
	None	
	Total possible marks (pass = 60)	**100**

Resources for Grade 1 Examination Preparation

Repertoire: *Celebration Series Perspectives®: Piano Repertoire 1*

Studies / Etudes: *Celebration Series Perspectives®: Piano Studies / Etudes 1*

Technique: *Technical Requirements for Piano 1*

Ear Training and Sight Reading: see p. 135 for ear-training and sight-reading resources.

Visit **www.frederickharrismusic.com** for information about publications.

1 Repertoire

Candidates must prepare *three* contrasting selections: *one* from each of List A, List B, and List C. Repertoire selections must be memorized. Please not that up to two memory marks will be deducted for each selection where music is used.

Bullets used to denote selections for examination purposes:

- ● one selection
- ▶ selection is found in *Celebration Series Perspectives®: Piano Repertoire 1 FHM*

List A
Baroque and Classical Repertoire

Anonymous
▶ Burlesque in G major (*Notebook for Wolfgang* OTT)

Bach, Johann Christian
Notenbuch der Anna Magdalena Bach WIE
▶ Aria in F major, BWV Anh. 131

Bach, Johann Christoph Friedrich
Musikalische Nebenstunden ABR
● Minuet in C major
● Schwäbisch in D major

Bach, Johann Sebastian
Notenbuch der Anna Magdalena Bach WIE
● Chorale, BWV 514

Beethoven, Ludwig van
● Ukrainian Folk Song, op. 107, no. 3 (*Celebrate Beethoven, vol. 1 FHM*)

Clarke, Jeremiah
The Third Book of the Harpsichord Master
▶ Minuet in D major, T 460

Clementi, Muzio
Introduction to the Art of Playing the Piano Forte
● Pyrenese Melody (*Masterwork Classics, 4* ALF)

Duncombe, William
Progressive Lessons for the Harpsichord and Pianoforte
● Sonatina in C major (*Masterwork Classics, 3* ALF)

Dunhill, Thomas
First Year Pieces ABR
● Gavotte in G major

Gossec, François-Joseph
● An Old French Dance (arr. Margaret Parsons, in *Legacy Collection, 2 FHM*)

Graupner, Christoph
Notebook for Wolfgang OTT
▶ Bourrée in D minor

Hässler, Johann Wilhelm
Fifty Pieces for Beginners, op. 38 ABR
▶ Minuet in C major (no. 4)

Haydn, Franz Joseph
- Capriccio (arr., from Caprice, Hob. XVII:1)
- German Dance in G major, Hob. IX:22, no. 3
- ▶ Minuet in G major (attr. trio section of the 2nd movement of Piano Sonata, Hob. XVI:15)

Hook, James
Guida di Musica, op. 81
- Allegretto in C major (no. 4) (*James Hook Album* ELK)

Krieger, Johann
Sechs musicalische Partien
- ▶ Minuet in A minor

Mozart, Leopold
Notebook for Wolfgang OTT
- Bourrée in E minor (attr.)
- Minuet in D minor

Mozart, Wolfgang Amadeus
- ▶ Minuet in F major, K 2

Telemann, Georg Philipp
- ▶ Andante in G minor

Türk, Daniel Gottlob
Handstücke für angehende Klavierspieler, 1 ABR
- The Hunting Horns and the Echo
Zwölf Handstücke
- ▶ Arioso in F major

List B
Romantic, 20th-, and 21st-century Repertoire

Adair, Yvonne
Sketches from Hans Christian Andersen OUP [OP]
- ▶ The Bronze Bear

Alexander, Dennis
Especially for Boys ALF
- Frogs and Snakes
Just for You, 1 ALF
- Cinnamon Popcorn

Berlin, Boris
- Hopscotch (*Legacy Collection*, 1 FHM)

Blok, Vladimir
Twelve Pieces in Folk Modes FHM
- Happy Times

Bonis, Mel.
Album pour les tout-petites COM
- ▶ The Flea

Boyd, Bill
Jazz Starters 3 HAL
- Too Blue

Brown, Stephen
Six Pentatonic Preludes SWA
- Pentatonic Prelude no. 1

Chatman, Stephen
Amusements, 1 FHM
- ▶ Silly Argument

Chatman, Stephen (continued)
Escapades, 1 FHM
- Beaver Boogie
- A Forgotten Promise

Clark, Frances
- Daydreaming (*Contemporary Piano Literature*, 1 ALF)
- March of the Trolls (*Contemporary Piano Literature*, 1 ALF)

Crosby, Anne
In My Dreams FHM
- ▶ Robots

Dello Joio, Norman
Suite for the Young SCH; EDW; HAL
- Little Sister

Donkin, Christine
Comics & Card Tricks FHM
- ▶ Crafty Card Tricks
Legends & Lore FHM
- ▶ Dream Journey

Duke, David
- March (Lydian Mode) (*Music of Our Time*, 1 WAT)

Eurina, Ludmilla
- A Sad Song (*Ukrainian Echoes* FHM)

Fairbank, Nicholas
A Pentad for Piano FAI
- Pentatonic Lullaby

Frid, Grigori
Youthful Adventures FHM
- ▶ The Jolly Fiddler, op. 41, no. 5

Gallant, Pierre
Animal Fair FHM
- ▶ "Croc" the Curmudgeon

Garścia, Janina
Very Easy Piano Pieces for Children, op. 3 PWM
- Chris's Song
- The Doll's Horse

Gedike, Alexander
60 Simple Piano Pieces for Beginners, op. 36
- A Happy Tale (no. 31)
- A Sad Song (no. 39)

Gillock, William L.
Accent on Solos, 2 WIL
- Argentina
Collected Short Lyric Pieces WIL
- Drifting Clouds

Grechaninov, Alexandr T.
Children's Album, op. 98 OTT
- Fairy Tale (no. 1)

Gurlitt, Cornelius
The First Lessons, op. 117 KAL
- Rocking (no. 6)
- The Hunt (no. 15)

Kabalevsky, Dmitri
24 Pieces for Children, op. 39 SCH
- ▶ March (no. 10)
- Waltz (no. 13)

Kasemets, Udo
One Plus One, 2 BER
- ● Old MacDonald

Krausas, Veronika
The Bestiary KRA
- ▶ The Alligator

Lefeld, Jerzy
Little Frogs and Other Piano Pieces for Children PWM
- ● A Folk Tune

Niamath, Linda
Soda Pop and Other Delights FHM
- ● Big Teddy, Little Teddy
- ▶ Hide and Seek
- ● March of the Terrible Trolls
A Zoo for You FHM
- ● Bears

Norton, Christopher
Christopher Norton Connections for Piano™, 1 FHM
- ● No Worries
- ● Merry-Go-Round
- ● Four-Wheel Drive
The Microjazz Collection, 1 B&H
- ▶ Duet for One
- ▶ On the Right Lines
- ● Struttin'

Paterson, Lorna
- ▶ Gremlins (titled "Marmoset" in *Safari Suite* FHM)
Pianimals FHM
- ● Wallabies on Parade

Pearce, Elvina
- ● Camel Ride (*Celebrate Piano!*®, *Lesson and Musicianship* 3 FHM)

Poole, Clifford
- ● Cobwebs (*Legacy Collection,* 1 FHM)
- ● The Itchy Ant (first published under pseudonym Ernest Marsden) (*Legacy Collection,* 2 FHM)
- ▶ Mist (*Legacy Collection,* 1 FHM)
- ▶ Spooks (*Legacy Collection,* 2 FHM)

Reubart, Dale
- ▶ Square Dance (*Celebrate Piano!*®, *Solos* 3 & 4 FHM)

Rybicki, Feliks
I Begin to Play, op. 20 PWM
- ● Cradle Song

Schnittke, Alfred
Eight Pieces for Piano SIK
- ▶ Folk Song

Shostakovich, Dmitri
Six Children's Pieces, op. 69 SCH
- ● Waltz

Siegmeister, Elie
- ● Song of the Dark Woods (*Contemporary Piano Literature,* 2 ALF)

Silvester, Frederick
- ● Jig (*Legacy Collection,* 1 FHM)

Stravinsky, Soulima
Piano Music for Children, 1 PET
- ● For the Kid Next Door
- ● Stepping Stones

Tan, Chee-Hwa
A Child's Garden of Verses FHM
- ● My Shadow
- ● Pirate Story
- ● Where Go the Boats?

Taranta, Italo
Piano Miniatures WIL
- ▶ A Starry Night

Telfer, Nancy
My Bark Canoe FHM
- ● Monté sur un éléphant / Climb up on an Elephant

List C
Inventions

Archer, Violet
Eleven Short Pieces ALK
- ● Little Prelude

Christopher, Renée
- ▶ The Snake FHM

Duke, David (arr.)
- ▶ She's Like the Swallow (*Music of Our Time,* 2 WAT)

Dyson, George
Twelve Easy Pieces ABR
- ● Study in Canon

Gallant, Pierre
- ▶ Sur le pont d'Avignon / On the Bridge at Avignon (arr.)
Imitations and Inventions FHM
- ● Dancing Partners
- ● A Little Song between Friends

Garztecka, Irena
Little Frogs and Other Piano Pieces for Children PWM
- ▶ A Ball

Gurlitt, Cornelius
Fireside Fancies: 12 Little Tone-Pictures on Five Notes
- ● Little Conversation, op. 197, no. 8

Keveren, Phillip
Mouse on a Mirror HAL
- ● Mouse on a Mirror

Markow, Andrew
- ▶ Teapot Invention FHM
- ▶ Where Did the Sun Go? FHM

Norton, Christopher
Christopher Norton Connections for Piano™, 1 FHM
- ▶ Carol in Canon

2 Technical Requirements

Studies / Etudes

Candidates must prepare *one* selection from the following list of studies / etudes. Memorization is *not* required and will not be rewarded with extra marks.

Bullets used to denote selections for examination purposes:
▶ selection is found in *Celebration Series Perspectives®: Studies / Etudes 1* FHM

Chatman, Stephen
Away FHM
▶ Scaly Things

Crosby, Anne
In My Dreams FHM
▶ Celebration

Diabelli, Anton
The First Twelve Lessons, op. 125 PET
▶ Study in C major (no. 3)

Donkin, Christine
Comics & Card Tricks FHM
▶ Time Travel
Legends & Lore FHM
▶ Soaring

Gallant, Pierre
Animal Fair FHM
▶ Paper Tigers

George, Jon
Kaleidoscope Solos, 2 ALF
▶ Relay Race (Canon)

Kabalevsky, Dmitri
Children's Adventures, op. 89 EMB
▶ Skipping Rope (no. 17)

Le Couppey, Felix
The Alphabet, op. 17 MAS
▶ Study in C major (no. 6)

Norton, Christopher
The Final Frontier B&H
▶ Space Fleet
The Microjazz Collection, 2 B&H
▶ Two-Handed Blues

Tansman, Alexander
On s'amuse au piano / Happy Time, 1 WAR
▶ Both Ways

Wolfahrt, Franz
Kinder-Kavierschule, op. 36
▶ Study in G major

Substitutions

Candidates may substitute *one* repertoire selection or *one* study / etude selection with a musical work *not found* in the Repertoire Lists for Grade 1. See p. 130 for more information on substitutions.

Total Substitutions Permitted	Requires Prior Approval (Submit an Examination Substitute Piece Request)		Does Not Require Prior Approval		
	Repertoire Substitution		Repertoire Substitution		Study / Etude Substitution
one Repertoire selection or one Study / Etude	One repertoire selection from piano literature comparable in style and difficulty to the corresponding List A or B of Grade 1	*or*	One repertoire selection from the corresponding List of Grade 2	*or*	One study / etude from Grade 2 or One Teacher's Choice selection (must be of equal difficulty and a length of 30–60 seconds)

Technical Tests

Candidates must play all Technical Tests from memory, ascending and descending, with good tone and logical fingering, at a steady tempo. Metronome markings indicate minimum speeds. All scales are to be played *legato* unless otherwise indicated.

See "Technical Patterns" on p. 19 for examples.

Keys for Grade 1   Major C, G, F
　　　　　　　　　 Minor A, E, D

Scales	Keys	Played	Tempo	Note values
Scales	C, G, F major A, E, D minor (natural and harmonic)	HS 2 octaves	♩ = 69	♫
Staccato	C, G, F major	HS 1 octave	♩ = 69	♫
Contrary Motion	C major	HT 2 octaves	♩ = 69	♫
Chromatic	beginning on C	HS tonic to dominant	♩ = 69	♫

Chords	Keys	Played	Tempo	Note values
Triads (root position and inversions) broken	C, G, F major A, E, D minor	HS 1 octave	♩ = 50	♫♫
solid (blocked)	C, G, F major A, E, D minor	HS 1 octave	♩ = 100	♪𝄽

3 Ear Tests

Clapback

Candidates will choose to either clap, tap, or sing the rhythm of a short melody after the examiner has played it *twice*.

Time signature	Approximate length
$\frac{2}{4}$ $\frac{3}{4}$	three to four measures

Example only

Playback

Candidates will be asked to play back a melody based on the first three notes of a major scale. The examiner will name the key, play the tonic triad *once*, and play the melody *twice*.

Beginning note	Approximate length	Keys
tonic, supertonic, or mediant	four notes	C, G, F major

Example only

4 Sight Reading

Playing

Candidates will be asked to play a passage that is divided between the hands and lies within the compass of the staff. The melody will include half and quarter notes.

Time signature	Approximate length	Keys
$\frac{4}{4}$	four measures	C, G, F major

Clapping

Candidates will be asked to clap or tap a rhythm. A steady pace and rhythmic accentuation are expected.

Time signature	Approximate length
$\frac{4}{4}$	two measures

Example only

Grade 2

Candidates at the Grade 2 level continue to explore various historical styles. Character pieces allow for exploration of pedaling, expression, and balance of tone. Scales played hands together, including the formula pattern, are introduced to help candidates achieve facility with this repertoire.

	Grade 2 Requirements	Marks
1	**Repertoire**	**50**
	one selection from List A: Baroque and Classical Repertoire	18
	one selection from List B: Romantic, 20th-, and 21st-century Repertoire	18
	one selection from List C: Inventions	14
	Memory (2 marks per selection awarded for memory)	**6**
2	**Technical Requirements**	**24**
	Studies / Etudes: *one* study / etude from the *Syllabus* list	12
	Technical Tests	12
	Major keys: C G F B♭ Minor keys: A E D G – scales – *staccato* scales – parallel motion scales – contrary motion scale – formula pattern scale – chromatic scale – triads	
3	**Ear Tests**	**10**
	Clapback	3
	Intervals	3
	Playback	4
4	**Sight Reading**	**10**
	Playing	7
	Clapping	3
	Theory Co-requisites	
	None	
	Total possible marks (pass = 60)	**100**

Resources for Grade 2 Examination Preparation

Repertoire: *Celebration Series Perspectives®: Piano Repertoire 2*

Studies / Etudes: *Celebration Series Perspectives®: Piano Studies / Etudes 2*

Technique: *Technical Requirements for Piano 2*

Ear Training and Sight Reading: see p. 135 for ear-training and sight-reading resources.

Visit **www.frederickharrismusic.com** for information about publications.

1 Repertoire

Candidates must prepare *three* contrasting selections: *one* from each of List A, List B, and List C. Repertoire selections must be memorized. Please note that up to two memory marks will be deducted for each selection if music is used.

Bullets used to denote selections for examination purposes:
● one selection
▲ part or section of a larger work
▶ selection is found in *Celebration Series Perspectives®: Piano Repertoire 2* FHM

List A

Baroque and Classical Repertoire

Anonymous
- ● Bourrée in D minor (*Notebook for Wolfgang* OTT)
- ▶ Entrée in A minor (*Notebook for Wolfgang* OTT)

Arnold, Samuel
- ▶ Gavotte in C major, op. 12, no. 2

Bach, Carl Philipp Emanuel
- ● Minuet in E flat major, H 171
- ▶ Minuetto II in F minor, H 196/2

Bach, Johann Sebastian
- ● Suite in G minor, BWV 822
  - ▲ VII: Minuet III in G major

Notenbuch der Anna Magdalena Bach WIE
- ● Aria in D minor, BWV 515

Beethoven, Ludwig van
- ▶ Écossaise in G major, WoO 23 (*Celebrate Beethoven, vol.* 1 FHM)

Ten National Airs with Variations, op. 107
- ● Russian Folk Song: Beautiful Minka (no. 7) (arr., in *Celebrate Beethoven, vol.* 1 FHM)

Clarke, Jeremiah
- ● King William's March (*Legacy Collection*, 2 FHM)

Couperin, François

Premier livre de clavecin, 2e ordre (*François Couperin: Complete Keyboard Works*, 1 DOV)
- ● Fanfare pour la suite de la Diane

Second livre de pièces de clavecin, 6e ordre (*François Couperin: Complete Keyboard Works*, 1 DOV)
- ● Les moissonneurs

Diabelli, Anton
- ● Sonatina in C major, op. 151, no. 2
  - ▲ 2nd movement

Handel, George Frideric
- ▶ Impertinence, HWV 494

Partita in G major, HWV 450
- ● Menuet in G major

Haydn, Franz Joseph
- ● German Dance in G major, Hob. IX: 12/7 (*Celebrate Haydn, vol.* 1 FHM)

Five Contradances and One Quadrille, Hob. IX:29 (*Il Mio Primo Haydn* RIC)
- ● Quadrille

Hook, James
Guida di musica, op. 81
- Gavotta in D major no. 3 (*James Hook Album* ELK)

Krebs, Johann Ludwig
- ▶ Minuet in B minor

Mozart, Wolfgang Amadeus
- Allegro in F major, K 1c (*Celebrate Mozart, vol. I* FHM)
- Minuet in G major, K 1e (*Celebrate Mozart, vol. I* FHM)
- ▶ Menuetto I in C major (from Sonata in C Major for Keyboard or Keyboard and Violin, K 6)

Neefe, Christian Gottlob
- ▶ Allegretto in C major

Purcell, Henry
- Hornpipe, Z T685 (*Essential Keyboard Repertoire, 4* ALF)

Rameau, Jean-Philippe
Pièces de clavecin (1724)
- ▶ Menuet en rondeau / Minuet in Rondo Form

Scarlatti, Domenico
- Sonata in C minor, L 217, K 73b (*Celebrate Scarlatti, vol. I* FHM)

Schubert, Franz
- Écossaise, D 299, no. 8

Telemann, Georg Philipp
- Fantasia in D major, TWV 33:16 ABR
  - ▲ 3rd section: Vite

Türk, Daniel Gottlob
Handstücke für angehende Klavierspieler, 1 ABR
- ▶ A Cheerful Spirit
- Contentment

List B

Romantic, 20th-, and 21st-century Repertoire

Barenboim, L.
- Polish Song (*From Russia for Youth* FHM)

Bartók, Béla
For Children, 1 B&H
- Children at Play (no. 1)
- Children's Song (no. 2)
- Allegretto (no. 3)

Berkovich, Isak
- ▶ Mazurka

Berlin, Boris
- ▶ March of the Goblins (*Legacy Collection, 2* FHM)
- The Merry-Go-Round (*Legacy Collection, 2* FHM)

Berr, Bruce
- Venetian Boat Song (*Hal Leonard Student Piano Library, Piano Solos 4* HAL)

Blok, Vladimir
Twelve Pieces in Folk Modes FHM
- A Little Ballad

Bonis, Mel.
Album pour les tout-petites COM
- ▶ Madrigal

Brown, Stephen
Five Extremities SWA
- Extremity no. 1

Byers, Rosemary
- Cheshire Cat Cool (*Hal Leonard Student Piano Library, Showcase Solos* HAL)

Caramia, Tony
- Porch Swing (*Hal Leonard Student Piano Library, Piano Solos 4* HAL)

Carroll, Walter
The Countryside FOR
- The Wood Fairies (no. 11)

Chatman, Stephen
Amusements, 2 FHM
- Ping Pong Party

Coulthard, Jean
- Alexa's Bell Song (*Music of Our Time, 1* WAT)
- Alexa's Music Box (*Music of Our Time, 1* WAT)
- First Little Dance (Lavender's Blue) (*Music of Our Time, 1* WAT)
- Grandmother's Nonsense Song (*Music of Our Time, 2* WAT)
- Lullaby for a Baby Seal (*Music of Our Time, 2* WAT)

Crosby, Anne
In My Dreams FHM
- Can't Catch Me!
In the Mermaid's Garden FHM
- ▶ The Banshee's Ball

Duke, David
- Butterflies (*Music of Our Time, 3* WAT)

Frid, Grigori
Youthful Adventures FHM
- I'm Sad
- The Teddy Bear

Garścia, Janina
Very Easy Piano Pieces for Children, op. 3 PWM
- ▶ The Clock
- A Joke (Zarcik)

Grechaninov, Alexandr T.
Children's Album, op. 98 OTT
- Farewell (no. 4)
Glass Beads, op. 123 OTT
- Little Beggar (no. 2)

Harmer, Daniel
- The Toy-maker BER

Joachim, Otto
12 Twelve Tone Pieces for Children BER
- Snowy Morning (no. 4)
- Gossip (no. 7)

Kabalevsky, Dmitri
30 Pieces for Children, op. 27 SCH
- Valse (no. 1)
- ▶ A Little Song (no. 2)

Khachaturian, Aram
24 Easy Piano Pieces for Children
- An Evening Tale

Kraehenbuehl, David
   ● March of the Trolls (*Contemporary Piano Literature*, 1 ALF)

Last, Joan
On the Move B&H
   ▶ Sailing by Moonlight

Lea, William
   ● Popcorn (*Meet Canadian Composers at the Piano*, 1 GVT [OP])

Mana Zucca (pseud. Augusta Zuckermann)
   ● A Slumber Song, op. 63, no. 6 JCC

Mrozinski, Mark
   ▶ Turkish Bazaar (*Celebrate Piano!*®, Lesson and Musicianship 4 FHM)

Nakada, Yoshinao
Children's Dreams KAW
   ▶ So Long, See You Tomorrow
Japanese Festival WAR
   ● A Short Story

Niamath, Linda
All Year Round FHM
   ▶ Autumn Leaves
A Zoo for You FHM
   ▶ Penguins

Norton, Christopher
Christopher Norton Connections for Piano™, 2 FHM
   ● Sidewalk Café
   ● Toronto Tango
   ● Trumpet Blues
The Microjazz Collection, 1 B&H
   ▶ Rag Time

Paterson, Lorna
Pianimals FHM
   ● Clown Fish

Perry, Nina
Through the Kaleidoscope OUP
   ● Lullaby (no. 5)

Pinto, Octavio
Festa de Crianças (Children's Festival) SCH
   ● Prelude (no. 1)

Poole, Clifford
   ▶ The Mouse in the Coal Bin (first published under pseudonym Charles Peerson) (*Legacy Collection*, 2 FHM)
   ● Parade (*Legacy Collection*, 2 FHM)

Reinecke, Carl
Serenade in G major, op. 183, no. 2
   ● Elegy (*Discovering Piano Literature*, 3 ALF)

Schumann, Robert
Album für die Jugend, op. 68
   ● Soldiers March (no. 2)

Stravinsky, Soulima
Piano Music for Children, 1 PET
   ● Tag

Szelényi, István
Musical Picture-Book EMB
   ▶ Faraway Regions

Tan, Chee-Hwa
A Child's Garden of Verses FHM
   ● The Land of Nod

Tansman, Alexandre
On s'amuse au piano / Happy Time, 1 WAR
   ● En Valsant / Waltzing

Tchaikovsky, Pyotr Il'yich
Album for the Young, op. 39
   ● The Sick Doll (no. 7)

Telfer, Nancy
I'm Not Scared FHM
   ▶ Skeleton Dance
Land of the Silver Birch FHM
   ● Land of the Silver Birch (arr.)
My Bark Canoe FHM
   ● Donkey Riding
Put On Your Dancing Shoes NSM
   ● Teaching a Bear to Waltz
The Sun and the Moon FHM
   ▶ The Silent Moon

List C

Inventions

Bartók, Béla
Mikrokosmos, 1 B&H
   ● Little Dance in Canon Form (no. 31)

Champagne, Claude
   ▶ Petit canon No. 2 CFP

Christopher, Renée
   ▶ Invention in C major

Dello Joio, Norman
Suite for the Young EDW
   ● Invention (on a Major and Minor Triadic Melody)

Gallant, Pierre
   ▶ Jazz Invention No. 1
   ▶ Jazz Invention No. 2
Imitations and Inventions FHM
   ● Changing Voices
   ● Lullaby for Two
   ● Mixolydian Mix-up

Gedike, Alexander
60 Piano Pieces for Beginners, op. 36 PET
   ● Fugato (no. 40)

Gurlitt, Cornelius
   ▶ Canon

Hässler, Johann Wilhelm
Fifty Pieces for Beginners, op. 38 ABR
   ▶ Moderato in C major (no. 5)

McKinnon, Gordon A.
   ▶ The Argument FHM

Niamath, Linda
Watermelon and Friends FHM
   ● Banana

Silvester, Frederick
   ▶ Invention in A minor

2 Technical Requirements

Studies / Etudes

Candidates must prepare *one* selection from the following list of studies / etudes. Memorization is *not* required and will not be rewarded with extra marks.

Bullets used to denote selections for examination purposes:
▶ selection is found in *Celebration Series Perspectives®: Piano Studies / Etudes 2* FHM

Czerny, Carl
▶ Study in C major, op. 261, no. 3

Donkin, Christine
Comics & Card Tricks FHM
▶ Crazy Comics

Gallant, Pierre
Clowning Around FHM
▶ Little Lopsided Waltz

Gurlitt, Cornelius
Die ersten Schritte des jungen Klavierspielers, op. 82
▶ Etude in D minor (no. 65)

Kabalevsky, Dmitri
24 Pieces for Children, op. 39 SCH
▶ Scherzo (no. 12)

Kadosa, Pál
Fourteen Little Pieces, in vol. 1 of *55 Small Piano Pieces* EMB
▶ Study in A minor

Köhler, Christian Louis Heinrich
Die allerleichtesten Übungsstücke für den Clavierunterricht, op. 190
▶ Study in F major (no. 27)

Krausas, Veronika
▶ Kangaroos

Niamath, Linda
All Year Round FHM
▶ Baseball Practice
▶ Celebration

Norton, Christopher
The Final Frontier B&H
▶ Asteroids

Tan, Chee-Hwa
A Child's Garden of Verses FHM
▶ The Wind

Telfer, Nancy
I'm Not Scared FHM
▶ Crocodile Teeth

Substitutions

Candidates may substitute *one* repertoire selection or *one* study / etude selection with a musical work *not found* in the Repertoire Lists for Grade 2. See p. 130 for more information on substitutions.

Total Substitutions Permitted	Requires Prior Approval (Submit an Examination Substitute Piece Request)		Does Not Require Prior Approval		
	Repertoire Substitution		**Repertoire Substitution**		**Study / Etude Substitution**
one Repertoire selection *or* *one* Study / Etude	One repertoire selection from piano literature comparable in style and difficulty to the corresponding List A or B of Grade 2	*or*	One repertoire selection from the corresponding List A or B only of Grade 3	*or*	One study / etude from Grade 3 *or* One Teacher's Choice selection (must be of equal difficulty and a length of 30–60 seconds)

Technical Tests

Candidates must play all Technical Tests from memory, ascending and descending, with good tone and logical fingering, at a steady tempo. Metronome markings indicate minimum speeds. All scales are to be played *legato* unless otherwise indicated.

See "Technical Patterns" on p. 19 for examples.

Keys for Grade 2   Major C G F B♭
                    Minor A E D G

Scales	Keys	Played	Tempo	Note values
Scales	C, G, F, B♭ major A, E, D, G minor (natural, harmonic, and melodic)	HS 2 octaves	♩ = 80	♫
Staccato	C, G, F, B♭ major	HS 1 octave	♩ = 80	♫
Parallel Motion	C, G major	HT 1 octave	♩ = 80	♫
Contrary Motion	G major	HT 2 octaves	♩ = 80	♫
Formula Pattern	C major	HT 2 octaves	♩ = 80	♫
Chromatic	beginning on C	HS 1 octave	♩ = 80	♫

Triads	Keys	Played	Tempo	Note values
Triads (root position and inversions) broken	C, G, F, B♭ major A E D G minor	HS 1 octave	♩ = 60	♫♫
solid (blocked)	C, G, F, B♭ major A E D G minor	HS 1 octave	♩ = 112	♩ 𝄾

3 Ear Tests

Clapback

Candidates will choose to either clap, tap, or sing the rhythm of a short melody after the examiner has played it *twice*.

Time signature	Approximate length
$\frac{2}{4}$, $\frac{3}{4}$	three to four measures

Example only
1

2

Intervals

Candidates will be asked to identify the following intervals. The examiner will play each interval *once* in broken form.
or
Candidates may choose to sing or hum the following intervals. The examiner will play the first note *once*.

Above a given note
major 3rd
perfect 5th

Playback

Candidates will be asked to play back a melody based on the first five notes of a major scale. The melody may include skips of a 3rd. The examiner will name the key, play the tonic triad *once*, and play the melody *twice*.

Beginning note	Approximate length	Keys
tonic or dominant	five notes	C, G, F major

Example only
1

2

4 Sight Reading

Playing

Candidates will be asked to play a passage that is divided between the hands and lies within the compass of the staff. The melody will include whole notes, half notes, quarter notes, and eighth notes.

Time signature	Approximate length	Keys
$\frac{4}{4}$	four measures	C, G, F major

Clapping

Candidates will be asked to clap or tap a rhythm. A steady pace and rhythmic accentuation are expected.

Time signature	Approximate length
$\frac{4}{4}$	two measures

Example only

Grade 3

At the Grade 3 level, candidates continue to explore Baroque dances as well as two- and three-part forms. Selections in List B introduce the Classical sonatina and its characteristic figures: scale passages, cadence patterns, and accompaniment styles. The *Popular Selection List* is also introduced, and candidates may substitute a popular selection for one study / etude.

	Grade 3 Requirements	Marks
1	**Repertoire**	**50**
	one selection from List A: Baroque Repertoire	18
	one selection from List B: Classical and Classical-style Repertoire	18
	one selection from List C: Romantic, 20th-, and 21st-century Repertoire	14
	Memory (2 marks per selection awarded for memory)	**6**
2	**Technical Requirements**	**24**
	Studies / Etudes: *two* studies / etudes from the *Syllabus* list	6 + 6
	Technical Tests	12
	Major keys: G D F B♭	
	Minor keys: E B D G	
	– scales	
	– *staccato* scales	
	– parallel motion scales	
	– formula pattern scale	
	– chromatic scale	
	– triads	
3	**Ear Tests**	**10**
	Clapback	3
	Intervals	3
	Playback	4
4	**Sight Reading**	**10**
	Playing	7
	Clapping	3
	Theory Co-requisites None	
	Total possible marks (pass = 60)	**100**

Resources for Grade 3 Examination Preparation

Repertoire: *Celebration Series Perspectives®: Piano Repertoire 3*

Studies / Etudes: *Celebration Series Perspectives®: Piano Studies / Etudes 3*

Technique: *Technical Requirements for Piano 3*

Popular Selections: *Popular Selection List*

Ear Training and Sight Reading: see p. 135 for ear-training and sight-reading resources.

Ear Training and Sight Reading: see p. 135 for ear-training and sight-reading resources.

> Visit **www.frederickharrismusic.com** for information about publications.

1 Repertoire

Candidates must prepare *three* contrasting selections: *one* from each of List A, List B, and List C. Repertoire selections must be memorized. Please note that up to two memory marks will be deducted for each selection if music is used.

Bullets used to denote selections for examination purposes:

- ● one selection
- ▲ part or section of a larger work
- ▶ selection is found in *Celebration Series Perspectives®: Piano Repertoire 3* FHM
- ▲ part or section of a larger work is found in *Celebration Series Perspectives®: Piano Repertoire 3* FHM

List A

Baroque Repertoire

Bach, Johann Sebastian
Notenbuch der Anna Magdalena Bach WIE
- ▶ Musette in D major, BWV Anh. 126 (attr.)
- ● Polonaise in G minor, BWV Anh. 119

Handel, George Frideric
- ● Air in D minor, HWV 461 (*Celebrate Handel* FHM)
- ▶ Gavotte in G major, HWV 491 (*Celebrate Handel* FHM)
- ● Minuet in F major HWV 516a (*Celebrate Handel* FHM)

Kirnberger, Johann Philipp
Recueil d'airs de danse caractéristiques
- ▶ Bourrée in D major (no. 3)

Krebs, Johann Ludwig
- ▶ Harlequinade

Mozart, Leopold
- ● Minuet in E minor (*Notebook for Wolfgang* OTT)

Petzold, Christian
- ▶ Minuet in G major, BWV Anh. 114 (*Notenbuch der Anna Magdalena Bach* WIE)
- ● Minuet in G minor, BWV Anh. 115 (*Notenbuch der Anna Magdalena Bach* WIE)

Purcell, Henry
- ▶ Hornpipe in B flat major, Z T683

List B

Classical and Classical-style Repertoire

Attwood, Thomas
Easy Progressive Lessons ABR
- Sonatina in G major

Beethoven, Ludwig van
Zwei Klaviersonatinen, Anh. 5 (*Celebrate Beethoven*,vol. I FHM)
- Sonatina in G major (attr.)
  - 1st movement *or* 2nd movement: Romanze

Biehl, Albert
- Sonatina in G major, op. 57, no. 4
  - 1st *or* 2nd movement (*The Easiest Sonatina Album* FHM)

Clementi, Muzio
- Sonatina in C major, op. 36, no. I
  - any *one* movement

Gedike, Alexander
60 Simple Piano Pieces for Beginners, op. 36
- Sonatina in C major (no. 20)

Gurlitt, Cornelius
Six Sonatinas, op. 76
- Sonatina in A minor (no. 5) (*Joy of Sonatinas* YOR)
  - 3rd movement

Hässler, Johann Wilhelm
Fifty Pieces for Beginners, op. 38
- Andantino in A major (no. 31)

Haydn, Franz Joseph
- German Dance in G Hob.IX:12/1 (*Celebrate Haydn*, vol. I FHM)

Mozart, Wolfgang Amadeus
- Allegro in B flat major, K 3 (*Celebrate Mozart*, vol. I FHM)
- Menuetto II in F major (from Sonata in C Major for Keyboard or Keyboard and Violin, K 6)
- Minuet in D major, K 7 (*Celebrate Mozart*, vol. I FHM)

Türk, Daniel Gottlob
Handstücke für angehende Klavierspieler, 1 ABR
- Carefree Happiness

List C

Romantic, 20th-, and 21st-century Repertoire

Alcon, Susan
Carefree Days FHM
- Summer at Last

Archer, Violet
Eleven Short Pieces ALK
- Little Canon (no. 9)

Bartók, Béla
For Children, 1 B&H
- Play (no. 5)
- Allegro moderato (no. 15)
For Children, 2 B&H
- Sorrow (no. 7)

Berkovich, Isaak
Discovering Piano Literature, 3 ALF
- Variations on a Russian Folksong

Berlin, Boris
- The Haunted Castle (*Legacy Collection*, 3 FHM)
- Rosemary Skating Waltz (*Legacy Collection*, 3 FHM)
Holiday in Canada MAY
- Prairie Song

Bernstein, Seymour
Moodscapes MAN
- The Elegant Toreador

Blok, Vladimir
Twelve Pieces in Folk Modes FHM
- Melancholy Song

Bonis, Mel.
Album pour les tout-petites COM
- Compliment à grand'maman
- Douce amie / Sweet Friend
- Monsieur Vieuxbois

Chatman, Stephen
- Echoes of November (*British Columbia Suite* FHM)

Coulthard, Jean
- A Little Joke (*Music of Our Time*, 1 WAT)
Early Pieces for Piano CMC; ALK
- The Song of the Shepherdess (no. 3)
- The Sad Story (no. 6)
- A Happy Day (no. 9)

Crawley, Clifford
Exchanges FHM
- Have a good day!
- Yes Sir!
- You're welcome

Crosby, Anne
In My Dreams FHM
- Funny Puppy
- In My Dreams
- Little Elves and Pixies
- The Stormy Sea

Fine, Irving
Music of Irving Fine B&H
- Lullaby for a Baby Panda

Fleming, Robert
- Happy Days (*Legacy Collection*, 3 FHM)

Fredrich, Frank
Cream of the Crop, 1 SUM
- Legerdemain (The Magician)

George, Jon
A Day in the Forest SUM
- Rain... and the Rainbow

Grechaninov, Alexandr T.
Children's Album, op. 98 SCH
- In Camp (no. 2)
- In the Woodland Glade (no. 6)
- Cradle Song (Lullaby) (no. 9)
- A Little Dance (no. 10)
- ▶ After the Ball (no. 13)
Glass Beads, op. 123 SCH
- Morning Walk (no. 1)
- Sad Song (no. 4)

Gurlitt, Cornelius
Little Flowers, op. 205 ABR
- Little Flower in E minor (no. 1)

Huang, An-Lun
A Chinese Festival, 1 BEL
- Pastures

Joachim, Otto
12 Twelve Tone Pieces for Children BER
- Plastic Soldier (no. 5)

Kabalevsky, Dmitri
30 Pieces for Children, op. 27 SCH
- Night on the River
24 Pieces for Children, op. 39 SCH
- ▶ Clowns (no. 20)

Lea, William
- Snoopy (*Meet Canadian Composers at the Piano*, 2 GVT [OP])

Liebermann, Lowell
Album for the Young PRE
- Song (no. 11)

Linn, Jennifer
- Tarantella HAL

Milhaud, Darius
L'enfant aime / A Child Loves, op. 289 UNI
- Les fleurs / Flowers

Moss, Earle
- In a Canoe (*Legacy Collection*, 3 FHM)
- Little Lamb (*Legacy Collection*, 3 FHM)

Nakada, Yoshinao
Japanese Festival WAR
- A Green Caterpillar and a Butterfly
- ▶ The Song of Twilight

Niamath, Linda
Here We Go! FHM
- Carousel

Norton, Christopher
Christopher Norton Connections for Piano™, 3 FHM
- Breezy
- Gentle Touch
- Up and Away
- ▶ White Sand
The Microjazz Collection, 2 B&H
- ▶ Coconut Rag

Ouchterlony, David
- Kickin' Stones (*Legacy Collection*, 2 FHM)

Paterson, Lorna
Pianimals FHM
- Doves
- Waltzing Pandas
- Whale's Lament

Persichetti, Vincent
Little Piano Book, op. 60 ELK
- Dialogue (no. 3)

Poole, Clifford
- Pop Goes the Weasel! (*Legacy Collection*, 5 FHM)

Schumann, Robert
Album für die Jugend, op. 68
- Melody (no. 1)

Scott, Cyril
For My Young Friends MAS
- Seesaw

Shostakovich, Dmitri
Six Children's Pieces, op. 69 SCH
- A Happy Tale (no. 4)

Siegmeister, Elie
- Street Games (*Contemporary Piano Literature*, 2 ALF)

Stravinsky, Soulima
Piano Music for Children, 1 PET
- Cops and Robbers

Tansman, Alexandre
Pour les enfants, 1 ESC
- Figurines de Sèvres / Dresden China Figures
- Le petit ours en peluche / The Dancing Bear

Taranta, Italo
- Folk Dance (*Hal Leonard Student Piano Library, Piano Solos* 4 HAL)

Tarp, Svend Erik
Mosaik, op. 31 MMB
- Flute and Bassoon Play a Duet (no. 6)

Tchaikovsky, Pyotr Il'yich
Album for the Young, op. 39
- ▶ Morning Prayer (no. 1)

Tcherepnin, Alexander
- Prelude SUM

Telfer, Nancy
I'm Not Scared FHM
- Giant Insects
- ▶ The Sleeping Dragon
Land of the Silver Birch FHM
- À la claire fontaine
Planets and Stars FHM
- Star Cluster

2 Technical Requirements

Studies / Etudes

Candidates must prepare *two contrasting* selections from the following list of studies / etudes. Memorization is *not* required and will not be rewarded with extra marks.

Bullets used to denote selections for examination purposes:
▶ selection is found in *Celebration Series Perspectives®*: *Piano Studies / Etudes 3* FHM

Bartók, Béla
The First Term at the Piano EMB
▶ Minuet

Bonis, Mel.
Album pour les tout-petits COM
▶ Marionnettes

Burgmüller, Johann Friedrich
25 Études faciles et progressives, op. 100
▶ Arabesque (no. 2)

Carroll, Walter
The Countryside: First Piano Lessons, 2 FOR
▶ The Village Band

Czerny, Carl
▶ Study in C major, op. 261, no. 81
▶ Study in D minor, op. 261, no. 53
▶ Study in E flat major, op. 139, no. 49

Donkin, Christine
Comics & Card Tricks FHM
▶ Computer Chatter
Legends & Lore FHM
▶ Witches and Wizards

Fitch, Gem
▶ Chinese Kites

Gurlitt, Cornelius
Technik und Melodie Elementar-Klavierschule, op. 228
▶ Study in A minor

Niamath, Linda
Fancy Free FHM
▶ Bike Ride
Here We Go! FHM
▶ All Aboard!

Norton, Christopher
The Microjazz Collection, 1 B&H
▶ Inter-city Stomp

Paterson, Lorna
Just a Second! FHM
▶ Rush Hour

Schytte, Ludwig
25 kleinen Etüden, op. 108
▶ Study in A minor (no. 5)

Telfer, Nancy
Planets and Stars FHM
▶ The Milky Way

> Candidates may substitute a popular selection for one of the studies / etudes. See p. 130 for details.

Substitutions

Candidates may substitute *one* repertoire selection or *one* study / etude selection with a musical work *not found* in the Repertoire Lists for Grade 3. See p. 130 for more information on substitutions.

Total Substitutions Permitted	Requires Prior Approval (Submit an Examination Substitute Piece Request)		Does Not Require Prior Approval		
	Repertoire Substitution		**Repertoire Substitution**		**Study / Etude Substitution**
one Repertoire selection *or* *one* Study / Etude	One repertoire selection from piano literature comparable in style and difficulty to the corresponding List A, B, or C of Grade 3	*or*	One selection from the corresponding List of Grade 4	*or*	One study / etude from Grade 4 *or* One Teacher's Choice selection (must be of equal difficulty and a length of 1–1.5 minutes) *or* One selection from the *Popular Selection List* for Grade 3 or Grade 4

46

Technical Tests

Candidates must play all Technical Tests from memory, ascending and descending, with good tone and logical fingering, at a steady tempo. Metronome markings indicate minimum speeds. All scales are to be played *legato* unless otherwise indicated.

See "Technical Patterns" on p. 19 for examples.

Keys for Grade 3   Major G, D, F, B♭
Minor E, B, D, G

Scales	Keys	Played	Tempo	Note values
Scales	G, D, F, B♭ major E, B, D, G minor (harmonic and melodic)	HS 2 octaves	♩ = 92	♫
Staccato	G, D, F, B♭ major	HS 2 octaves	♩ = 92	♫
Parallel Motion	G, D, F, B♭ major E, B, D, G minor (harmonic and melodic)	HT 1 octave	♩ = 80	♫
Formula Pattern	G major	HT 2 octaves	♩ = 80	♫
Chromatic	beginning on G	HS 1 octave	♩ = 92	♫

Triads	Keys	Played	Tempo	Note values
Triads (root position and inversions) broken	G, D, F, B♭ major E, B, D, G minor	HS 2 octaves	♩ = 69	♫
		HT 1 octave	♩ = 50	♫
solid (blocked)	G, D, F, B♭ major E, B, D, G minor	HS 2 octaves	♩ = 120	♩ 𝄽

Grade 3

3 Ear Tests

Clapback

Candidates will choose to either clap, tap, or sing the rhythm of a short melody after the examiner has played it *twice*.

Time signature	Approximate length
$\frac{2}{4}$ $\frac{3}{4}$	four measures

Example only
1

2

Intervals

Candidates will be asked to identify the following intervals. The examiner will play each interval *once* in broken form.
or
Candidates may choose to sing or hum the following intervals. The examiner will play the first note *once*.

Above a given note	Below a given note
major 3rd	minor 3rd
perfect 5th	perfect 5th
perfect octave	

Playback

Candidates will be asked to play back a melody based on the first five notes of a major scale. The examiner will name the key, play the tonic triad *once*, and play the melody *twice*.

Beginning note	Approximate length	Keys
Tonic or mediant	five notes	C, G, D, F major

Example only
1

2

4 Sight Reading

Playing

Candidates will be asked to play a short passage, hands together. The right-hand part will be in quarter notes, half notes, or eighth notes; the left-hand part will be in whole notes and half notes.

Time signature	Approximate length	Keys
$\frac{4}{4}$	four measures	G, D, F major

Clapping

Candidates will be asked to clap or tap a rhythm. A steady pace and rhythmic accentuation are expected.

Time signature	Approximate length
$\frac{3}{4}$ $\frac{4}{4}$	four measures

Example only

Grade 4

At the Grade 4 level, candidates are exposed to new accompaniment styles, independent in Baroque repertoire, and an array of figurations in Classical sonatinas. Selections from the Romantic period focus on melody, balance, and expression, while those of the contemporary era offer interesting rhythmic challenges. The technical requirements are expanded to include arpeggios, and cadences at the ends of triads.

	Grade 4 Requirements	Marks
1	**Repertoire**	**50**
	one selection from List A: Baroque Repertoire	18
	one selection from List B: Classical and Classical-style Repertoire	18
	one selection from List C: Romantic, 20th-, and 21st-century Repertoire	14
	Memory (2 marks per selection awarded for memory)	**6**
2	**Technical Requirements**	**24**
	Studies / Etudes: *two* studies / etudes from the *Syllabus* list	6 + 6
	Technical Tests	12
	Major keys: D A B♭ E♭	
	Minor keys: B F♯ G C	
	– parallel motion scales	
	– *staccato* scales	
	– formula pattern scale	
	– chromatic scale	
	– triads	
	– tonic arpeggios	
3	**Ear Tests**	**10**
	Clapback	3
	Intervals	3
	Playback	4
4	**Sight Reading**	**10**
	Playing	7
	Clapping	3
	Theory Co-requisites None	
	Total possible marks (pass = 60)	**100**

Resources for Grade 4 Examination Preparation

Repertoire: *Celebration Series Perspectives®: Piano Repertoire 4*

Studies / Etudes: *Celebration Series Perspectives®: Piano Studies / Etudes 4*

Technique: *Technical Requirements for Piano 4*

Popular Selections: *Popular Section List*

Ear Training and Sight Reading: see p. 135 for ear-training and sight-reading resources.

Visit **www.frederickharrismusic.com** for information about publications.

1 Repertoire

Candidates must prepare *three* contrasting selections: *one* from each of List A, List B, and List C. Repertoire selections must be memorized. Please note that up to two memory marks will be deducted for each section where music is used.

Bullets used to denote selections for examination purposes:

- ● one selection
- ▲ part or section of a larger work
- ▶ selection is found in *Celebration Series Perspectives®: Piano Repertoire 4 FHM*
- ◣ part or section of a larger work is found in *Celebration Series Perspectives®: Piano Repertoire 4 FHM*

List A
Baroque Repertoire

Babell, William
- ▶ Rigadoon in A minor

Bach, Carl Philipp Emanuel
- ▶ March in D major, BWV Anh. 122 (*Notenbuch der Anna Magdalena Bach* WEI)

Bach, Johann Sebastian
- ● English Suite no. 3 in G minor, BWV 808
  - ▲ Musette
Notenbuch der Anna Magdalena Bach WEI
- ● Minuet in F major, BWV Anh. 113
- ● Minuet in G major, BWV Anh. 116
- ● Minuet in C minor, BWV Anh. 121
- ▶ Minuet in D minor, BWV Anh. 132 (attr.)

Handel, George Frideric
- ▶ Air in D minor, HWV 461
- ● Air in B flat major, HWV 471 (*Celebrate Handel* FHM)
- ● Sonata in G major, op. 1, no. 5, HWC 363b
  - ▲ Bourrée (*Celebrate Handel* FHM)

Hässler, Johann Wilhelm
Fifty Pieces for Beginners, op. 38
- ▶ Allegro in E minor (no. 24)

Mozart, Wolfgang Amadeus
- ● Minuet in D major, K 94/37h (*Mozart: Piano Music from His Early Years* ALF)

Scarlatti, Domenico
- ● Sonata in D minor, L 423, K 32 (*Celebrate Scarlatti, vol. I* FHM)

Stölzel, Gottfried Heinrich
- ● Partita in G minor (*Clavierbüchlein vor Wilhelm Friedemann Bach* BAR)
  - ▲ Italian Air

Telemann, Georg Philipp
- ● Fantasia in E minor, TWV 33:21
  - ▲ 3rd section: Très vite
- ● Fantasia in G major, TWV 33:7
  - ▲ 2nd section: Largo

List B

Classical and Classical-style Repertoire

André, Johann Anton
- Sonatina in C major, op. 34, no. 1
  - 3rd movement: Rondo
- Sonatina in F major, op. 34, no. 5
  - 3rd movement: Rondo

Beethoven, Ludwig van
Twelve German Dances, WoO13 OTT; SCH
- No. 9 in E flat major

Biehl, Albert
- Sonatina in A minor, op. 94, no. 4
  - 1st movement

Clementi, Muzio
- Sonatina in G major, op. 36, no. 2
  - 2nd movement *or*
  - 3rd movement

Diabelli, Anton
- Sonatina in G major, op. 151, no. 1
  - *one* movement
- Sonatina in F major, op. 168, no. 1
  - 1st movement

Gurlitt, Cornelius
Six Sonatinas, op. 188
- Sonatina in G major (no. 3)
  - 1st movement

Haydn, Franz Joseph
- Sonata in F major, Hob. XVI:9
  - 3rd movement: Scherzo

Mayer, Charles
- Exercise (Übungsstück), op. 340, no. 2 (*A Romantic Sketchbook for Piano*, 2 ABR; *Graded Pianoforte Studies, First Series, Grade 3* ABR)

Melartin, Erkki
- Sonatina

Schmitt, Jacob
- Sonatina in G major, op. 83, no. 1
  - 2nd movement
- Sonatina in G major, op. 249, no. 2
  - 1st movement

Türk, Daniel Gottlob
Sixty Pieces for Aspiring Players, 1 ABR
- German Song

Wesley, Samuel
- Sonatina in B flat major, op. 4, no. 8

List C

Romantic, 20th-, and 21st-century Repertoire

Alcon, Susan
Wind Chimes FHM
- Feeling Lucky

Archer, Violet
- Waltzing Along (*Rainbows* ALK)
Eleven Short Pieces ALK
- Rondino (no. 4)
- Wide Open Spaces (no. 5)

Barrell, Bernard
Five Bagatelles, op. 87 FRE
- Intrada (no. 1) (*Studio 21*, 2 UNI)

Bartók, Béla
For Children, 1 B&H
- Children's Game (no. 8)
- Allegretto (no. 22)
- Allegro non troppo (no. 33)
For Children, 2 B&H
- Andante, molto rubato (no. 28)
- Dance (no. 8)
- The Highway Robber (no. 31)
- Farewell (no. 34)

Benedict, Robert C.
Watercolours for Piano WAT
- Shallows

Berlin, Boris
- Monkeys in the Tree (*Meet Canadian Composers at the Piano*, 1 GVT [OP])
- Squirrels at Play (*Legacy Collection*, 3 FHM)
- Yanina Polish Dance (*Legacy Collection*, 3 FHM)

Berr, Bruce
Explorations in Style HAL
- Droplets

Boyd, Bill
Bill Boyd: Jazz Sketches HAL
- Home Fried Potatoes

Burgmüller, Johann Friedrich Franz
- Ballade, op. 100, no. 15

Champagne, Claude
- Petit scherzo (*Meet Canadian Composers at the Piano*, 2 GVT [OP])

Chatman, Stephen
Amusements, 3 FHM
- Game of Hypnosis

Coulthard, Jean
Four Piano Pieces BER
- Pleading

Crosby, Anne
In the Mermaid's Garden FHM
- Dreamcatcher

50

Decoursey, Ralph
- ⬤ Steamboat's A-Comin'! BER

Dello Joio, Norman
Suite for the Young EDW
- ⬤ Little Brother (no. 4)
- ⬤ Small Fry (no. 11)

Duke, David
- ▶ Barcarole (*Music of Our Time, 4* WAT)

Evans, Lee
- ⬤ Spooky Spirits (*Hal Leonard Student Piano Library, Showcase Solos* HAL)

Fiala, George
- ⬤ Mood in the Dorian Mode (*Horizons, 1* WAT)
- ⬤ Miniature Suite BER
  - ▲ Almost a Waltz

Filtz, Bohdana
- ⬤ A Lost Toy (*Ukrainian Echoes* FHM)
- ⬤ Playing Ball (*Childhood Memories* FHM)

Gillock, William L.
Lyric Preludes in Romantic Style SUM
- ⬤ Interlude

Goldston, Margaret
The Magic Typewriter ECS
- ⬤ The Magic Typewriter

Grechaninov, Alexandr T.
Grandfather's Album, op. 119 OTT
- ⬤ An Old Romance (no. 2)
- ⬤ On the Meadow (no. 4)
- ▶ Happy Meeting (no. 15)
- ⬤ Returning Home (no. 16)

Gurlitt, Cornelius
Der erste Vortrag, op. 210
- ▶ Dancing on the Green
Little Flowers, op. 205 ABR
- ⬤ Little Flower in F major (no. 8)

Hanson, Howard
- ⬤ Enchantment FIS

Haughton, Alan
Rhythm and Rag ABR
- ⬤ Freeway

Ishchenko, Yuri
- ⬤ Trembitas in the Distance (*Ukrainian Echoes* FHM)

Kabalevsky, Dmitri
30 Pieces for Children, op. 27 SCH
- ⬤ A Sad Story (no. 6) (also titled "A Sad Little Tale")
- ⬤ Dance on the Lawn (no. 17)
24 Pieces for Children, op. 39 SCH
- ⬤ Hopping (no. 18) (also titled "Galop")
Children's Adventures, op. 89
- ▶ Chastushka (no. 25)

Kirchner, Theodor Fürchtegott
New Scenes of Childhood, op. 55 ABR
- ⬤ Andantino (no. 3)

Kisbey-Hicks, Marjory
- ⬤ Three-legged Race BER

Klein, Lothar
Spring Folio CMC
- ⬤ Ballet Lesson
- ⬤ Dots

Klose, Carol
- ⬤ Dance of the Trolls (*Hal Leonard Student Piano Library, Showcase Solos* HAL)

Lea, William
- ⬤ One-Two-Three O'Leary (*Meet Canadian Composers at the Piano, 2* GVT [OP])
- ⬤ On the Mountain Stands a Lady (*Meet Canadian Composers at the Piano, 2* GVT [OP])

Linn, Jennifer
- ⬤ Wizard's Wish (*Hal Leonard Student Piano Library, Showcase Solos* HAL)

Maikapar, Samuil
- ⬤ Dewdrops, op. 33, no. 12 MCA

Milhaud, Darius
L'enfant aime / A Child Loves, op. 289 UNI
- ⬤ Les bonbons / Candy

Muczynski, Robert
Fables: Nine Pieces for the Young, op. 21 SCH
- ▶ Fable (no. 3)

Nakada, Yoshinao
Children's Dreams
- ▶ A Winter Melody KAW

Norton, Christopher
Christopher Norton Connections for Piano™, 4 FHM
- ⬤ Deep in Thought
- ⬤ Open Window
- ⬤ Positively Swinging
The Microjazz Collection, 2 B&H
- ▶ Play It Again

Olson, Lynn Freeman
Audience Pleasers, 3 ALF
- ⬤ Whirligig

Papp, Lajos
Images LEM
- ▶ The Rooster Crows

Paterson, Lorna
Just a Second FHM
- ⬤ Lullaby
Pianimals FHM
- ⬤ The Loon

Pearce, Elvina
Seven Preludes in Seven Keys BEL
- ⬤ Prelude no. 2 in D minor

Pentland, Barbara
Music of Now, 3 AVO; CMC
- Aubade

Pozzoli, Ettore
Piccole scintille RIC
- The Cuckoo (no. 6)
- Before the Crib (no. 7)
- Soldier's March (no. 12)

Rebikov, Vladimir Ivanovich
Silhouettes, op. 31 ALF; SCH
- The Little Shepherd (no. 8)

Reubart, Dale
Parodies FHM
- Thinguma Jig

Schumann, Robert
Album für die Jugend, op. 68
- The Wild Horseman (no. 8)
- The Happy Farmer (no. 10)
- The First Loss (no. 16)

Sheftel, Paul
Interludes: Mood Studies for Piano FIS
- Nocturne

Shostakovich, Dmitri
Six Children's Pieces, op. 69 SCH
- A Sad Fairy Tale (no. 5)

Silvester, Frederick
- Twilight (*Legacy Collection*, 3 FHM)

Starer, Robert
Games with Names, Notes and Numbers SCH
- Twelve Notes Twelve Times

Szelényi, István
Vierzig kleine Klavierstücke für Anfänger, 2 EMB
- Changing Bars

Tansman, Alexandre
On s'amuse au piano / Happy Time, 1 WAR
- Little Prelude
- Mélodie
Pour les enfants, 1 ESC
- Fin de vacances
Pour les enfants, 2 ESC
- Petite solemnité
Pour les enfants, 3 ESC
- Réveil (no. l)

Taranta, Italo
Piano Miniatures WIL
- Creole Lullaby

Tchaikovsky, Pyotr Il'yich
Album for the Young, op. 39
- The Doll's Funeral (no. 7)
- Italian Song (no. 15)
- Old French Song (no. 16)

Telfer, Nancy
She's Like the Swallow FHM
- Feller from Fortune (arr.)

Vandall, Robert D.
Bagatelles, 1 MYK
- Bagatelle no. 8

Zhuravytsky, Vadim
- The Detective (*Postcards from Ukraine* FHM)

Substitutions

Candidates may substitute *one* repertoire selection or *one* study / etude selection with a musical work *not found* in the Repertoire Lists for Grade 4. See p. 130 for more information on substitutions.

Total Substitutions Permitted	*Requires* Prior Approval (Submit an Examination Substitute Piece Request)		*Does Not Require* Prior Approval		
	Repertoire Substitution		Repertoire Substitution		Study / Etude Substitution
one Repertoire selection *or* *one* Study / Etude	One repertoire selection from piano literature comparable in style and difficulty to the corresponding List A, B, or C of Grade 4	*or*	One selection from the corresponding List of Grade 5	*or*	One study / etude from Grade 5 *or* One Teacher's Choice selection (must be of equal difficulty and a length of 1–1.5 minutes) *or* One selection from the *Popular Selection List* for Grade 4 or Grade 5

2 Technical Requirements

Studies / Etudes

Candidates must prepare *two contrasting* selections from the following list of studies / etudes. Memorization is *not* required and will not be rewarded with extra marks.

Bullets used to denote selections for examination purposes:
▶ selection is found in *Celebration Series Perspectives*®: *Piano Studies / Etudes 4* FHM

Balázs, Árpád
Fourteen Pieces for Piano EMB
▶ Game

Bonis, Mel.
Album pour les tout-petits COM
▶ La toupie / The Top

Burgmüller, Johann Friedrich
25 Études faciles et progressives, op. 100
▶ The Wagtail (no. 11)

Chatman, Stephen
Preludes for Piano, 3 FHM
▶ Hotshot

Crawley, Clifford
Exchanges FHM
▶ You're Joking!

Czerny, Carl
▶ Study in B flat major, op. 599, no. 83

Duvernoy, Jean-Baptiste
Elementary Studies, op. 176
▶ Study in A major (no. 15)
▶ Study in C major (no. 24)

Gillock, William L.
Lyric Preludes in Romantic Style SUM
▶ Dragon Fly

Hässler, Johann Wilhelm
Cinquante pièces à l'usage des commensans, op. 38
▶ Allegro in G major (no. 19)

Heller, Stephen
25 Études faciles, op. 45
▶ The Avalanche (no. 2)

Loeschhorn, Carl Albert
Etuden für Anfanger, op. 65
▶ Study in E minor (no. 42)

Niamath, Linda
Fancy Free FHM
▶ Masquerade

Norton, Christopher
The Microjazz Collection, 2 B&H
▶ Blues No. 1

Reubart, Dale
Kaleidoscope FHM
▶ Bike Ride

Candidates may substitute a popular selection for one of the studies / etudes. See p. 130 for details.

Technical Tests

Candidates must play all Technical Tests from memory, ascending and descending, with good tone and logical fingering, at a steady tempo. Metronome markings indicate minimum speeds. All scales are to be played *legato* unless otherwise indicated.

See "Technical Patterns" on p. 19 for examples.

Keys for Grade 4   Major D, A, B♭, E♭
                    Minor B, F♯, G, C

Scale	Keys	Played	Tempo	Note values
Parallel Motion	D, A, B♭, E♭ major B, F♯, G, C minor (harmonic and melodic)	HT 2 octaves	♩ = 92	♫
Staccato	D, B♭ major B, G minor (harmonic)	HS 2 octaves	♩ = 104	♫
Formula Pattern	C minor (harmonic)	HT 2 octaves	♩ = 92	♫
Chromatic	beginning on D	HS 1 octave	♩ = 104	♫

Chords	Keys	Played	Tempo	Note values
Triads (root position and inversions) broken	D, A, B♭, E♭ major B, F♯, G, C minor	HS 2 octaves (no cadence)	♩ = 76	♫
		HT 1 octave (ending with V–I cadence)	♩ = 60	♫
solid (blocked)	D, A, B♭, E♭ major B, F♯, G, C minor	HS 2 octaves (no cadence)	♩ = 132	♩ 𝄽
		HT 1 octave (ending with V–I cadence)	♩ = 120	♩ 𝄽

Arpeggios	Keys	Played	Tempo	Note values
Tonic (root position only)	D, A major G, C minor	HS 2 octaves	♩ = 72	♫

3 Ear Tests

Clapback

Candidates will choose to either clap, tap, or sing the rhythm of a short melody after the examiner has played it *twice*.

Time signature	Approximate length
$\frac{2}{4}$ $\frac{6}{8}$	two to three

Example only

Intervals

Candidates will be asked to identify the following intervals. The examiner will play each interval *once* in broken form.
or
Candidates may choose to sing or hum the following intervals. The examiner will play the first note *once*.

Above a given note	Below a given note
major and minor 3rds	minor 3rd
perfect 4th	
perfect 5th	perfect 5th
perfect octave	perfect octave

Playback

Candidates will be asked to play back a melody based on the first five notes of a major scale. The examiner will name the key, play the tonic triad *once*, and play the melody *twice*.

Beginning note	Approximate length	Keys
tonic, mediant, or dominant	six notes	C, F, G, D major

Example only

Visit **www.frederickharrismusic.com** for information about publications.

4 Sight Reading

Playing

Candidates will be asked to play a short passage, hands together. The right-hand part will be in eighth notes, quarter notes, or half notes; the left-hand part will be in half notes.

Difficulty	Time signature	Approximate length	Keys
Grade 1 repertoire	$\frac{4}{4}$ $\frac{3}{4}$	six measures	G, F, D major E, D minor

Clapping

Candidates will be asked to clap or tap the rhythm of a melody. A steady pace and rhythmic accentuation are expected.

Time signature	Approximate length
$\frac{3}{4}$ $\frac{4}{4}$	four measures

Example only

Grade 5

At the Grade 5 level, candidates encounter longer and more varied forms as well as ornamentation, thicker harmonic textures, and an increasingly sophisticated interplay of melody and accompaniment. Technical requirements expand the candidate's harmonic vocabulary to include dominant 7th and diminished 7th chords.

	Grade 5 Requirements	Marks
1	**Repertoire**	**50**
	one selection from List A: Baroque Repertoire	18
	one selection from List B: Classical and Classical-style Repertoire	18
	one selection from List C: Romantic, 20th-, and 21st-century Repertoire	14
	Memory (2 marks per selection awarded for memory)	**6**
2	**Technical Requirements**	**24**
	Studies / Etudes: *two* studies / etudes from the *Syllabus* list	6 + 6
	Technical Tests	12
	Major keys: A E E♭ A♭	
	Minor keys: F♯ C♯ C F	
	– parallel motion scales	
	– *staccato* scales	
	– formula pattern scales	
	– chromatic scale	
	– triads	
	– dominant 7th and diminished 7th chords	
	– tonic arpeggios	
3	**Ear Tests**	**10**
	Clapback	3
	Intervals	3
	Playback	4
4	**Sight Reading**	**10**
	Playing	7
	Clapping	3
	Theory Co-requisites	
	Basic Rudiments [Preliminary Rudiments]	
	Total possible marks (pass = 60)	**100**

Resources for Grade 5 Examination Preparation

Repertoire: *Celebration Series Perspectives®: Piano Repertoire 5*

Studies / Etudes: *Celebration Series Perspectives®: Piano Studies / Etudes 5*

Technique: *Technical Requirements for Piano 5*

Popular Selections: *Popular Selection List*

Ear Training and Sight Reading: see p. 135 for ear-training and sight-reading resources.

1 Repertoire

Candidates must prepare *three* contrasting selections: *one* from each of List A, List B, and List C. Repertoire selections must be memorized. Please not that up to two memory marks will be deducted for each selection where music is used.

Bullets used to denote selections for examination purposes:

- ◉ one selection
- ▲ part or section of a larger work
- ▶ selection is found in *Celebration Series Perspectives®: Piano Repertoire 5* FHM
- ▲ part or section of a larger work is found in *Celebration Series Perspectives®: Piano Repertoire 5* FHM

List A
Baroque Repertoire

Arnold, Samuel
- ◉ Sonata in D major, op. 12, bk 2, no. 3 (*English Piano Music 1780–1800* ABR)
- ▲ 2nd movement: Siciliana

Bach, Carl Philipp Emanuel
- ◉ March in G major, BWV Anh. 124 (*Notenbuch der Anna Magdalena Bach* WEI)

Bach, Johann Christoph Friedrich
Musikalische Nebenstunden ABR
- ◉ Angloise in D major

Bach, Johann Sebastian
- ▶ Allemande in G minor, BWV 836
- ◉ French Suite no. 6 in E major, BWV 817
  - ▲ Minuet
- ▶ Little Prelude in C major, BWV 939

Dieupart, Charles
Six suittes de clavessin (1701)
- ◉ Suite no. 2 in D major
  - ▲ Passepied

Graupner, Christoph
- ◉ Intrada in C major (*Baroque Piano* ALF)

Handel, George Frideric
- ◉ Fuga (Sonatina) in G major, HWV 582 (*Celebrate Handel* FHM)
- ◉ Sonatina in B flat major, HWV 585 (*Celebrate Handel* FHM)

Kirnberger, Johann Philipp
Recueil d'airs de danse caractéristiques
- ▶ Gigue in D major (no. 10)

Rameau, Jean-Philippe
Pièces de clavecin (1724)
- ◉ Suite no. 1
  - ▲ Deux rigaudons

56

Scarlatti, Domenico
- Sonata in C minor, L 357, K 40 (*Celebrate Scarlatti, vol. I* FHM)
- Sonata in D minor, LS 7, K 34 (*Celebrate Scarlatti, vol. I* FHM)
- Sonata in B flat, LS 36, K42 (*Celebrate Scarlatti, vol. I* FHM)

Stölzel, Gottfried Heinrich
Partita (*Clavierbüchlein vor Wilhelm Friedemann Bach* BAR)
- ▶ Bourrée in G minor

Telemann, Georg Philipp
- Fantasia in C major, TWV 33:14
  - ▲ 2nd section: Gaiment in C major
- Fantasia in E flat major, TWV 33:35
  - ▲ 2nd section: Moderato in C minor

Zipoli, Domenico
Sonate d'intavolatura per organo e cimbalo, parte prima, op. 1
- ▶ Verso in E minor

List B

Classical and Classical-style Repertoire

Bach, Johann Christoph Friedrich
Musikalische Nebenstunden ABR
- ▶ Allegretto in F major

Beethoven, Ludwig van
- Minuet in G major, WoO 10, no. 2 (*Celebrate Beethoven, vol. I* FHM)
Zwei Klaviersonatinen, Anh. 5
- Sonatina in F major
  - ▲ 1st *or* 2nd movement
Twelve German Dances, WoO13 OTT; SCH
- No. 1 in D major
- No. 5 in F major

Cimarosa, Domenico
- Sonata no. 17 in D minor (*Melodious Masterpieces, 3* ALF)

Clementi, Muzio
- Sonatina in G major, op. 36, no. 2
  - ▲ 1st movement
- Sonatina in C major, op. 36, no. 3
  - ▲ 3rd movement
- Sonatina in G major, op. 36, no. 5
  - ▲ 3rd movement: Rondo

Diabelli, Anton
- Sonatina in F major, op. 168, no. 1
  - ▲ 2nd movement
- Sonatina in G major, op. 168, no. 2
  - ▲ 1st movement
- Sonatina in C major, op. 168, no. 3
  - ▲ 1st *or* 3rd movement

Gurlitt, Cornelius
Four Sonatinas, op. 214
- ▶ Sonatina in A minor, op. 214, no. 4
  - ▲ 1st movement *or*
  - ▲ 2nd *and* 3rd movements

Hässler, Johann Wilhelm
Fifty Pieces for Beginners, op. 38 ABR
- Capriccio in C major

Haydn, Franz Joseph
- Divertimento in G major, Hob. XVI:8
  - ▲ 1st movement *or*
  - ▲ 3rd *and* 4th movements

Kuhlau, Friedrich
- Six Variations in G major, op. 42, no. 1

Lichner, Heinrich
- Sonatina in F major, op. 4, no. 2 KJO; SCH
  - ▲ 1st movement

Mozart, Wolfgang Amadeus
- Minuet in F major, K 5
Viennese Sonatinas, K 439b
- Viennese Sonatina no. 1 in C major
  - ▲ Minuetto and Trio

Spindler, Fritz
- Sonatina in C major, op. 157, no. 4 ALF
  - ▲ 2nd movement

Wesley, Samuel
- Sonata in A major, op. 5, no. 1 (*English Piano Music 1780–1800* ABR)
  - ▲ 2nd movement: Waltz

List C

Romantic, 20th-, and 21st-century Repertoire

Agay, Denes
Petit Trianon Suite SCH
- Sarabande d'amour

Archer, Violet
Three Scenes (Habitant Sketches) BER
- ▶ Jig

Bartók, Béla
For Children, 1 B&H
- Children's Dance (no. 10)
- Ballad (no. 13)
- Moderato (no. 26)
- ▶ Jest (no. 27)
- Choral (no. 28)
For Children, 2 B&H
- Lento (no. 11)
- Teasing Song (no. 18)
- Romance (no. 19)
- Game of Tag (no. 20)

Beach, Amy
Children's Carnival, op. 25 HIL
- Pierrot and Pierrette (no. 4)

Grade 5

Beckwith, John
Six Mobiles, 2 BER
- Minor or Major?
- Two and Three are Five
- What Goes Up Must Come Down

Bortkiewicz, Sergei
Andersen's Fairy Tales, op. 30 SIM
- The Hardy Tin Soldier (no. 3)

Bruce, Robert
Picture Studies for the Piano CEL
- Rag Doll

Carroll, Walter
Sea Idylls FOR
- From the Cliffs (no. 1)
- Sea-Nymphs (no. 3)
- Moon Beams (no. 6)
- A Passing Storm (no. 7)
- To a Sea-Bird (no. 8)
- The Lifeboat (no. 9)
- Alone at Sunset (no. 10)

Chatman, Stephen
Preludes for Piano, 3 FHM
- Poltergeist

Cherney, Brian
- Elegy for a Misty Afternoon (*Horizons, 1* WAT)

Copland, Aaron
- Sunday Afternoon Music (*Masters of Our Day* FIS)

Coulthard, Jean
- The Rocking Chair (*Music of Our Time, 5* WAT)
- ▶ Star Gazing (*Music of Our Time, 6* WAT)
Four Piano Pieces BER
- Little Song of Long Ago

Creston, Paul
Five Little Dances SCH
- Rustic Dance (no. 1)

Eurina, Ludmilla
- Pastorale (*Town and Country* FHM)

Faith, Richard
Finger Paintings for Piano SHA
- Moonless Night

Fiala, George
Australian Suite, op. 2 BER
- Black Swan
- Emu
- Koala
- Lyre Byrd
- Platypus
Ten Postludes for Young Students, op. 7 WAT
- ▶ Postlude no. 6 (à la Shostakovich)

Filtz, Bohdana
- A Song about Grandmother (*Childhood Memories* FHM)

Fleming, Robert
Bag-o-Tricks WAT
- Gently (no. 1)

Frid, Grigori
A Day in the Country FHM
- Garmoshka
Russian Tales FHM
- Chastushka
- A Little Song

Gillock, William L.
Lyric Preludes in Romantic Style SUM
- Legend
- Serenade

Gretchaninov, Alexander
Glass Beads, op. 123 OTT
- Waltz

Grieg, Edvard
Lyric Pieces, op. 12
- ▶ Waltz (no. 2)

Griesdale, Susan
Piano Mime OCE
- Dancing Clowns
- Sleepwalking

Hansen, Joan
- Traffic (*Music of Our Time, 5* WAT)

Harmer, Daniel
- Hop, Skip and Jump BER

Haughton, Alan
Rhythm and Rag ABR
- Lazy

Huang, An-Lun
A Chinese Festival, 1 BEL
- Cradle Song

Ibert, Jacques
Petite suite en quinze images FOE
- Berceuses aux étoiles (no. 4)

Jaque, Rhené
- Marionnette / Puppet (*Meet Canadian Composers at the Piano, 2* GVT [OP])
- Rustic Dance GVT

Kabalevsky, Dmitri
30 Pieces for Children, op. 27 SCH
- Cradle Song (no. 8)
- Sonatina in A minor (no. 18)
24 Pieces for Children, op. 39 SCH
- ▶ A Slow Waltz (no. 23)
Easy Variations for Piano, op. 51
- Five Happy Variations on a Russian Folk Song (no. 1)

Karganov, Génari
- ▶ Arabesque, op. 6, no. 2

Kenins, Talivaldis
Two Little Pieces (*Meet Canadian Composers at the Piano, 2* GVT [OP])
- ▶ Little March
- Tenderness

Kirchner, Theodor F.
Miniaturen, op. 62 ABR
- Miniature in C minor (no. 15)

Koechlin, Charles
Dix petites pièces faciles, op. 61c SAL
- La maison heurese (no. 3)

Kuzmenko, Larysa
- ▶ Romance

Lebeda, Miroslav
Music for Young Pianists FHM
- March
- Mood

McLean, Edwin
Impressions on Rock, Bone, Wood, Earth FJH
- Bird Whistle (Bone)

Merath, Siegfried
Tanz-Typen, 1 OTT
- ▶ Cha-Cha

Mier, Martha
Jazz, Rags & Blues, 2 ALF
- Red Rose Rendezvous

Mould, Warren
- Jamaican Serenade (*Legacy Collection*, 3 FHM)

Muczynski, Robert
Fables: Nine Pieces for the Young SCH
- Allegro (no. 1)

Niemann, Walter
Im Kinderland, op. 46 PET
- Cradle Song

Norton, Christopher
Christopher Norton Connections for Piano™, 5 FHM
- ▶ Scamp
- Moonscape
- Boxcar Blues
The Microjazz Collection, 3 B&H
- In a Hurry

Papineau-Couture, Jean
- Aria BER

Papp, Lajos
Petite suite EMB
- Cock-crow

Pinto, Octavio
Festa de Crianças (Children's Festival) SCH
- Little March
- Serenade

Previn, André
Impressions for Piano WAR
- Trees at Twilight (no. 7)

Reinecke, Carl
Hausmusik, op. 77
- Romanza (no. 8)

Rejino, Mona
Portraits in Style HAL
- Nocturne

Ridout, Godfrey
- Prelude in F major (*Meet Canadian Composers at the Piano*, 1 GVT [OP])

Rowley, Alec
- ▶ The Lake, op. 42, no. 9

Schoenmehl, Mike
Piano Studies in Pop SIK
- ▶ Melancholy Reflections

Schumann, Robert
Album für die Jugend, op. 68
- Hunting Song (no. 7)
- Little Folk Song (no. 9)
- Sicilienne (no. 11)
- A Little Romance (no. 19)
- Nordic Song (no. 40)

Shostakovich, Dmitri
- The Barrel-Organ Waltz (from film score for *The Gadfly*, op. 97) SCH
Seven Doll's Dances SCH; SIK
- Hurdy-Gurdy (no. 6)
Six Children's Pieces, op. 69 SCH
- The Mechanical Doll

Starer, Robert
Sketches in Color WAR
- Shades of Blue (no. 2)
- Black and White (no. 3)

Takács, Jenő
Klänge und farben, op. 95 DOB
- ▶ Sounding the Accordion

Tansman, Alexandre
On s'amuse au piano / Happy Time, 1 WAR
- Petite promenade
On s'amuse au piano / Happy Time, 2 WAR
- Valse – Boston
On s'amuse au piano / Happy Time, 3 WAR
- Souvenir de George Gershwin, 1925
Pour les enfants, 3 ESC
- Petite rêverie (no. 4)

Tchaikovsky, Pyotr Il'yich
Album for the Young, op. 39
- Polka (no. 10)
- Mazurka (no. 11)
- Sweet Dreams (no. 21)

Telfer, Nancy
Planets and Stars FHM
- ▶ When Rivers Flowed on Mars

Volkmann, Robert
Lieder des Grossmütter, op. 27
- ▶ Grandmother's Song (no. 10)

2 Technical Requirements

Studies / Etudes

Candidates must prepare *two contrasting* selections from the following list of studies / etudes. Memorization is *not* required and will not be rewarded with extra marks.

Bullets used to denote selections for examination purposes:
▶ selection is found in *Celebration Series Perspectives*®: *Piano Studies / Etudes 5* FHM

Bertini, Henri Jérôme
25 *Primary Etudes for the Piano*, op. 166
▶ Study in G major (no. 7)

Burgmüller, Johann Friedrich
25 *Études faciles et progressives*, op. 100
▶ Sweet Sorrow (no. 16)

Crosby, Anne
In the Mermaid's Garden FHM
▶ Dragonfly Scherzo

Czerny, Carl
▶ Study in G major, op. 139, no. 38

Fuchs, Robert
Jugendklänge: Leichte Stücke für Pianoforte, op. 32
▶ The Little Trumpeter (no. 4)

Gedike, Alexander
Twelve Melodious Studies for Beginners, op. 32
▶ Study in C major (no. 16)

Gnesina, Yelena Fabianovna
Small Pieces – Tableaux
▶ Skipping Rope

Gurlitt, Cornelius
Der erste Vorträg, op. 210
▶ The Merry Wanderer (no. 29)

Kabalevsky, Dmitri
24 *Pieces for Children*, op. 39 SCH
▶ Prelude (no. 19)

Kadosa, Pál
Eight Little Piano Pieces EMB
▶ Vivo

Maikapar, Samuil
▶ Staccato Prelude, op. 31, no. 6

Rohde, Eduard
▶ Dance of the Dragonflies, op. 76, no. 7

Schoenmehl, Mike
Piano Studies in Pop SIK
▶ Chicken Talk

Takács, Jenő
Für mich, op. 76 DOB
▶ The Little Fly

Tchaikovsky, Pyotr Il'yich
Album for the Young, op. 39
▶ In Church (no. 24)

Telfer, Nancy
Planets and Stars FHM
▶ Supernova

> Candidates may substitute a popular selection for one of the studies / etudes. See p. 130 for details.

Substitutions

Candidates may substitute *one* repertoire selection or *one* study / etude selection with a musical work *not found* in the Repertoire Lists for Grade 5. See p. 130 for more information on substitutions.

Total Substitutions Permitted	Requires Prior Approval (Submit an Examination Substitute Piece Request)		Does Not Require Prior Approval		
	Repertoire Substitution		Repertoire Substitution		Study / Etude Substitution
one Repertoire selection *or* *one* Study / Etude	One repertoire selection from piano literature comparable in style and difficulty to the corresponding List A, B, or C of Grade 5	*or*	One selection from the corresponding List of Grade 6	*or*	One study / etude from Grade 6 *or* One Teacher's Choice selection (must be of equal difficulty and a length of 1.5–2 minutes) *or* One selection from the *Popular Selection List* for Grade 5 or Grade 6

Technical Tests

Candidates must play all Technical Tests from memory, ascending and descending, with good tone and logical fingering, at a steady tempo. Metronome markings indicate minimum speeds. All scales are to be played *legato* unless otherwise indicated.

See "Technical Patterns" on p. 19 for examples.

Keys for Grade 5   Major A, E, Eb, Ab
                    Minor F#, C#, C, F

Scales	Keys	Played	Tempo	Note values
Parallel Motion	A, E, Eb, Ab major F#, C#, C, F minor (harmonic and melodic)	HT 2 octaves	♩ = 104	♫
Staccato	A, Eb major F#, C minor (harmonic)	HS 2 octaves	♩ = 112	♬
Formula Pattern	Eb major C minor (harmonic)	HT 2 octaves	♩ = 104	♫
Chromatic	beginning on A	HT 1 octave	♩ = 104	♫

Chords	Keys	Played	Tempo	Note values
Triads (root position and inversions) broken	A, E, Eb, Ab major F#, C#, C, F minor	HT 2 octaves (ending with V–I cadence)	♩ = 66	♫
solid (blocked)			♩ = 132	♩ 𝄾
Dominant 7th (root position and inversions) broken	A, E, Eb, Ab major	HS 1 octave	♩ = 72	♫
solid (blocked)			♩ = 120	♩ 𝄾
Diminished 7th (root position and inversions) broken	F#, C#, C, F minor	HS 1 octave	♩ = 72	♫
solid (blocked)			♩ = 120	♩ 𝄾

Arpeggios	Keys	Played	Tempo	Note values
Tonic (root position only)	A, E, Eb, Ab major F#, C#, C, F minor	HS 2 octaves	♩ = 80	♫

3 Ear Tests

Clapback

Candidates will choose to either clap, tap, or sing the rhythm of a short melody after the examiner has played it *twice*.

Time signature	Approximate length
$\frac{3}{4}$ $\frac{6}{8}$	two to four measures

Example only

1

2

Intervals

Candidates will be asked to identify the following intervals. The examiner will play each interval *once* in broken form.
or
Candidates may choose to sing or hum the following intervals. The examiner will play the first note *once*.

Above a given note	Below a given note
major and minor 3rds	major and minor 3rds
major and minor 6ths	
perfect 4th	
perfect 5th	perfect 5th
perfect octave	perfect octave

Playback

Candidates will be asked to play back a melody based on the first five notes and upper tonic of a major scale. The examiner will name the key, play the tonic triad *once*, and play the melody *twice*.

Beginning note	Approximate length	Keys
tonic, mediant, or dominant	seven notes	C, G, D, F major

Example only

4 Sight Reading

Playing

Candidates will be asked to play a passage of music by sight.

Difficulty	Time signature	Approximate length	Keys
Grade 2 repertoire	$\frac{3}{4}$ $\frac{4}{4}$ $\frac{6}{8}$	eight measures	major and minor keys up to two sharps or two flats

Clapping

Candidates will be asked to clap or tap the rhythm of a melody. Tied notes may be included. A steady pace and rhythmic accentuation are expected.

Time signature	Approximate length
$\frac{3}{4}$ $\frac{4}{4}$ $\frac{6}{8}$	four measures

Example only

Grade 6

At the Grade 6 level, candidates explore intermediate-level repertoire from the major style periods. Challenges include the control of polyphonic textures, command of tempo in longer sonatina movements, and the incorporation of *rubato* in Romantic repertoire. Technical requirements introduce the four-note broken chord and dominant 7th and diminished 7th arpeggios.

	Grade 6 Requirements	Marks
1	**Repertoire**	**50**
	one selection from List A: Baroque Repertoire	18
	one selection from List B: Classical and Classical-style Repertoire	18
	one selection from List C: Romantic, 20th-, and 21st-century Repertoire	14
	Memory (2 marks per selection awarded for memory)	**6**
2	**Technical Requirements**	**24**
	Studies / Etudes: *two* studies / etudes from the *Syllabus* list	6 + 6
	Technical Tests	12
	Major keys: G E F A♭ D♭	
	Minor keys: G E F G♯ C♯	
	– parallel motion scales	
	– *staccato* scales	
	– formula pattern scales	
	– chromatic scales	
	– triads	
	– tonic four-note chords	
	– dominant 7th and diminished 7th chords	
	– tonic arpeggios	
	– dominant 7th and diminished 7th arpeggios	
3	**Ear Tests**	**10**
	Clapback	2
	Intervals	3
	Chords	2
	Playback	3
4	**Sight Reading**	**10**
	Playing	7
	Clapping	3
	Theory Co-requisites	
	Intermediate Rudiments [Grade 1 Rudiments]	
	Total possible marks (pass = 60)	**100**

Resources for Grade 6 Examination Preparation

Repertoire: *Celebration Series Perspectives®: Piano Repertoire 6*

Studies / Etudes: *Celebration Series Perspectives®: Piano Studies / Etudes 6*

Technique: *Technical Requirements for Piano 6*

Popular Selections: *Popular Selection List*

Ear Training and Sight Reading: see p. 135 for ear-training and sight-reading resources.

1 Repertoire

Candidates must prepare *three* contrasting selections. Repertoire selections must be memorized. Please note that up to two memory marks will be deducted for each selection where music is used.

Bullets used to denote selections for examination purposes:
- one selection
- ▲ part or section of a larger work
- ▶ selection is found in *Celebration Series Perspectives®: Piano Repertoire 6 FHM*
- ▲ part or section of a larger work is found in *Celebration Series Perspectives®: Piano Repertoire 6 FHM*

List A
Baroque Repertoire

Bach, Carl Philipp Emanuel
- Polonaise in G minor, BWV Anh. 123 (*Notenbuch der Anna Magdalena Bach* WEI)
- Polonaise in G minor, BWV Anh. 125 (*Notenbuch der Anna Magdalena Bach* WEI)

Bach, Johann Christoph Friedrich
Musikalische Nebenstunden ABR
- Angloise in A major
- ▶ Scherzo in C major

Bach, Johann Sebastian
- Overture in the French Style in B minor, BWV 831
  - ▲ Bourrée
- French Suite no. 1 in D minor, BWV 812
  - ▲ Sarabande
- Little Prelude in D minor, BWV 926
- Little Prelude in C minor, BWV 934
- ▶ Little Prelude in E minor, BWV 941
- Prelude in C minor, BWV 999 (*Celebrate Bach, vol. 1* FHM)
Clavierbüchlein vor Wilhelm Friedemann Bach BAR
- Allemande in G minor, BWV 837
- Minuet no. 3 in G major, BWV 843
Notenbuch der Anna Magdalena Bach WIE
- March in E flat major, BWV Anh. 127
- Polonaise in G major, BWV Anh. 130

Handel, George Frideric
- Allemande in A minor, HWV 478 (*Celebrate Handel* FHM)
- Suite no. 4 in D minor, HWV 437 (*Celebrate Handel* FHM)
  - ▲ Sarabande *or* Gigue
- Suite no. 9 in G major, HWV 442
  - ▲ Prelude

Kirnberger, Johann Philipp
Klavierübungen, erste Sammlung DIA
- Minuet in E major
Recueil d'airs de danse caractéristique
- ▶ Les Carillons (no. 20)

Krebs, Johann Ludwig
- Suite no. 1 in D major
  - ▲ Burlesca in D major (6th movement)
- Toccata in E flat major (*Essential Keyboard Repertoire*, 7 ALF)

Scarlatti, Domenico
- Sonata in A major, LS 31, K 83b (*Celebrate Scarlatti, vol. I FHM*)
- Sonata in G major, L 84, K 63 (*Celebrate Scarlatti, vol. I FHM*)
- Sonata in B flat major, L 97, K 440 (*Celebrate Scarlatti, vol. I FHM*)

Seixas, José Antonio Carlos de
- ▶ Toccata in C minor

Stölzel, Gottfried Heinrich
- Partita in G minor (*Clavierbüchlein vor Wilhelm Friedemann Bach BAR*)
  - ▲ Minuet in G minor (6th movement)

Telemann, Georg Philipp
- ▶ Aria
- Fantasia in C minor, TWV 33:30

Zipoli, Domenico
Sonate d'intavolatura per organo e cimbalo, parte seconda, op. 1 BAR
- Suite in G minor
  - ▲ Sarabanda in G minor

List B
Classical and Classical-style Repertoire

Bach, Carl Philipp Emanuel
Sechs Sonaten für Kenner und Liebhaber OTT
- Sonata no. 5 in F major, H 243
  - ▲ 3rd movement

Beethoven, Ludwig van
- Lustig und Traurig, WoO 54

Benda, Jiří Antonín (George Anton)
Sammlung vermischter Clavierstücke (Benda: 17 Sonatas for Piano OUP)
- Sonatina in D minor (no. 6)
- Sonatina in A minor ALF

Cimarosa, Domenico
- ▶ Sonata in A minor, F 55

Clementi, Muzio
- Sonatina in F major, op. 36, no. 4
  - ▲ *one* movement

Diabelli, Anton
- Sonatina in F major, op. 168, no. 1
  - ▲ 3rd movement: Rondo
- Sonatina in G major, op. 168, no. 6
  - ▲ 3rd movement: Rondo

Dussek, Jan Ladislav
Six Sonatinas, op. 20 ABR
- Sonatina in G major (no. 1)
  - ▲ 1st movement *or*
  - ▲ 2nd movement: Rondo

Gurlitt, Cornelius
Four Sonatinas, op. 214
- Sonatina in G major (no. 3)
  - ▲ 1st movement

Haydn, Franz Joseph
- Divertimento in C major, Hob. XVI:3
  - ▲ 2nd movement: Minuetto and Trio
- Divertimento in G major, Hob. XVI:G1
  - ▲ 1st movement
- Sonata [Divertimento] in D major, Hob. XVI:4
  - ▲ 2nd movement: Minuet and Trio
- Sonata in G major, Hob. XVI:8
  - ▲ 1st movement

Hook, James
- Sonata in D major, op. 12, no. 1
  - ▲ 1st movement

Kuhlau, Friedrich
- Sonatina in C major, op. 20, no. 1
  - ▲ 1st movement
- Sonatina in G major, op. 55, no. 2
  - ▲ 1st movement
- Sonatina in G major, op. 88, no. 2
  - ▲ 1st movement

Lichner, Heinrich
- Sonatina in G major, op. 4, no. 3 KJO; SCH
  - ▲ last movement: Rondo

Mozart, Wolfgang Amadeus
- Andantino, K 236/588b
- German Dance, K 600
Viennese Sonatinas, K 439b
- Viennese Sonatina no. 6 in C major
  - ▲ last movement

Rosetti, Antonio
Vier Klaviersonaten
- Sonata in G major, RWV E2
  - ▲ 2nd movement: Romance

Wesley, Samuel
- ▶ Sonatina in E flat major, op. 4, no. 7

List C
Romantic, 20th-, and 21st-century Repertoire

Alexander, Dennis
24 Character Preludes ALF
- Zigzag

Archer, Violet
Three Scenes (Habitant Sketches) BER
- Church Scene

Bartók, Béla
For Children, 1 B&H
- Jeering Song (no. 30)
- Andante (no. 32)
- Drunkard's Song (no. 36)
For Children, 2 B&H
- Variations (no. 5)
- Round Dance 1 (no. 6)
- Bagpipe 2 (no. 30)
Mikrokosmos, 3 B&H
- Merriment (no. 84)
Ten Easy Pieces EMB
- Dawn

Berlin, Boris
Holiday in Canada MAY
- In the Grotto (*Meet Canadian Composers at the Piano, 1* GVT [OP])
- Winter Scene

Bernstein, Leonard
Five Anniversaries
- ▶ For Susanna Kyle B&H

Bloch, Ernest
Enfantines FIS
- Melody (no. 6)
- Pastorale (no. 7)
- Teasing (no. 9)

Bouchard, Rémi
- Au jour de l'an (*Golden Anniversary Collection* WAT)

Boyd, Bill
Jazz Sketches HAL
- Oh So Blue

Byers, Rosemary Barrett
- Seaside Morning HAL

Carroll, Walter
Sea Idylls FOR
- Early Morning
- Ebb Tide

Chatman, Stephen
Fantasies FHM
- Melancholy Song
Preludes for Piano, 3 FHM
- Prairie Sky
- Rose-cheek'd Tara

Chopin, Frédéric
- Prelude in C minor, op. 28, no. 20
- Waltz in A minor, op. posth., B 150

Copland, Aaron
- The Young Pioneers (*Masters of Our Day* FIS)

Coulthard, Jean
Pieces for the Present WAT
- Where the Trade Winds Blow

Dahlgren, David F.
- Jazz Cat ALK

Dolin, Samuel
- A Slightly Square Round Dance BER

Duke, David
- Cape Breton Lullaby (*Music of Our Time, 5* WAT)

Dunhill, Thomas
- The Irish Boy LEG

Faith, Richard
Finger Paintings for Piano SHA
- Celebration

Fiala, George
Australian Suite, op. 2 BER
- Kangaroo

Fibich, Zdeněk
- ▶ Childhood – Spring (Hudek 55)

Finch, Douglas
- ▶ Cancan FHM

Filtz, Bohdana
- ▶ An Ancient Tale (*Town and Country* FHM)

Flagello, Nicholas
Episodes for Piano GEN
- March

Fleming, Robert
Bag-O-Tricks WAT
- Bright-Dancy (no. 2)
- Quiet Mood (no. 3)
Four Modernistics CMC
- Marching

Gardiner, Mary
Turnabout STU
- no. 1
- no. 4

Gillock, William L.
Lyric Preludes in Romantic Style SUM
- ▶ Winter Scene

Glick, Srul Irving
Four Preludes GVT
- Prelude no. 2 (*Meet Canadian Composers at the Piano, 2* GVT [OP])

Glière, Reinhold
Eight Easy Piano Pieces, op. 43 ABR
- ▶ Prayer (no. 2)

Greaves, Terrence
More Swinging Rhymes ABR
- Baa, Baa, Blue Sheep's Waltz (no.5)

Grieg, Edvard
Lyric Pieces, op. 12
- ▶ Arietta (no. 1)
- Watchman's Song (no. 3)
- Folksong (no. 5)
- Patriotic Song (no. 8)

Haughton, Alan
Rhythm and Rag ABR
- You and Me

Heller, Stephen
Notenbuch für Klein und Gross, op. 138
- ▶ Barcarolle (no. 5) (*Celebrate Heller* FHM)

Hofmann, Heinrich
Skizzen, op. 77 ABR
- ▶ On the Lake (no. 12)
- ▶ Little Wood-bird (no. 15) (*Hofmann: 17 Miscellaneous Pieces* ABR)

Ibert, Jacques
Petite suite en quinze images FOE
- ▶ Parade (no. 6)
- ▶ Romance (no. 8)

Jaque, Rhené
- ▶ Jesting GVT
- ▶ Jeux / Games (*Meet Canadian Composers at the Piano*, 2 GVT [OP])

Kabalevsky, Dmitri
30 Pieces for Children, op. 27 SCH
- ▶ Song of the Cavalry (no. 29) (also titled "Cavalry Gallop")
- ▶ Warrior's Dance (no. 19)
- ▶ Fairy Tale (no. 20)

Kenins, Talivaldis
- ▶ Toccata-Dance (*Legacy Collection*, 4 FHM)

Khachaturian, Aram
Adventures of Ivan ALF; MCA
- ▶ Ivan Sings

Klose, Carol
- ▶ Vaudeville Repartée (*Hal Leonard Student Piano Library, Piano Solos 5* HAL)

Koechlin, Charles
Dix petites pieces faciles, op. 61c SAL
- ▶ La jolie fleur (no. 2)
- ▶ Berceuse

Kolodub, Janna
- ▶ Carpathian Waterfall (*Postcards from Ukraine* FHM)

Kullak, Theodor
Scenes from Childhood, set 2, op. 81 PET; SCH
- ▶ Grandmother Tells a Ghost Story (no. 3)

Louie, Alexina
Star Light, Star Bright FHM
- ▶ Distant Star

Lutosławski, Witold
Folk Mélodies (Most Beautiful Lutosławski PWM)
- ▶ Master Michael

Mendelssohn, Felix
- ▶ Lied ohne Worte, op. 19, no. 4
Sechs Kinderstrücke, op.72
- ▶ Allegro non troppo (no. 1)

Menotti, Gian Carlo
Poemetti per Maria Rosa: 12 Pieces for Children BEL
- ▶ Lullaby
- ▶ The Shepherd

Muczynski, Robert
Fables: Nine Pieces for the Young SCH
- ▶ Presto (no. 6)

Norton, Christopher
Christopher Norton Connections for Piano™, 6 FHM
- ▶ Bahama Beach
- ▶ In Between
- ▶ Mississauga Rag
Microstyles 1 B&H
- ▶ Oriental Flower

Pachulski, Henryk
Six Preludes, op. 8
- ▶ Prelude in C minor (no. 1) (*A Romantic Sketchbook for Piano*, 3 ABR)

Papp, Lajos
Images LEM
- ▶ Hungarian Dance

Pinto, Octavio
Festa de Crianças (Children's Festival) SCH
- ▶ Playing Marbles (no. 5)

Previn, André
Impressions for Piano WAR
- ▶ By a Quiet Stream (no. 5)
- ▶ Roundup (no. 11)

Prokofiev, Sergei
Music for Children, op. 65 SCH
- ▶ Promenade (no. 2)

Rebikov, Vladimir Ivanovich
- ▶ Valse miniature, op. 10, no. 10

Reinecke, Carl
- ▶ Serenade in G major, op. 183, no. 2 ABR
  - ▲ Pastorale

Reubart, Dale
Pantomimes FHM
- ▶ March of the Buffoons
- ▶ Prelude

Rorem, Ned
A Quiet Afternoon PER
- ▶ A New Game

Scharwenka, Xaver
Album for the Young, op. 62
- ▶ A Tale (no. 3)

Schubert, Franz
Valses sentimentales, op. 50, D 797
- ▶ Valse sentimentale no. 13

Schumann, Robert
Album für die Jugend, op. 68
- ▶ Mignon (no. 35)
Albumblätter, op. 124
- ▶ Waltz in A minor (no. 4)
Kinderszenen, op. 15
- ▶ From Foreign Lands and People (no. 1)

Southam, Ann
- ▶ Sea Flea BER

Starer, Robert
Sketches in Color WAR
- ⬤ Purple (no. 1)
- ▶ Bright Orange (no. 4)

Tansman, Alexandre
Ten Diversions for the Young Pianist MCA
- ⬤ Prayer

Tchaikovsky, Pyotr Il'yich
Album for the Young, op. 39
- ⬤ Waltz (no. 8)

Telfer, Nancy
- ▶ Fantasy CMC
She's Like the Swallow FHM
- ⬤ She's Like the Swallow (arr.)
- ⬤ Vive la canadienne! (arr.)

Tsitsaros, Christos
- ⬤ Song of the Fisherman (*Hal Leonard Student Piano Library, Piano Solos 5* HAL)
Cinderella Suite FHM
- ⬤ Cinderella's Sorrow

Wuensch, Gerhard
A Winter Foursome, op. 39 WAT
- ⬤ Frosted Windows (no. 1)

2 Technical Requirements

Studies / Etudes

Candidates must prepare *two contrasting* selections from the following list of studies / etudes. Memorization is *not* required and will not be rewarded with extra marks.

Bullets used to denote selections for examination purposes:
- ▶ selection is found in *Celebration Series Perspectives®*: *Piano Studies / Etudes 6* FHM

Bertini, Henri Jérôme
Etudes for the Piano, op. 29
- ▶ Study in E minor (no. 14)

Concone, Giuseppe
Twenty-five Melodic Studies, Easy and Progressive, op. 24
- ▶ Study in B flat major (no. 5)
- ▶ Study in C major (no. 10)

Czerny, Carl
- ▶ Study in A flat major, op. 139, no. 51

Finney, Ross Lee
24 Piano Inventions PET
- ▶ Playing Ball

Gnesina, Yelena Fabianovna
Small Pieces – Tableaux
- ▶ Song of the Brook

Heller, Stephen
30 Études progressives, op. 46
- ▶ Fluttering Leaves (no. 11)

Kabalevsky, Dmitri
30 Pieces for Children, op. 27 SCH
- ▶ Toccatina (no. 12)

Karganov, Génari
Jugend-Album, op. 25
- ▶ Game of Patience (no. 2)

Nakada, Yoshinao
Japanese Festival WAR
- ▶ The Gear Wheels of a Watch

Nölck, August
Melodische Studien für Klavier
- ▶ Good Humoured

Papp, Lajos
Aquarium: 11 Piano Pieces EMB
- ▶ Pebbles in the Water

Schoenmehl, Mike
Little Stories in Jazz OTT
- ▶ The Broken Record

Shostakovich, Dmitri
Dances of the Dolls SIK
- ▶ Dance

Substitutions

Candidates may substitute *one* repertoire selection or *one* study / etude selection with a musical work *not found* in the Repertoire Lists for Grade 6. See p. 130 for more information on substitutions.

Total Substitutions Permitted	Requires Prior Approval (Submit an Examination Substitute Piece Request)		Does Not Require Prior Approval		
	Repertoire Substitution		**Repertoire Substitution**		**Study / Etude Substitution**
one Repertoire selection *or* *one* Study / Etude	One repertoire selection from piano literature comparable in style and difficulty to the corresponding List A, B, or C of Grade 6	*or*	One selection from the corresponding List of Grade 7	*or*	One study / etude from Grade 7 *or* One Teacher's Choice selection (must be of equal difficulty and a length of 1.5–2 minutes) *or* One selection from the *Popular Selection List* for Grade 6 or Grade 7

Technical Tests

Candidates must play all Technical Tests from memory, ascending and descending, with good tone and logical fingering, at a steady tempo. Metronome markings indicate minimum speeds. All scales are to be played *legato* unless otherwise indicated.

See "Technical Patterns" on p. 19 for examples.

Keys for Grade 6   Major G, E, F, A♭, D♭
                    Minor G, E, F, G♯, C♯

Scales	Keys	Played	Tempo	Note values
Parallel Motion	G, E, F, A♭, D♭ major G, E, F, G♯, C♯ minor (harmonic and melodic)	HT 2 octaves	♩ = 60	(four sixteenth notes beamed)
Staccato	E, F major E minor (harmonic and melodic)	HT 2 octaves	♩ = 60	(four staccato sixteenth notes)
Formula Pattern	E, F major E minor (harmonic)	HT 2 octaves	♩ = 60	(four sixteenth notes beamed)
Chromatic	beginning on E, D♭	HT 2 octaves	♩ = 60	(four sixteenth notes beamed)

Chords	Keys	Played	Tempo	Note values
Triads (root position and inversions) broken	G, E, F, A♭, D♭ major G, E, F, G♯, C♯ minor	HT 2 octaves (ending with V–I cadence)	♩ = 80	(triplet eighth notes)
solid (blocked)		HT 2 octaves (ending with V–I cadence)	♩ = 80	(two quarter notes)
Tonic Four-note Chords (root position and inversions) broken	G, E, F, A♭, D♭ major G, E, F, G♯, C♯ minor	HS 1 octave (no cadence)	♩ = 88	(two eighth notes)
Dominant 7th (root position and inversions) broken	G, E, F, A♭, D♭ major G, E, F, G♯, C♯ minor	HS 2 octaves	♩ = 88	(two eighth notes)
solid (blocked)			♩ = 72	(two quarter notes)
Diminished 7th (root position and inversions) broken	G, E, F, G♯, C♯ minor	HS 2 octaves	♩ = 88	(two eighth notes)
solid (blocked)			♩ = 72	(two quarter notes)

Arpeggios	Keys	Played	Tempo	Note values
Tonic (root followed by 1st inversion)	G, E, F, A♭, D♭ major	HS 2 octaves	♩ = 92	(two eighth notes)
Dominant 7th (root position only)	G, E, F, G♯, C♯ minor			
Diminished 7th (root position only)	G, E, F, G♯, C♯ minor			

3 Ear Tests

Clapback

Candidates will choose to either clap, tap, or sing the rhythm of a short melody after the examiner has played it *twice*.

Time signature	Approximate length
2/4 3/4 6/8	two to four measures

Example only

1

2

Intervals

Candidates will be asked to identify the following intervals. The examiner will play each interval *once* in broken form.
or
Candidates may choose to sing or hum the following intervals. The examiner will play the first note *once*.

Above a given note	Below a given note
major 2nd	
major and minor 3rds	major and minor 3rds
major and minor 6ths	minor 6th
perfect 4th	perfect 4th
perfect 5th	perfect 5th
perfect octave	perfect octave

Chords

Candidates will be asked to identify any of the following chords after the examiner has played the chord once in solid (blocked) form, close position.

Chords	Position
major and minor triads	root position

Playback

Candidates will be asked to play back a melody based on the complete major scale (tonic to tonic, mediant to mediant, dominant to dominant). The examiner will name the key, play the tonic triad *once*, and play the melody *twice*.

Beginning note	Approximate length	Keys
tonic, mediant, or dominant	nine notes	C, G, D, F major

Example only

4 Sight Reading

Playing

Candidates will be asked to play a passage of music at sight.

Difficulty	Time signature	Approximate length	Keys
Grade 3 repertoire	2/4 3/4 4/4 6/8	eight measures	major and minor keys up to three sharps or three flats

Clapping

Candidates will be asked to clap or tap the rhythm of a melody. A steady pace and rhythmic accentuation are expected.

Time signature	Approximate length
3/4 4/4 6/8	four measures

Example only

Grade 7

The Grade 7 level is an important transitional point in a candidate's musical development. The Baroque repertoire selections require independence of the hands and ease with ornamentation. The Classical sonatinas demand fluency of rhythmic and technical elements. Pedaling becomes integral to the performance of lyrical Romantic repertoire, and chromaticism, modality, changing meters, and dynamic extremes accompany the post-1900 repertoire.

	Grade 7 Requirements	Marks
1	**Repertoire**	**50**
	one selection from List A: Baroque Repertoire	18
	one selection from List B: Classical and Classical-style Repertoire	18
	one selection from List C: Romantic, 20th-, and 21st-century Repertoire	14
	Memory (2 marks per selection awarded for memory)	6
2	**Technical Requirements**	**24**
	Studies / Etudes: *two* studies / etudes from the *Syllabus* list	6 + 6
	Technical Tests	12
	Major keys: C D B F B♭ A♭ D♭	
	Minor keys: C D B F B♭ G♯ C♯	
	– parallel motion scales	
	– *staccato* scales	
	– formula pattern scales	
	– chromatic scales	
	– scale in 6ths *or* octaves	
	– tonic four-note chords	
	– dominant 7th and diminished 7th chords	
	– tonic arpeggios	
	– dominant 7th and diminished 7th arpeggios	
3	**Ear Tests**	**10**
	Clapback	2
	Intervals	3
	Chords	2
	Playback	3
4	**Sight Reading**	**10**
	Playing	7
	Clapping	3
	Theory Co-requisites	
	Advanced Rudiments [Grade 2 Rudiments]	
	Total possible marks (pass = 60)	**100**

Resources for Grade 7 Examination Preparation

Repertoire: *Celebration Series Perspectives®: Piano Repertoire* 7

Studies / Etudes: *Celebration Series Perspectives®: Piano Studies / Etudes* 7

Technique: *Technical Requirements for Piano* 7

Popular Selections: *Popular Selection List*

Ear Training and Sight Reading: see p. 135 for ear-training and sight-reading resources.

1 Repertoire

Candidates must prepare *three* contrasting selections: *one* from each of List A, List B, and List C. Repertoire selections must be memorized. Please note that up to two memory marks will be deducted for each selection where music is used.

Bullets used to denote selections for examination purposes:
- ● one selection
- ▲ part or section of a larger work
- ▶ selection is found in *Celebration Series Perspectives®: Piano Repertoire* 7 FHM
- ▲ part or section of a larger work is found in *Celebration Series Perspectives®: Piano Repertoire* 7 FHM

List A

Baroque Repertoire

Alcock, John
Six Suites of Easy Lessons ABR
- ● Suite no. 1 in A major
  - ▲ Minuet

Bach, Carl Philipp Emanuel
- ● Sonata in E minor, Wq 62/12, H 66
  - ▲ 3rd movement: Sarabande

Bach, Johann Sebastian
- ● French Suite no. 4 in E flat major, BWV 815
  - ▲ Allemande
- ● French Suite no. 5 in G major, BWV 816
  - ▲ Gavotte
- ● French Suite no. 6 in E major, BWV 817
  - ▲ Polonaise
- ▶ Invention no. 1 in C major, BWV 772
- ● Little Prelude in F major, BWV 927
- ● Little Prelude in C major, BWV 933
- ● Little Prelude in D minor, BWV 935
- ● Little Prelude in A minor, BWV 942

Couperin, François
L'art de toucher le clavecin
- ● Allemande in D minor

Fiocco, Joseph-Hector
- ● Suite in G major, op. 1, no. 1
  - ▲ 11th movement

Handel, George Frideric
- ● Air in G minor, HWV 467 BAR
- ● Suite no. 4 in D minor, HWV 437
  - ▲ 3rd movement: Courante (*Celebrate Handel* FHM)
- ● Suite no. 7 in G minor, HWV 432
  - ▲ Allegro
- ● Suite no. 8 in G major, HWV 441 (*Celebrate Handel* FHM)
  - ▲ 1st movement: Allemande *or*
  - ▲ 2nd movement: Allegro *or*
  - ▲ 4th movement: Aria

Kirnberger, Johann Philipp
Recueil d'airs de danse caractéristiques
  ▶ Passepied in D major (no. 1)

Krebs, Johann Ludwig
  ● Sonatina No. 4 in B flat major
    ▲ 3rd movement

Scarlatti, Domenico
  ● Sonata in A minor, L 93, K 149 (*Celebrate Scarlatti,* *vol.* 1 FHM)
  ● Sonata in F major, L 297, K 274
  ● Sonata in A major, L 483, K 322 (*Celebrate Scarlatti,* *vol.* 1 FHM)

Telemann, Georg Philipp
  ● Fantasia in B flat major, TWV 33:18
    ▲ 2nd movement: Gaiment
  ● Fantasia in B flat major, TWV 33:36
    ▲ Vivace
  ● Fantasia in G minor, TWV 33:29
    ▲ 1st section: Allegro
Essercizii Musici, TWV 32
  ● Solo in F major, TWV 32:4
    ▲ 2nd movement: Bourrée

List B

Classical and Classical-style Repertoire

Albéniz, Mateo
  ● Sonata in D major ALF

Beethoven, Ludwig van
  ● Bagatelle in D major, op. 33, no. 6
  ▶ Bagatelle, op. 119, no. 1
  ▶ Für Elise, WoO 59

Clementi, Muzio
  ● Sonatina in C major, op. 36, no. 3
    ▲ 1st movement
  ● Sonatina in D major, op. 36, no. 6
    ▲ 1st movement *or* 2nd movement: Rondo

Diabelli, Anton
  ● Sonatina in C major, op. 151, no. 2
    ▲ 1st movement
  ● Sonatina in C major, op. 168, no. 3
    ▲ 1st movement

Haydn, Franz Joseph
  ● Sonata [Divertimento] in C major, Hob. XVI:1
    ▲ 2nd movement
  ● Sonata [Divertimento] in G major, Hob. XVI:27
    ▲ 2nd movement: Menuet and Trio
  ● Sonata [Divertimento] in E flat major, Hob. XVI:28
    ▲ 3rd movement
  ● Sonata in D major, Hob XVII:D1
    ▲ 3rd movement: Finale

Hummel, Johann Nepomuk
Anweisung zum Piano-forte Spiel
  ● Scherzo in A major (no. 45) (*Sixteen Short Pieces* ABR)

Kuhlau, Friedrich
  ● Sonatina in G major, op. 20, no. 2
    ▲ 2nd movement
  ● Sonatina in C major, op. 55, no. 3
    ▲ 1st movement
  ● Sonatina in C major, op. 88, no. 1
    ▲ 1st movement
  ● Sonatina in A minor, op. 88, no. 3
    ▲ 3rd movement

Mozart, Wolfgang Amadeus
Viennese Sonatinas, K 439b
  ● Viennese Sonatina no. 1 in C major
    ▲ 4th movement: Allegro
  ● Viennese Sonatina no. 2 in A major
    ▲ 1st movement
  ● Viennese Sonatina no. 5 in F major
    ▲ 1st movement
  ● Viennese Sonatina no. 6 in C major
    ▲ 1st movement

Schumann, Robert
  ● Children's Sonata, op. 118a, no. 1
    ▲ 1st movement *or* 2nd movement: Theme and variations

Storace, Stephen
  ● Sonatina no. 5 in D major
    ▲ 1st movement

Vorisek, Jan Václav
  ● Rondo in G major, op. 18, no. 1

List C

Romantic, 20th-, and 21st-century Repertoire

Alexander, Dennis
24 Character Preludes ALF
  ● Longing

Bartók, Béla
For Children, 1 B&H
  ● Allegro (no. 12)
  ▶ Pentatonic Tune (no. 29)
  ● Andante tranquillo (no. 31)
  ● Winter Solstice Song (no. 38)
For Children, 2 B&H
  ● Ballad (no. 35)

Benjamin, Arthur L.
  ● Romance-Impromptu ALF

Bernstein, Seymour
Birds, 1 MAN
  ● The Purple Finch and The Hummingbird

Bloch, Ernest
Enfantines FIS
  ● Dream (no. 10)

Blok, Vladimir
Twelve Pieces in Folk Modes FHM
  ● Bashkir Chastushka

Bober, Melody
Cyclone FJH
- Whirling Winds

Bonsor, Brian
Jazzy Piano, 2 UNI
- ▶ Feelin' Good

Brown, Stephen
West Coast Sundries SWA
- Ballade for Liliane

Buczynski, Walter
Ten Piano Pieces for Children CMC
- Mood Indigo

Chatman, Stephen
Amusements, 3 FHM
- Earthquake
Fantasies FHM
- Blue Angel
- ▶ Katherine
- Night Sounds
- Sunrise at Jericho Beach
Preludes for Piano, 3 FHM
- Ginger Snaps

Chopin, Frédéric
- Polonaise in B flat major, op. 71, no. 2 CT 160
- Polonaise in G minor, op. posth., CT 161
- ▶ Prelude in E minor, op. 28, no. 4

Coulthard, Jean
Pieces for the Present WAT
- Far Above the Clouds

Dello Joio, Norman
Lyric Pieces for the Young EDW
- ▶ Prayer of the Matador

Duncan, Martha
Isla Vista Suite
- Eucalyptus Grove (*Diamond Jubilee Collection* WAT)

Eckhardt-Gramatté, Sophie-Carmen
From My Childhood, 1: Alphabet Pieces WAT
- "P" Poissarde (Fisherwoman)

Eggleston, Anne
- Hurry! Hurry! Hurry! (*Horizons, 2* WAT)

Falla, Manuel de
- Récit du pêcheur [also titled The Fisherman's Story, The Magic Circle] (from El *amor brujo*) CHS

Fiala, George
Sonatina, op. 1 BER
- 1st movement

Frid, Grigori
Russian Tales FHM
- Nocturne
- A Sad Song

Fuchs, Robert
Jugendalbum, op. 47
- Mother Tells a Story (no. 16) (*Fuchs: Children's Pieces* ABR)

Gallant, Pierre
- ▶ A Joke (*Legacy Collection, 4* FHM)

Gillock, William L.
Lyric Preludes in Romantic Style SUM
- ▶ Moonlight Mood

Ginastera, Alberto
Dos canciones, op. 3 RIC
- Milonga

Glick, Srul Irving
- Caprice (*Meet Canadian Composers at the Piano, 2* GVT [OP])

Glière, Reinhold
Eight Easy Piano Pieces, op. 43 ABR
- ▶ Arietta (no. 7)
Pièces enfantines / Twelve Children's Pieces, op. 31 MAS
- Cradle Song (no. 3)
- Romance (no. 7)

Godard, Benjamin
- ▶ First Sorrow, op. 149, no. 6

Granados, Enrique
Cuentos de la juventud / Stories of the Young, op. 1 ABR; MAS
- La huerfana / The Little Orphan Girl (no. 9)

Grieg, Edvard
Lyric Pieces, op. 12
- Elfin Dance (no. 4)
- Album-leaf (no. 7)
Lyric Pieces, op. 43
- Solitary Traveller (no. 2)

Haughton, Alan
More Rhythm and Rag ABR
- Bread and Butter

Hofmann, Heinrich
Skizzen, op. 77
- ▶ Go to Sleep! (no. 9)

Ibert, Jacques
Petite suite en quinze images HUG
- Le cavalier Sans-Souci (no. 5)
- ▶ Sérénade sur l'eau (no. 10)

Jaque, Rhené
- ▶ Lutin / Goblin (*Meet Canadian Composers at the Piano, 2* GVT [OP])
- Suite no. 1 pour piano BER
  - ▲ L'heure d'angoisse

Kabalevsky, Dmitri
Easy Variations for Piano, op. 51
- Seven Good-Humoured Variations on a Ukrainian Folk Song (no. 4)
Four Rondos, op. 60
- ▶ Rondo–March (no. 1)
- Rondo–Dance (no. 2)
- Rondo–Song (no. 3)

Kenins, Talivaldis
- Little Romance (*Meet Canadian Composers at the Piano, 1* GVT [OP])
- Rondino (*Meet Canadian Composers at the Piano, 1* GVT [OP])

Khachaturian, Aram
Adventures of Ivan ALF; MCA
- Ivan Is Very Busy

Koechlin, Charles
Dix petites pièces faciles, op. 61c SAL
- L'enfant bien sage (no. 1)
- Sicilienne (no. 10)

Kossenko, Viktor
24 Pieces for Children, op. 15
- ▶ Waltz

Lebeda, Miroslav
Music for Young Pianists FHM
- Toccata

Louie, Alexina
Star Light, Star Bright FHM
- Blue Sky II
- Shooting Stars

Lutosławski, Witold
Bucolics PWM
- no. 4

MacDowell, Edward
Woodland Sketches, op. 51
- To a Wild Rose (no. 1)

Martinů, Bohuslav
Spring in the Garden BAR
- It Isn't Bad, Is It, To Pick a Few Flowers

Mendelssohn, Felix
Lieder ohne Worte, op. 30
- Consolation (no. 3)
- ▶ Venetian Boat Song (no. 6)

Menotti, Gian Carlo
Poemetti per Maria Rosa: 12 Pieces for Children BEL
- Giga
- War Song

Muczynski, Robert
Diversions SCH
- Allegro molto (no. 9)

Niemann, Walter
Im Kinderland, op. 46 PET
- The Little Mermaid in the Shell (no. 9)

Norton, Christopher
Christopher Norton Connections for Piano™, 7 FHM
- Fantasy Bossa
- Hanging Gardens
- Ringing Changes

Papp, Lajos
- ▶ Song and Dance
- Petite Suite EMB
  - ▲ Alpine Horn and Chamois

Pentland, Barbara
Hands across the C AVO
- Sparks (no. 1)
- Seashore (no. 3)

Pinto, Octavio
Scenas infantis SCH
- Sleeping Time

Poole, Clifford
- Ghost Town (*Legacy Collection, 4* FHM)
- Nocturne (*Legacy Collection, 4* FHM)

Poulenc, Francis
Villageoises SAL
- Valse tyrolienne (no. 1)
- Staccato (no. 2)

Prokofiev, Sergei
Music for Children, op. 65 SCH
- Regrets (no. 5)
- Waltz (no. 6)
- March of the Grasshoppers (no. 7)
- March (no. 10)
- Evening (no. 11)

Rebikov, Vladimir Ivanovich
Album of Easy Pieces
- ▶ Waltz (no. 6)

Rossi, Wynn-Anne
An Alaska Tour FJH
- Arctic Moon

Rybicki, Feliks
This Is Our Garden Fair PWM
- ▶ Our Little Garden

Schubert, Franz
Walzer, Ländler, und Ecossaisen, op. 18, D 145
- Waltz in B minor (no. 6)

Schumann, Robert
Albumblätter, op. 124
- Fantastic Dance (no. 5)
- Wiegenliedchen / Little Cradle Song (no. 6)

Stone, Court
- Ottawa Valley Song HOM

Takács, Jenő
From Far Away Places, op. 111 UNI
- Song and Alborada (no. 14)

Tchaikovsky, Pyotr Il'yich
Album for the Young, op. 39
- Chant de l'alouette / Song of the Lark (no. 22)

Telfer, Nancy
She's Like the Swallow FHM
- The Morning Dew (arr.)

Thompson, John
- Variations on Three Blind Mice WIL

Tsitsaros, Christos
Cinderella Suite FHM
- At the Prince's Ball

Nine Tales FHM
- Tap Dance

Wuensch, Gerhard
Twelve Glimpses into 20th Century Idioms, op. 37 B&H
- Beatless
- Quick March in Minor Sixths

2 Technical Requirements

Studies / Etudes

Candidates must prepare *two contrasting* selections from the following list of studies / etudes. Memorization is *not* required and will not be rewarded with extra marks.

Bullets used to denote selections for examination purposes:
▶ selection is found in *Celebration Series Perspectives®*: *Piano Studies / Etudes 7* FHM

Bertini, Henri Jérôme
Etudes for the Piano, op. 29
▶ Study in C minor (no. 7)

Concone, Giuseppe
Twenty-five Melodic Studies, Easy and Progressive, op. 24
▶ Study in C major (no. 22)

Gnesina, Yelena Fabianovna
Small Pieces – Tableaux
▶ Spinning Top

Hofmann, Heinrich
Skizzen, op. 77
▶ Elegie (no. 2)

Kabalevsky, Dmitri
30 Pieces for Children, op. 27 SCH
▶ Etude (no. 3)
▶ Dance (no. 27)

Maikapar, Samuil
Trifles, op. 8
▶ Toccatina (no. 1)

Norton, Christopher
Christopher Norton Connections for Piano™, 7 FHM
▶ Wound Up

Previn, André
Impressions for Piano WAR
▶ Mechanical Toy

Schoenmehl, Mike
Piano Studies in Pop SIK
▶ Cyclone

Swinstead, Felix
Six Studies for the Development of the Left Hand B&H
▶ Study in G major

Takács, Jenő
Klänge und Farben, op. 95 DOB
▶ In a Great Hurry (no. 3)

Tcherepnin, Alexander
Batagelles, op. 5
▶ Bagatelle (no. 9)

Candidates may substitute a popular selection for one of the studies / etudes. See p. 130 for details.

Substitutions

Candidates may substitute *one* repertoire selection or *one* study / etude selection with a musical work *not found* in the Repertoire Lists for Grade 7. See p. 130 for more information on substitutions.

Total Substitutions Permitted	Requires Prior Approval (Submit an Examination Substitute Piece Request)		Does Not Require Prior Approval		
	Repertoire Substitution		Repertoire Substitution		Study / Etude Substitution
one Repertoire selection *or* *one* Study / Etude	One repertoire selection from piano literature comparable in style and difficulty to the corresponding List A, B, or C of Grade 7	or	One selection from the corresponding List of Grade 8	or	One study / etude from Grade 8 *or* One Teacher's Choice selection (must be of equal difficulty and a length of 1.5–2 minutes) *or* One selection from the *Popular Selection List* for Grade 7 or Grade 8

Technical Tests

Candidates must play all Technical Tests from memory, ascending and descending, with good tone and logical fingering, at a steady tempo. Metronome markings indicate minimum speeds. All scales are to be played *legato* unless otherwise indicated.

See "Technical Patterns" on p. 19 for examples.

Keys for Grade 7   Major C, D, B, F, B♭, A♭, D♭
                    Minor C, D, B, F, B♭, G♯, C♯

Scales	Keys	Played	Tempo	Note values
Parallel Motion	C, D, B, F, B♭, A♭, D♭ major C, D, B, F, B♭, G♯, C♯ (harmonic and melodic)	HT 2 octaves	♩ = 76	♬♬
Staccato	C, D major C, D minor (harmonic and melodic)	HT 3 octaves	♩ = 76	♪♪♪³
Formula Pattern	C, D major C, D minor (harmonic)	HT 2 octaves	♩ = 76	♬♬
Chromatic	Beginning on D and A♭	HT 2 octaves	♩ = 76	♬♬
Scale in 6ths solid (blocked) *staccato* *or*	C major (beginning on tonic as upper note, mediant as lower note)	HS 1 octave	♩ = 88	♪♪
Scale in octaves broken *legato*	C major		♩ = 100	♪♪

Chords	Keys	Played	Tempo	Note values
Tonic Four-note Chords (root position and inversions) broken	C, D, B, F, B♭, A♭, D♭ major C, D, B, F, B♭, G♯, C♯ minor	HS 2 octaves (no cadence)	♩ = 69	♬♬
		HT 1 octave (ending with V–I cadence)	♩ = 60	♬♬
Dominant 7th (root position and inversions) broken	C, D, B, F, B♭, A♭, D♭ major C, D, B, F, B♭, G♯, C♯ minor	HT 2 octaves	♩ = 60	♬♬
solid (blocked)			♩ = 80	♩♩
Diminished 7th (root position and inversions) broken	C, D, B, F, B♭, G♯, C♯ minor	HT 2 octaves	♩ = 60	♬♬
solid (blocked)			♩ = 80	♩♩

Arpeggios	Keys	Played	Tempo	Note values
Tonic (root position followed by 1st and 2nd inversions)	C, D, B, F, B♭, A♭, D♭ major C, D, B, F, B♭, G♯, C♯ minor	HT 2 octaves	♩ = 60	♬♬
Dominant 7th (root position only)				
Diminished 7th (root position only)	C, D, B, F, B♭, G♯, C♯ minor			

3 Ear Tests

Clapback

Candidates will choose to either clap, tap, or sing the rhythm of a short melody after the examiner has played it *twice*.

Time signature	Approximate length
$\frac{2}{4}$ $\frac{3}{4}$ $\frac{6}{8}$	four measures

Example only

2

Intervals

Candidates will be asked to identify the following intervals. The examiner will play each interval *once* in broken form.
or
Candidates may choose to sing or hum the following intervals. The examiner will play the first note *once*.

Above a given note	Below a given note
major and minor 2nds	
major and minor 3rds	major and minor 3rds
major and minor 6ths	minor 6th
	major 7th
perfect 4th	perfect 4th
perfect 5th	perfect 5th
perfect octave	perfect octave

Chords

Candidates will be asked to identify any of the following chords after the examiner has played the chord once in solid (blocked) form, close position.

Chords	Position
major and minor triads	root position
dominant 7th	root position

Playback

Candidates will be asked to play back a melody based on the complete major scale (tonic to tonic, mediant to mediant, dominant to dominant). The examiner will name the key, play the tonic chord *once*, and play the melody *twice*.

Beginning note	Approximate length	Keys
tonic, mediant, dominant, or upper tonic	nine notes	C, G, D, F, B♭ major

Example only

4 Sight Reading

Playing

Candidates will be asked to play a short composition at sight.

Difficulty	Time signature	Approximate length	Keys
Grade 4 repertoire	$\frac{2}{4}$ $\frac{3}{4}$ $\frac{4}{4}$ $\frac{6}{8}$	twelve measures	major and minor keys up to three sharps or three flats

Clapping

Candidates will be asked to clap or tap the rhythm of a melody. A steady pace and rhythmic accentuation are expected.

Time signature	Approximate length
$\frac{2}{4}$ $\frac{3}{4}$ $\frac{4}{4}$ $\frac{6}{8}$	four measures

Example only

Grade 7

Grade 8

By the Grade 8 level, candidates have been exposed to repertoire from four historical style periods. From this level onwards, candidates encounter masterworks of the pianist's core repertoire. A greater command of texture and increased stylistic refinement will help candidates meet the technical and interpretive demands of this level.

	Grade 8 Requirements	Marks
1	**Repertoire**	**56**
	one selection from List A: Baroque Repertoire	16 (1.5)
	one selection from List B: Classical and Classical-style Repertoire	16 (1.5)
	one selection from List C: Romantic Repertoire	12 (1)
	one selection from List D: Post-Romantic, 20th-, and 21st-century Repertoire	12 (1)
	(The figures in parentheses indicate marks awarded for memory as a portion of the total mark for each selection.)	
2	**Technical Requirements**	**24**
	Studies / Etudes: *two* studies / etudes from the *Syllabus* list	6 + 6
	Technical Tests	12
	Major keys: C D A E B B♭ E♭ G♭	
	Minor keys: C D A E B B♭ E♭ F♯	
	– parallel motion scales	
	– *staccato* scales	
	– formula pattern scales	
	– chromatic scales	
	– scales in octaves	
	– tonic four-note chords	
	– dominant 7th and diminished 7th chords	
	– tonic arpeggios	
	– dominant 7th and diminished 7th arpeggios	
3	**Ear Tests**	**10**
	Intervals	3
	Chords	2
	Cadences	2
	Playback	3
4	**Sight Reading**	**10**
	Playing	7
	Clapping	3
	Theory Co-requisites	
	Advanced Rudiments [Grade 2 Rudiments]	
	Introductory Harmony (recommended)	
	Total possible marks (pass = 60)	**100**

Visit **www.frederickharrismusic.com**
for information about publications.

Resources for Grade 8 Examination Preparation

Repertoire: *Celebration Series Perspectives*®: *Piano Repertoire 8*

Studies / Etudes: *Celebration Series Perspectives*®: *Piano Studies / Etudes 8*

Technique: *Technical Requirements for Piano 8*

Popular Selections: *Popular Selection List*

Ear Training and Sight Reading: see p. 135 for ear-training and sight-reading resources.

1 Repertoire

Candidates must prepare *four* contrasting selections: *one* from each of List A, List B, List C, and List D. Repertoire selections must be memorized. Please note that marks will be deducted if music is used.

Bullets used to denote selections for examination purposes:

-   one selection
- ▲ part or section of a larger work
- ▶ selection is found in *Celebration Series Perspectives*®: *Piano Repertoire 8* FHM
- ▲ part or section of a larger work is found in *Celebration Series Perspectives*®: *Piano Repertoire 8* FHM

List A
Baroque Repertoire

Arne, Thomas
Eight Sonatas or Lessons for the Harpsichord
- Sonata no. 6
  - ▲ Gigue

Bach, Carl Philipp Emanuel
- Solfegietto

Bach, Johann Christoph Friedrich
Musikalische Nebenstunden ABR
- Allegro in G major

Bach, Johann Sebastian
- French Suite no. 2 in C minor, BWV 813
  - ▲ Air
- French Suite no. 3 in B minor, BWV 814
  - ▲ Minuet and Trio
Two-Part Inventions
- Invention no. 2 in C minor, BWV 773
- Invention no. 3 in D major, BWV 774
- Invention no. 4 in D minor, BWV 775
- Invention no. 5 in E flat major, BWV 776
- Invention no. 6 in E major, BWV 777
- Invention no. 7 in E minor, BWV 778
- Invention no. 8 in F major, BWV 779
- Invention no. 9 in F minor, BWV 780
- Invention no. 10 in G major, BWV 781
- Invention no. 11 in G minor, BWV 782
- Invention no. 12 in A major, BWV 783
- ▶ Invention no. 13 in A minor, BWV 784
- Invention no. 14 in B flat major, BWV 785

Bach, Johann Sebastian (continued)
- ● Invention no. 15 in B minor, BWV 786
- ▶ Little Prelude in D major, BWV 925 (*Clavierbüchlein vor Wilhelm Friedemann Bach* BAR)
- ● Little Prelude in F major, BWV 928
- ● Little Prelude in D major, BWV 936
- ● Little Prelude in E major, BWV 937
- ● Little Prelude in E minor, BWV 938

Handel, George Frideric
- ● Suite no. 4 in D minor, HWV 437
  - ▲ Allemande
- ● Suite no. 5 in E minor, HWV 438
  - ▲ Allemande
- ● Suite no. 7 in G minor, HWV 432
  - ▲ 5th movement: Gigue

Krebs, Johann Ludwig
- ● Suite no. 1 in D major
  - ▲ 8th movement: Gigue

Pescetti, Giovanni Battista
Six Sonatas (ca 1756)
- ● Sonata in C minor (*Baroque Spirit, 1* ALF)
  - ▲ 3rd movement

Purcell, Henry
- ● Suite no. 5 in C major, Z 666
  - ▲ Prelude

Scarlatti, Domenico
- ● Sonata in C major, L 218, K 398
- ● Sonata in E major, L 430, K 531
- ● Sonata in F minor, L 173, K 185

Telemann, Georg Philipp
- ▶ Fantasia in D minor, TWV 33:2
- ● Fantasia in G minor, TWV 33:8

List B

Classical and Classical-style Repertoire

Arnold, Samuel
- ● Sonata in D major, op. 12, bk 2, no. 3 (*English Piano Music 1780–1800* ABR)
  - ▲ 1st movement *or*
  - ▲ 3rd movement: Rondo

Beethoven, Ludwig van
- ● Bagatelle in F major, op. 33, no. 3
- ● Six Variations on a Swiss Theme in F major, WoO 64
- ● Sonata in G minor, op. 49, no. 1
  - ▲ Andante *or* Rondo
- ● Sonata in G major, op. 49, no. 2
  - ▲ 1st movement *or*
  - ▲ 2nd movement
- ● Sonatina in E flat major, WoO 47, no. 1
  - ▲ 1st movement

Cimarosa, Domenico
- ● Sonata in B flat major (no. 27 in *Sonatas vol. 1* BVP)
- ● Sonata in A major (no. 35 in *Sonatas vol. 1* BVP)

Clementi, Muzio
- ● Sonatina in G major, op. 36, no. 5
  - ▲ 1st movement
- ● Sonatina in E flat major, op. 37, no. 1
  - ▲ 1st or 2nd movement
- ● Sonatina in B flat major, op. 38, no. 2
  - ▲ 1st movement

Dussek, Jan Ladislav
Six Sonatinas, op. 20 ABR
- ● Sonatina in E flat major (no. 6)
  - ▲ 1st movement

Haydn, Franz Joseph
- ● Sonata [Divertimento] in D major, Hob. XVI:4
  - ▲ 1st movement
- ● Sonata [Divertimento] in G major, Hob. XVI:27
  - ▲ Finale
- ● Sonata in G major, Hob. XVI:39
  - ▲ 1st movement

Hummel, Johann Nepomuk
- ● Rondo in C major, op. 52, no. 6

Kuhlau, Friedrich
- ● Sonatina in G major, op. 20, no. 2
  - ▲ 1st movement
- ● Sonatina in F major, op. 20, no. 3
  - ▲ 1st movement
- ● Sonatina in C major, op. 55, no. 6
  - ▲ 1st movement
- ● Sonatina in A major, op. 59, no. 1
  - ▲ 1st movement *or*
  - ▲ 2nd movement
- ● Sonatina in A major, op. 60, no. 2
  - ▲ 1st movement

Mozart, Wolfgang Amadeus
- ● Sonata in C major, K 545
  - ▲ 1st movement
Viennese Sonatinas, K 439b
- ● Viennese Sonatina no. 2 in A major
  - ▲ Rondo

List C

Romantic Repertoire

Brahms, Johannes
Walzer, op. 39 (*Brahms' simplified version*)(*Celebrate Brahms* FHM)
- ● Waltz in A flat major (no. 15)

Chopin, Frédéric
- ● Mazurka in A minor, op. 7, no. 2
- ● Mazurka in G minor, op. 67, no. 2, CT 93
- ● Mazurka in A minor, op. 68, no. 2
- ● Nocturne in G minor, op. 15, no. 3
- ● Polonaise in A flat major, CT 162
- ▶ Prelude in B minor, op. 28, no. 6
- ● Prelude in E major, op. 28, no. 9
- ● Waltz in A flat major, op. 69, no. 1 ("L'adieu")
- ● Waltz in B minor, op. 69, no. 2

Field, John
- ● Nocturne no. 5 in B flat, H 37

Gade, Niels
Albumleaves
- Capriccio (*More Romantic Pieces for Piano*, 5 ABR)

Aquarelles, op. 19 ABR
- Intermezzo (no. 8)

Glière, Reinhold
- Melody, op. 34, no. 13

Eight Easy Piano Pieces, op. 43 ABR
- ▶ Prelude in D flat major (no. 1)

Grieg, Edvard
- Humoreske, op. 6, no. 3 PET

Lyric Pieces, op. 71
- Puck (no. 3)

Six Poetic Tone Pictures, op. 3 ABR
- ▶ Allegro, ma non troppo (no. 1)
- Allegro cantabile (no. 2)
- Andante con sentimento (no. 4)

Hofmann, Heinrich
Stimmungsbilder, op. 88
- ▶ Nocturne (no. 3)

Kalinnikov, Vasili Sergeievich
- ▶ Chanson triste / A Sad Song

Lyadov, Anatoli Konstantinovich
- Prelude in B flat minor, op. 31, no. 2 (*Preludes, Trifles and Other Pieces* PET)

Liszt, Franz
Six Consolations
- Andante con moto (no. 1)

Macdowell, Edward
Woodland Sketches
- At an Old Trysting-Place (no. 3)

Mendelssohn, Felix
- Gondola Song (Barcarolle) in A major
- Lied ohne Worte, op. 19, no. 2
- Lied ohne Worte, op. 62, no. 4
- Lied ohne Worte, op. 102, no. 2

Sechs Kinderstücke, op. 72
- ▶ Andante sostenuto (no. 2)

Rebikov, Vladimir Ivanovich
- Valse mélancolique, op. 3, no. 3 KJO

Reinecke, Carl
- Sonatina in B flat major, op. 47, no. 3
  - ▲ 2nd movement

Schubert, Franz
Zwei Scherzi, D 593
- Scherzo in B flat major

Schumann, Robert
Album für die Jugend, op. 68
- Knight Rupert (no. 12)
- The Horseman (no. 23)
- Remembrance (no. 28)
- The Stranger (no. 29)

Kinderszenen, op. 15
- ▶ An Important Event (no. 6)

Smetana, Bedřich
Sechs Albumblätter, op. 2 BAR
- Song (no. 2)

Tchaikovsky, Pyotr Il'yich
The Seasons, op. 37b
- March (Song of the Lark)

List D

Post-Romantic, 20th-, and 21st-century Repertoire

Albéniz, Isaac
España, op. 165
- Prelude (no. 1)
- Tango (no. 2)

Archer, Violet
Four Bagatelles WAT
- Forceful (no. 1)

Six Preludes WAT
- Prelude (no. 5)

Bartók, Béla
For Children, 1 B&H
- Allegro moderato (no. 39)
- Swine-herd's Dance (no. 40)

For Children, 2 B&H
- Revelry (no. 22)
- Canon (no. 29)

Ten Easy Pieces EMB
- ▶ Evening at the Village

Behrens, Jack
- New Year Waltz CMC

Benjamin, Arthur L.
Fantasies, 2 B&H
- Silent and Soft and Slow Descends the Snow

Bernstein, Seymour
Birds, 2 MAN
- The Nightingale (no. 7)

Brown, Stephen
Giant Things SWA
- Ukrainian Easter Egg

Casella, Alfredo
Eleven Children's Pieces, op. 35 MAS
- Bolero

Chatman, Stephen
Amusements, 3 FHM
- ▶ Sneaky

Coulthard, Jean
Early Pieces for Piano ALK
- The Rider on the Plain (no. 10)

Coutts, George
- Mazurka (*Meet Canadian Composers at the Piano*, 2 GVT [OP])

Debussy, Claude
- Page d'album

Children's Corner Suite
- Jimbo's Lullaby (no. 2)
- ▶ The Little Shepherd (no. 5)

Faith, Richard
- Souvenir (12 X 11: *Piano Music in 20th Century America* ALF)

Freedman, Harry
- Rent a Rag ANE

Gardiner, Mary
Short Circuits STU
- Currents
- Luminescence

Grovlez, Gabriel
L'almanach aux images S&B
- Berceuse de la poupée
- ▶ Petites litanies de Jésus / Little Litanies of Jesus

Ibert, Jacques
Histoires pour piano ALF; LED
- A Giddy Girl (no. 4)

Jaque, Rhené
- Caprice CHC
- Toccata (Sur touches blanches / On the White Keys) CHC

Kabalevsky, Dmitri
- Prelude, op. 38, no. 8

In the Pioneer Camp, op. 3/86
- ▶ Early Morning Exercises (no. 2)

Kenins, Talivaldis
- Bagatelle (*Legacy Collection*, 4 FHM)

Kodály, Zoltán
Children's Dances (Gyermektáncok) B&H
- Vivace (no. 3) *and* Moderato cantabile (no. 4)

Kuzmenko, Larysa
- ▶ Mysterious Summer's Night

Louie, Alexina
Star Light, Star Bright FHM
- Blue Sky I
- ▶ O Moon
- Rings of Saturn
- Star Gazing

Milhaud, Darius
L'enfant aime / A Child Loves, op. 289 UNI
- La vie / Life (no. 5)

Nakada, Yoshinao
Japanese Festival WAR
- ▶ Etude Allegro

Norton, Christopher
Christopher Norton Connections for Piano™, 8 FHM
- Celtic Lament
- Cuban Romance
- Hot Day
Rock Preludes B&H
- Prelude I: Wildcat
- Prelude VI: Blue Sneakers

Peterson, Oscar
- The Gentle Waltz (*Oscar Peterson Originals* HAL)
Jazz Piano for the Young Pianist, 3 HSN [OP]
- ▶ Jazz Exercise No. 2
- ▶ Jazz Exercise No. 3

Piazzolla, Astor
- ▶ Milonga del ángel LAG

Pinto, Octavio
Scenas infantis SCH
- March, Little Soldier!
- ▶ Roda-roda!

Ravel, Maurice
- Prélude DUR

Satie, Eric
- Gnossienne no. 3
Trois gymnopédies
- any *one*

Scriabin, Alexander
Twenty-Four Preludes, op. 11
- Prelude (no. 22)

Southam, Ann
Three in Blue: Jazz Preludes BER
- any *one*

Starer, Robert
Sketches in Color WAR
- ▶ Pink *and* Crimson

Thurgood, George
- Fissure CMC
- Saturday Night CMC

Torjussen, Trygve
- To the Rising Sun, op. 4, no. 1 ALF

Tsitsaros, Christos
Nine Tales FHM
- Mayflowers

Turina, Joaquín
Miniaturas, op. 52 OTT
- La aldea duerme/ The Sleeping Village

Wuensch, Gerhard
- Scherzo (*Horizons*, 2 WAT)
Twelve Glimpses into 20th Century Idioms, op. 37 B&H
- Oliver's Twist

2 Technical Requirements

Studies / Etudes

Candidates must prepare *two contrasting* selections from the following list of studies / etudes. Memorization is *not* required and will not be rewarded with extra marks.

Bullets used to denote selections for examination purposes:
► selection is found in *Celebration Series Perspectives®: Piano Studies / Etudes* 8 FHM

Burgmüller, Johann Friedrich
18 Characteristic Studies, op. 109
► The Gypsies (no. 4)

Chatman, Stephen
Preludes for Piano, 3 FHM
► Chromatic Etude

Heller, Stephen
25 Études faciles, op. 45
► Etude in D minor (no. 15)

Hofmann, Heinrich
Stimmungsbilder, op. 88
► Lyric Song (no. 7)

Kabalevsky, Dmitri
30 Pieces for Children, op. 27 SCH
► Etude (no. 24)

Loeschhorn, Carl Albert
► Song of the Waterfall

Norton, Christopher
Christopher Norton Connections for Piano™, 8 FHM
► Jane's Song

Previn, André
Impressions for Piano WAR
► In Perpetual Motion

Rowley, Alec
Thirty Melodic and Rhythmic Studies, op. 42
► Lied (no. 13)

Schoenmehl, Mike
Piano Studies in Pop SIK
► Classical Pop Tune

Stamaty, Camille Marie
Vingt études de moyenne difficulté, op. 38 (Paris, 1859)
► Etude in F major (no. 2)

Swinstead, Felix
Six Studies for the Development of the Left Hand B&H
► Study in D major

Takács, Jenő
Klänge und Farben, op. 95 DOB
► Toccatina (no. 12)

Tarenghi, Mario
Three Small Scenes for Children RIC
► Dance of the Marionettes

Candidates may substitute a popular selection for *one* of the studies / etudes. See p. 130 for details.

Substitutions

Candidates may substitute *one* repertoire selection or *one* study / etude selection with a musical work *not found* in the Repertoire Lists for Grade 8. See p. 130 for more information on substitutions.

Total Substitutions Permitted	Requires Prior Approval (Submit an Examination Substitute Piece Request)		Does Not Require Prior Approval		
	Repertoire Substitution		Repertoire Substitution		Study / Etude Substitution
one Repertoire selection *or* *one* Study / Etude	One repertoire selection from piano literature comparable in style and difficulty to the corresponding List A, B, C, or D of Grade 8	*or*	One selection from the corresponding List of Grade 9	*or*	One study / etude from Grade 9 *or* One Teacher's Choice selection (must be of equal difficulty and a length of 2–2.5 minutes) *or* One selection from the *Popular Selection List* for Grade 8 or Grade 9

Technical Tests

Candidates must play all Technical Tests from memory, ascending and descending, with good tone and logical fingering, at a steady tempo. Metronome markings indicate minimum speeds. All scales are to be played *legato* unless otherwise indicated.

See "Technical Patterns" on p. 19 for examples.

Keys for Grade 8   Major C, D, A, E, B, B♭, E♭, G♭
                    Minor C, D, A, E, B, B♭, E♭, F♯

Scales	Keys	Played	Tempo	Note values
Parallel Motion	C, D, A, E, B, B♭, E♭, G♭ major C, D, A, E, B, B♭, E♭, F♯ minor (harmonic and melodic)	HT 4 octaves	♩ = 88	♬♬
Staccato	A, B, B♭ major B minor (harmonic and melodic)	HT 3 octaves	♩ = 88	♩♩♩³
Formula Pattern	A, B, B♭ major B minor (harmonic)	HT 4 octaves	♩ = 88	♬♬
Chromatic	beginning on A and B♭	HT 2 octaves	♩ = 88	♬♬
Scales in octaves solid (blocked) *staccato* *or*	A, B♭ major	HS 1 octave	♩ = 88	♫
Scales in octaves broken *legato*			♩ = 108	♫

Chords	Keys	Played	Tempo	Note values
Tonic Four-note Chords (root position and inversions) broken	C, D, A, E, B, B♭, E♭, G♭ major C, D, A, E, B, B♭, E♭, F♯ minor	HT 2 octaves (ending with I–IV–V–I chord progression)	♩ = 80	♬♬
Dominant 7th (root position and inversions) broken	C, D, A, E, B, B♭, E♭, G♭ major C, D, A, E, B, B♭, E♭, F♯ minor	HT 2 octaves	♩ = 80	♬♬
solid (blocked)			♩ = 100	♩ ♩
Diminished 7th (root position and inversions) broken	C, D, A, E, B, B♭, E♭, F♯ minor	HT 2 octaves	♩ = 80	♬♬
solid (blocked)			♩ = 100	♩ ♩

Arpeggios	Keys	Played	Tempo	Note values
Tonic (root position followed by inversions in sequence)	C, D, A, E, B, B♭, E♭, G♭ major C, D, A, E, B, B♭, E♭, F♯ minor	HT 4 octaves	♩ = 69	♬♬
Dominant 7th (root position only)				
Diminished 7th (root position only)	C, D, A, E, B, B♭, E♭, F♯ minor			

3 Ear Tests

Intervals

Candidates will be asked to identify the following intervals. The examiner will play each interval *once* in broken form.
or
Candidates may choose to sing or hum the following intervals. The examiner will play the first note *once*.

Above a given note	Below a given note
major and minor 2nds	major 2nd
major and minor 3rds	major and minor 3rds
major and minor 6ths	minor 6th
minor 7th	major 7th
perfect 4th	perfect 4th
perfect 5th	perfect 5th
perfect octave	perfect octave

Chords

Candidates will be asked to identify any of the following chords after the examiner has played the chord once in solid (blocked) form, close position.

Chords	Position
major and minor triads	root position
dominant 7th	root position
diminished 7th	root position

Cadences

Candidates will be asked to identify the following cadences by name or symbols. The examiner will play the tonic chord *once*, and then play a short phrase ending in a cadence *twice*

Name of Cadence	Symbols
perfect or authentic	V–I
plagal	IV–I

Example only

Perfect (Authentic)

Playback

Candidates will be asked to play back a melody approximately one octave in range. The examiner will name the key, play the tonic chord *once*, and play the melody *twice*.

Approximate length	Keys
nine notes	C, G, D, F, B♭ major

Example only

4 Sight Reading

Playing

Candidates will be asked to play a short composition at sight.

Difficulty	Time signature	Keys
Grade 5 repertoire	any time signature	major and minor keys up to five sharps or five flats

Clapping

Candidates will be asked to clap or tap the rhythm of a melody. A steady pace and rhythmic accentuation are expected.

Time signature	Approximate length
$\frac{2}{4}$ $\frac{3}{4}$ $\frac{4}{4}$ $\frac{6}{8}$	four measures

Example only

The Junior Musicianship examination can be substituted for the Ear Tests and Sight Reading sections of the Grade 8 piano examination (see p. 123).

Grade 9

Reaching the Grade 9 level is a considerable accomplishment that brings new musical demands for the hand, ear, and mind: thick textures, delicate balances, and subtle articulations, as well as complex harmonies and forms. Baroque three-part contrapuntal works, larger-scale Classical sonata movements, and Romantic and contemporary character pieces all present candidates with a wide range of challenges and rewards.

Candidates who plan to take an ARCT in Piano Performance examination must include a Prelude and Fugue by J.S. Bach in the examination program for their Grade 9, Grade 10, or ARCT examination.

	Grade 9 Requirements	Marks
1	**Repertoire**	**56**
	one selection from List A: Baroque Repertoire	16 (1.5)
	one selection from List B: Classical Repertoire	16 (1.5)
	one selection from List C: Romantic Repertoire	12 (1)
	one selection from List D: Post-Romantic, 20th-, and 21st-century Repertoire	12 (1)
	(The figures in parentheses indicate marks awarded for memory as a portion of the total mark for each selection.)	
2	**Technical Requirements**	**24**
	Studies / Etudes: two studies / etudes from the Syllabus list	6 + 6
	Technical Tests	12
	Major keys: all	
	Minor keys: all	
	– parallel motion scales	
	– staccato scales	
	– formula pattern scales	
	– chromatic scales	
	– scales in octaves	
	– chromatic scales in octaves	
	– tonic four-note chords	
	– dominant 7th and diminished 7th chords	
	– tonic arpeggios	
	– dominant 7th and diminished 7th arpeggios	
3	**Ear Tests**	**10**
	Intervals	3
	Chords	2
	Cadences	2
	Playback	3
4	**Sight Reading**	**10**
	Playing	7
	Clapping	3
	Theory Co-requisites	
	Advanced Rudiments [Grade 2 Rudiments]	
	Basic Harmony or Basic Keyboard Harmony [Grade 3 Harmony or Grade 3 Keyboard Harmony]	
	History 1: An Overview [Grade 3 History]	
	Total possible marks (pass = 60)	**100**

Resources for Grade 9 Examination Preparation

Repertoire: *Celebration Series Perspectives®: Piano Repertoire* 9

Studies / Etudes: *Celebration Series Perspectives®: Piano Studies / Etudes* 9

Popular Selections: *Popular Selection List*

Ear Training and Sight Reading: see p. 135 for ear-training and sight-reading resources.

1 Repertoire

Candidates must prepare *four* contrasting selections: *one* from each of List A, List B, List C, and List D. Repertoire selections must be memorized. Please note that marks will be deducted if music is used. Candidates are encouraged to consider the overall length and balance of their programs within the time allotted for the examination.

Bullets used to denote selections for examination purposes:

- ● one selection
- ▲ part or section of a larger work
- ▶ selection is found in *Celebration Series Perspectives®: Piano Repertoire* 9 FHM
- ▲ part or section of a larger work is found in *Celebration Series Perspectives®: Piano Repertoire* 9 FHM

List A
Baroque Repertoire

Bach, Johann Sebastian
- ● Capriccio sopra la lontananza del fratello dilettissimo, BWV 992
  - ▲ 1st movement: Adagissimo
- ● Fugue in C major, BWV 952
- ● Fugue in C major, BWV 953 (*Klavierbüchlein vor Wilhelm Friedemann Bach* BAR)

Das wohltemperierte Klavier, 1
- ▶ Prelude and Fugue in C minor, BWV 847

Three-part Inventions (Sinfonias)
- ● Sinfonia no. 1 in C major, BWV 787
- ● Sinfonia no. 2 in C minor, BWV 788
- ● Sinfonia no. 3 in D major, BWV 789
- ● Sinfonia no. 4 in D minor, BWV 790
- ● Sinfonia no. 5 in E flat major, BWV 791
- ▶ Sinfonia no. 6 in E major, BWV 792
- ▶ Sinfonia no. 7 in E minor, BWV 793
- ● Sinfonia no. 8 in F major, BWV 794
- ● Sinfonia no. 9 in F minor, BWV 795
- ● Sinfonia no. 10 in G major, BWV 796
- ● Sinfonia no. 11 in G minor, BWV 797
- ● Sinfonia no. 12 in A major, BWV 798
- ● Sinfonia no. 13 in A minor, BWV 799
- ● Sinfonia no. 14 in B flat major, BWV 800
- ● Sinfonia no. 15 in B minor, BWV 801

Daquin, Louis-Claude
Premier livre de pièces de clavecin
- Troisième suite
  - ▲ Le coucou (Rondeau)

Handel, George Frideric
- Suite no. 1 in B flat major, HWV 434
  - ▲ Air with variations
- Suite no. 4 in E minor, HWV 429
  - ▲ 2nd movement: Allemande

Krebs, Johann Ludwig
- Suite no. 3 in E flat major
  - ▲ 10th movement: Gigue

Scarlatti, Domenico
- Sonata in C major, L 104, K 159
- Sonata in G minor, L 128, K 426
- ▶ Sonata in F minor, L 187, K 481
- Sonata in B minor, L 263, K 377
- Sonata in F minor, L 281, K 239
- Sonata in E minor, L 321, K 263
- Sonata in D minor, L 413, K 9
- ▶ Sonata in D major, L 463, K 430
- Sonata in G major, L 486, K 13

List B
Classical Repertoire

Bach, Carl Philipp Emanuel
Sei sonate per cembalo (Prussian Sonatas)
- Sonata in C minor, Wq 48/4, H 27
  - ▲ 3rd movement
Clavier-Sonatenbebst einegen Rondos
- Sonata in F minor, Wq 57/6, H 173
  - ▲ 1st movement: Allegro assai

Bach, Johann Christian
- Sonata in D major, op. 5, no. 2
  - ▲ 1st movement
- Sonata in B flat major, op. 17, no. 6
  - ▲ 1st movement

Beethoven, Ludwig van
- Bagatelle in E flat major, op. 33, no. 1
- Neun Variationen über das Thema "Quant' è più bello," WoO 69
- ▶ Rondo in C major, op. 51, no. 1
- ▶ Six Easy Variations on an Original Theme, WoO 77
- Six Variations on "Nel cor più non mi sento" (*La Molinara* by Paisiello), WoO 70 (*Celebrate Beethoven, vol. I* FHM)
- Sonata in G major, op. 79
  - ▲ 1st movement

Clementi, Muzio
- Sonata in E flat major, op. 37, no. 1
  - ▲ 2nd movement: Presto

Haydn, Franz Joseph
- Sonata in F major, Hob. XVI:23
  - ▲ 1st movement
- ▶ Sonata in E minor, Hob. XVI:34
  - ▲ 1st movement *or*
  - ▲ 2nd movement *or*
  - ▲ 3rd movement
- Sonata in D major, Hob. XVI:37
  - ▲ 1st movement
  - ▲ 2nd *and* 3rd movements

Mozart, Wolfgang Amadeus
- ▶ Fantasia in D minor, K 397 (385g)
- Sonata in G major, K 283 (189h)
  - ▲ 1st *or* 2nd movement
- Sonata in C major, K 330 (300h)
  - ▲ 1st movement *or*
  - ▲ 2nd movement
- Sonata in B flat major, K 570
  - ▲ 1st movement

Soler, Antonio
- Sonata in D minor, EA no. 25 HEN

List C
Romantic Repertoire

Brahms, Johannes
- Intermezzo in B flat major, op. 76, no. 4
- ▶ Intermezzo in A minor, op. 76, no. 7

Chopin, Frédéric
- Mazurka in F sharp minor, op. 6, no. 1
- Mazurka in A minor, op. posth. 67, no. 4
- Mazurka in C major, op. 68, no. 1
- Nocturne in E flat major, op. 9, no. 2
- Nocturne in B major, op. 32, no. 1
- Nocturne in G minor, op. 37, no. 1
- Nocturne in F minor, op. 55, no. 1
- ▶ Nocturne in C sharp minor, op. posth. KK IVa 16
- Prelude in F sharp major, op. 28, no. 13
- Prelude in D flat major, op. 28, no. 15
- Waltz in D flat major, op. 64, no. 1 ("Minute")
- Waltz in C sharp minor, op. 64, no. 2
- Waltz in A flat major, op. 64, no. 3
- ▶ Waltz in G flat major, op. posth. 70, no. 1, CT 217
- Waltz in F minor, op. posth. 70, no. 2
- Waltz in D flat major, op. posth. 70, no. 3

Glinka, Mikhail Ivanovich
- Variations on a Russian Song (A minor) KON

Grieg, Edvard
Lyric Pieces, op. 43
- Butterfly (no. 1)
- Erotik (no. 5)
- To Spring (no. 6)
Lyric Pieces, op. 54
- ▶ Notturno (no. 4)

Liszt, Franz
- En rêve, S 207
Six Consolations HEN
- Consolation no. 2: Un poco più mosso
- ▶ Consolation no. 3: Lento placido
- Consolation no. 4: Quasi adagio

MacDowell, Edward
- Scotch Poem, op. 31, no. 2

Woodland Sketches, op, 51
- Will o' the Wisp (no. 2)

Mendelssohn, Felix
- Lied ohne Worte, op. 19, no. 1
- ▶ Lied ohne Worte, op. 30, no.1
- Lied ohne Worte, op. 38, no. 1
- Lied ohne Worte, op. 38, no. 2
- Lied ohne Worte, op. 38, no. 6 (Duetto)
- Lied ohne Worte, op. 53, no. 2
- Lied ohne Worte, op. 62, no. 1
- Lied ohne Worte, op. 85, no. 1
- Lied ohne Worte, op. 102, no. 4

Schubert, Franz
Moments musicaux, op. 94, D 780
- no. 3 in F minor: Allegretto moderato
- no. 6 in A flat major: Allegretto

Vier Impromptus für Klavier, op. 142, D 935
- ▶ Impromptu in A flat major (no. 2)

Schumann, Robert
- Romance in F sharp major, op. 28, no. 2

Fantasiestücke, op. 12
- Grillen (no. 4)

Waldszenen: neun Klavierstücke, op. 82
- Herberge (no. 6)

Albumblätter, op. 124
- ▶ Schlummerlied / Slumber Song (no. 16)

Tchaikovsky, Pyotr Il'yich
The Seasons, op. 37b
- April (Snowdrop) (no. 4)
- June (Barcarolle) (no. 6)
- October (Autumn Song) (no. 10)
- December (Christmas) (no. 12)

List D

Post-Romantic, 20th-, and 21st-century Repertoire

Archer, Violet
Four Bagatelles WAT
- Capricious (no. 2)
- Introspective (no. 3)
- Festive (no. 4)

Arlen, Harold
- ▶ Over the Rainbow (arr. George Shearing) ALF

Bartók, Béla
Ten Easy Pieces EMB
- Bear Dance

Beach, Amy
- Scottish Legend, op. 54, no. 1 (*Piano Music: Amy Beach* DOV)

Copland, Aaron
Four Piano Blues B&H
- no. 1
- no. 2
- no. 3

Coulthard, Jean
- White Caps BER

Twelve Preludes for Piano BER
- Prelude no. 1 (Leggiero)

Debussy, Claude
- Mazurka PET
- Rêverie

Children's Corner Suite
- Golliwogg's Cake-Walk

Préludes, 1
- ▶ La fille aux cheveux de lin (no. 8)

Préludes, 2
- Canope (no. 10)

Dolin, Samuel
- Prelude for John Weinzweig CMC

Duncan, Martha Hill
Isla Vista Suite CMC
- Monarchs
- Santa Ana Winds

Fauré, Gabriel
- ▶ Romance sans paroles, op. 17, no. 3

Huit pièces brèves, op. 84 LED
- Improvisation (no. 5)

Fleming, Robert
- Toccatina WAT

Gardiner, Mary
- Footloose ALK

Two for D CMC
- no. 1 *or* no. 2

Gershwin, George
- Prelude (Melody no. 17) ALF

Granados, Enrique
Danzas españolas
- Andaluza (Playera), op. 5, no. 5 ALF; SAL

Grechaninov, Alexandr T.
Sonatina in F major, op. 110, no. 2
- 1st movement

Griffes, Charles T.
Three Tone Pictures, op. 5 SCH
- The Lake at Evening (no. 1)

Grovlez, Gabriel
L'almanach aux images S&B
- Les ânes
- Chanson de l'escarpolette
- La sarabande

A Child's Garden CHS
- Chanson (no. 5)
- Pepita (no. 6)

Henderson, Ruth Watson
- ▶ Ocean Vista

Hovhaness, Alan
- Mystic Flute PET

Ibert, Jacques
Histoires pour piano ALF; LED
- La cage de cristal
- Le petit âne blanc

Ireland, John
- The Darkened Valley S&B

Kabalevsky, Dmitri
- Sonatina in C major, op. 13, no. 1
  - ▲ 1st movement
- Variations in D major, op. 40, no. 1

Easy Variations for Piano, op. 51
- Six Variations on a Ukrainian Folk Song (no. 5)

24 Preludes, op. 38
- Prelude no. 1 *and* Prelude no. 2
- Prelude no. 12

Six Pieces for Piano, op. 88
- ▶ Dreams (no. 1)

Six Preludes and Fugues, op. 61
- Prelude and Fugue no. 5 in C minor
- Prelude and Fugue no. 6 in F major

Kenins, Talivaldis
Diversities CMC
- *two* of nos. 5, 9, 12

Khachaturian, Aram
- Sonatina SCH
  - ▲ 1st *or* 3rd movement

Louie, Alexina
Music for Piano GVT
- Changes
- ▶ Distant Memories
- The Enchanted Bells
- Once upon a Time

Star Light, Star Bright FHM
- Moonlight Toccata

Manzano, Miguel
Spanish Preludes B&H
- ▶ Decadent Sentimental Song

Mompou, Federico
Cancións y Danzas SAL
- Cantabile expressivo (no. 6)

Morawetz, Oskar
- Scherzino CMC

Muczynski, Robert
Six Preludes, op. 6 (Muczynski: Collected Piano Pieces SCH)
- Prelude (no. 6)

Palmgren, Selim
- May Night, op. 27, no. 4 ALF; SCH

Pépin, Clermont
Three Short Pieces for the Piano CMC
- Le nez

Peterson, Oscar
Canadiana Suite HAL
- Laurentide Waltz (no. 2)

Pinto, Octavio
Scenas infantis SCH
- Run, Run!
- ▶ Salta, Salta

Poulenc, Francis
- Valse (*Album des six* ESC; MAS)

Prokofiev, Sergei
Four Pieces, op. 32
- Gavotte (no. 3)

Tales of the Old Grandmother, op. 31
- Sostenuto (no. 4)

Ravel, Maurice
Le tombeau de Couperin DUR
- Menuet

Schafer, R. Murray
- Polytonality ARC

Schwantner, Joseph
- Veiled Autumn (**K**indertoteslied) (*Changing Faces: New Piano Works* OTT)

Scriabin, Alexander
24 Preludes, op. 11
- *two* of nos. 9, 10, and 13

Shchedrin, Rodion Konstantinovich
- ▶ Humoreske

Shostakovich, Dmitri
24 Preludes, op. 34
- Prelude no. 24 in D minor

Sibelius, Jean
Ten Pieces, op. 24; KAL; MAS
- ▶ Romance (no. 9)

Starer, Robert
Five Preludes MCA
- Prelude no. 2 *and* Prelude no. 3

Stevens, Halsey
- Notturno (*12 X 11: Piano Music in 20th Century America* ALF)

Stone, Court
- Old Country Suite HOM
  - ▲ Mist

Strauss, Richard
Fünf Stimmungsbilder, op. 9 UNI
- Träumerei (no. 4)

Takács, Jenő
- Kleine Sonate, op. 51 DOB

Wenn der Frosch auf Reisen geht DOB
- ▶ Merry Andrew

Tcherepnin, Alexander
Bagatelles, op. 5 ALF; HEU; SCH
- no. 1 *and* no. 4
- no. 3 *and* no. 5
- no. 8
- no. 10

Turina, Joaquín
Niñeras (Petite suite), op. 21
- Procession of the Tin Soldiers (no. 3) SAL

El circo / The Circus OTT
- Trapeze Artists (no. 6)

Cuentos d'España, op. 20
- In the Garden of Murcia (no. 4) SAL

Turina, Joaquín (continued)
Cinco danzas gitanas I, op. 55 SAL
- ● Sacro-Monte (no. 5)
Miniaturas, op. 52 SCH; OTT
- ● *two* of:
  - – Caminando (no. 1)
  - – Se acercan soldados (no. 2)
  - – Amanecer (no. 4)
  - – El mercando (no. 5)
  - – Duo sentimental (no. 6)
  - – Fiesta (no. 7)
  - – La Vuelta (no. 8)

Villa-Lobos, Heitor
Prole do bebê ALF
- ● O Polinchinello (Punch)

Weiner, Leo
Three Hungarian Rural Dances EMB
- ● Fox Dance (no. 1) PRE

Wuensch, Gerhard
Mini-Suite no. 1 B&H
- ● Prelude
- ● Tarantella
Mini-Suite no. 2 B&H
- ● Prelude

2 Technical Requirements

Studies / Etudes

Candidates must prepare *two contrasting* selections from the following list of studies / etudes. Memorization is *not* required and will not be rewarded with extra marks.

Bullets used to denote selections for examination purposes:
- ▶ selection is found in *Celebration Series Perspectives*®: *Piano Studies / Etudes 9* FHM

Bartók, Béla
Fourteen Bagatelles, op. 6 EMB
- ▶ Bagatelle no. 2

Berens, Hermann
Neueste Schule der Geläfigkeit, op. 61
- ▶ Study in A minor (no. 13)

Concone, Giuseppe
20 Études chantantes, op. 30
- ▶ Study in C major (no. 20)

Cramer, Johann Baptist
Studio per il pianoforte, 1
- ▶ Study in E minor (no. 2)

Czerny, Carl
- ▶ Study in C major, op. 553, no. 1

Duvernoy, Jean-Baptiste
École de mécanisme, op. 120
- ▶ Study in C major (no. 10)

Gade, Niels
Aquarelles, op. 19 ABR
- ▶ Scherzo (no. 2)

Heller, Stephen
25 études pour former au sentiment du rythme et à l'expression, op. 47
- ▶ Etude in G major (no. 24)

Hofmann, Heinrich
Nachklänge, op. 37
- ▶ To the Lute (no. 1)

Ibert, Jacques
Petite suite en quinze images FOE
- ▶ La promenade en traîneau

Kabalevsky, Dmitri
Six Pieces for Piano, op. 88
- ▶ Who'll Win the Argument? (no. 2)

Moszkowski, Moritz
Dexterity and Style: 20 Melodic Studies for the Piano, op. 91
- ▶ Study in E flat major (no. 17)

Schytte, Ludwig
25 Études modernes, faciles et progressives
- ▶ Study in A major, op. 68, no. 7

Substitutions

Candidates may substitute *one* repertoire selection or *one* study / etude selection with a musical work *not found* in the Repertoire Lists for Grade 9. See p. 130 for more information on substitutions.

Total Substitutions Permitted	Requires Prior Approval (Submit an Examination Substitute Piece Request)		Does Not Require Prior Approval		
	Repertoire Substitution		Repertoire Substitution		Study / Etude Substitution
one Repertoire selection *or* *one* Study / Etude	One repertoire selection from piano literature comparable in style and difficulty to the corresponding List A, B, or C of Grade 9	*or*	One selection from the corresponding List of Grade 10 *or* One Own Choice selection may replace a piece from List D	*or*	One study / etude from Grade 10 *or* One selection from the *Popular Selection List* for Grade 9

Technical Tests

Candidates must play all Technical Tests from memory, ascending and descending, with good tone and logical fingering, at a steady tempo. Metronome markings indicate minimum speeds. All scales are to be played *legato* unless otherwise indicated.

See "Technical Patterns" on p. 19 for examples.

Keys for Grade 9: all major keys; all minor keys

Scales	Keys	Played	Tempo	Note values
Parallel Motion	all major keys all minor keys (harmonic and melodic)	HT 4 octaves	♩ = 104	♬♬
Staccato	B, A♭, D♭ major G♯, F, B♭ minor (harmonic and melodic)	HT 3 octaves	♩ = 104	♪♪♪ (triplet)
Formula Pattern	B, A♭, D♭ major G♯, F, B♭ minor (harmonic)	HT 4 octaves	♩ = 96	♬♬
Chromatic	beginning on any note	HT 4 octaves	♩ = 96	♬♬
Scales in Octaves solid (blocked) *staccato* *or*	B, A♭, D♭ major F minor (harmonic and melodic)	HT 2 octaves	♩ = 60	♬♬
broken *legato*			♩ = 72	
Chromatic Scales in Octaves solid (blocked) *staccato* *or*	beginning on any note	HT 2 octaves	♩ = 60	♬♬
broken *legato*			♩ = 72	

Chords	Keys	Played	Tempo	Note values
Tonic Four-note Chords (root position and inversion) broken	all keys	HT 2 octaves (ending with I–IV–I$^6_4$–V–I chord progression)	♩ = 104	♬♬
solid (blocked) *or*			♩ = 80	♩ ♩
broken alternate-note pattern			♩ = 80	♬♬
Dominant 7th (root position and inversion) broken	all keys	HT 2 octaves	♩ = 104	♬♬
solid (blocked)			♩ = 104	♩ ♩
Diminished 7th (root position and inversion) broken	all minor keys	HT 2 octaves	♩ = 104	♬♬
solid (blocked)			♩ = 104	♩ ♩

Arpeggios	Keys	Played	Tempo	Note values
Tonic (Candidates may be asked to play all inversions in sequence beginning in root position or any inversion, *or* to play root position or any one inversion only)	all keys	HT 4 octaves	♩ = 84	♬♬
Dominant 7th (root position followed by inversions in sequence)				
Diminished 7th (root position followed by inversions in sequence)				

Grade 9

3 Ear Tests

Intervals

Candidates will be asked to identify the following intervals. The examiner will play each interval *once* in broken form.

or

Candidates may choose to sing or hum the following intervals. The examiner will play the first note *once*.

Above a given note	Below a given note
any interval within the octave	any interval within the octave *except* diminished 5th / augmented 4th

Chords

Candidates will be asked to identify any of the following chords and their inversion or position after the examiner has played the chord *once* in solid (blocked) form, close position.

Chords	Position
major and minor triads	root position, 1st inversion
dominant 7th	root position
diminished 7th	root position

Cadences

Candidates will be asked to identify the following cadences by name or symbols. The examiner will play the tonic chord *once*, and then play a short phrase ending in a cadence *twice*.

Name of Cadence	Symbols
perfect or authentic	V–I
plagal	IV–I
imperfect	I–V

Example only

I   V

Imperfect

Playback

Candidates will be asked to play back the upper voice of a two-voice phrase. The examiner will name the key, play the tonic chord *once*, and play the melody *twice*.

Approximate length	Keys
two or three measures	C, G, D, F, B♭ major

Example only

4 Sight Reading

Playing

Candidates will be asked to play a short composition at sight.

Difficulty	Time signature	Keys
Grade 6 repertoire	any time signature	major and minor keys up to six sharps or six flats

Clapping

Candidates will be asked to clap or tap the rhythm of a melody. A steady pace and rhythmic accentuation are expected.

Time signature	Approximate length
$\frac{2}{4}$ $\frac{3}{4}$ $\frac{4}{4}$ $\frac{6}{8}$	five measures

Example only

The intermediate Musicianship examination can be submitted for the Ear Tests and Sight Reading sections of the Grade 9 piano examination (see p. 123).

Grade 10

Having arrived at the highest graded level (before the ARCT diploma), Grade 10 candidates are challenged and rewarded with repertoire by the greatest composers of the piano literature. Three- and four-part contrapuntal texture, contrasting movements of Classical sonatas, and more technically and interpretively demanding Romantic and contemporary character pieces form the basis of candidates' developing artistry.

Grade 10 candidates who wish to pursue an ARCT in Piano Performance or ARCT in Piano Pedagogy must achieve either an overall mark of 75 or a minimum of 70 percent in each section of the Grade 10 examination. Figures in bold parentheses next to the total mark allotted for each section indicate the minimum number of marks required to receive 70 percent.

Candidates who plan to take an ARCT in Piano Performance examination must include a Prelude and Fugue by J.S. Bach in the examination program for their Grade 9, Grade 10, or ARCT examinations.

	Grade 10 Requirements	Marks
1	**Repertoire**	**56 (39)**
	one selection from List A: Works of J.S. Bach	12 (1.5)
	one selection from List B: Classical Repertoire	14 (1.5)
	one selection from List C: Romantic Repertoire	10 (1)
	one selection from List D: Post-Romantic and Early 20th-century Repertoire	10 (1)
	one selection from List E: 20th- and 21st-century Repertoire	10 (1)
	(The figures in parantheses indicate marks awarded for memory as a portion of the total mark for each selection)	
2	**Technical Requirements**	**24 (17)**
	Studies / Etudes: *two* studies / etudes from the *Syllabus* list	6 + 6
	Technical Tests	12
	Major keys: all	
	Minor keys: all	
	– parallel motion scales	
	– *staccato* scales	
	– major scales separated by 3rds, 6ths, and 10ths	
	– formula pattern scales	
	– chromatic scales	
	– scales in octaves	
	– chromatic scales in octaves	
	– tonic four-note chords	
	– dominant 7th and diminished 7th chords	
	– tonic arpeggios	
	– dominant 7th and diminished 7th arpeggios	
	– *one* exercise of candidate's choice (see p. 96)	

3	**Ear Tests**	**10 (7)**
	Intervals	2
	Chords	2
	Cadences	3
	Playback	3
4	**Sight Reading**	**10 (7)**
	Playing	7
	Clapping	3
	Theory Co-requisites	
	Advanced Rudiments [Grade 2 Rudiments] History 1: An Overview [Grade 3 History] History 2: Middle Ages to Classical [Grade 4 History] Intermediate Harmony *or* Intermediate Keyboard Harmony [Grade 4 Harmony *or* Grade 4 Keyboard Harmony]	
	Total possible marks (pass = 60)	**100**

Resources for Grade 10 Examination Preparation

Repertoire: *Celebration Series Perspectives®: Piano Repertoire 10*

Studies / Etudes: *Celebration Series Perspectives®: Piano Studies / Etudes 10*

Ear Training and Sight Reading: see p. 135 for ear-training and sight-reading resources.

1 Repertoire

Candidates must prepare *five* contrasting selections: *one* from each of List A, List B, List C, List D, and List E. Repertoire selections must be memorized. Please note that marks will be deducted if music is used.

Bullets used to denote selections for examination purposes:

● one selection

▲ part or section of a larger work

▶ selection is found in *Celebration Series Perspectives®: Piano Repertoire 10 FHM*

⧊ part or section of a larger work is found in *Celebration Series Perspectives®: Piano Repertoire 10 FHM*

List A
Works of J.S. Bach

Bach, Johann Sebastian
● Capriccio sopra la lontananza del fratello dilettissimo, BWV 992
   ▲ 4th, 5th, *and* 6th movements

Bach, Johann Sebastian (continued)
- English Suite no. 2 in A minor, BWV 807
  - ▲ Allemande *and* Gigue
- English Suite no. 4 in F major, BWV 809
  - ▲ Allemande *and* Gigue
- ▶ Fantasia in C minor, BWV 906
- French Suite no. 3 in B minor, BWV 814
  - ▲ Allemande *and* Gigue
- French Suite no. 5 in G major, BWV 816
  - ▲ Allemande *and* Gigue
- French Suite no. 6 in E major, BWV 817
  - ▲ Allemande *and* Gigue

Das wohltemperierte Klavier, 1
- Prelude and Fugue in D major, BWV 850
- Prelude and Fugue in D minor, BWV 851
- Prelude and Fugue in E major, BWV 854
- Prelude and Fugue in E minor, BWV 855
- Prelude and Fugue in F major, BWV 856
- Prelude and Fugue in F sharp major, BWV 858
- Prelude and Fugue in F sharp minor, BWV 859
- Prelude and Fugue in G minor, BWV 861
- Prelude and Fugue in A flat major, BWV 862
- Prelude and Fugue in G sharp minor, BWV 863
- Prelude and Fugue in B flat major, BWV 866
- Prelude and Fugue in B major, BWV 868

Das wohltemperierte Klavier, 2
- Prelude and Fugue in C major, BWV 870
- Prelude and Fugue in C minor, BWV 871
- Prelude and Fugue in C sharp major, BWV 872
- Prelude and Fugue in D minor, BWV 875
- ▶ Prelude and Fugue in E flat major, BWV 876
- Prelude and Fugue in D sharp minor, BWV 877
- Prelude and Fugue in E major, BWV 878
- Prelude and Fugue in E minor, BWV 879
- Prelude and Fugue in F minor, BWV 881
- Prelude and Fugue in G major, BWV 884
- Prelude and Fugue in A major, BWV 888
- Prelude and Fugue in A minor, BWV 889
- Prelude and Fugue in B minor, BWV 893

List B

Classical Repertoire

Beethoven, Ludwig van
- Sonata in F minor, op. 2, no. 1
  - ▲ 1st *and* 2nd movements *or* 3rd *and* 4th movements
- Sonata in C minor, op. 10, no. 1
  - ▲ 1st *and* 2nd movements *or* 2nd *and* 3rd movements
- Sonata in F major, op. 10, no. 2
  - ▲ 1st *and* 2nd movements *or* 2nd *and* 3rd movements
- ▶ Sonata in E major, op. 14, no. 1
  - ▲ 1st *and* 2nd movements *or*
  - ▲ 2nd *and* 3rd movements
- Sonata in G major, op. 14, no. 2
  - ▲ 1st *and* 2nd movements *or* 2nd *and* 3rd movements
- Sonata in D major, op. 28
  - ▲ 1st *and* 2nd movements *or* 3rd *and* 4th movements

Clementi, Muzio
- Sonata in B flat major, op. 47, no. 2 (identified as op. 24 no. 2 in PET)
  - ▲ 1st *and* 2nd movements *or* 2nd *and* 3rd movements

Haydn, Franz Joseph
- Sonata in D major, Hob. XVI:19
  - ▲ 1st *and* 2nd movements
- Sonata in B minor, Hob. XVI:32
- ▶ Sonata in D major, Hob. XVI:33
- Sonata in C major, Hob. XVI:35
- Sonata in C sharp minor, Hob. XVI:36
- Sonata in G minor, Hob. XVI:44
- Sonata in D major, Hob. XVI:51

Mozart, Wolfgang Amadeus
- Fantasia in C minor, K 396
- Rondo in D major, K 485
- Rondo in A minor, K 511
- Sonata in F major, K 280 (189e)
  - ▲ 1st *and* 2nd movements *or* 2nd *and* 3rd movements
- Sonata in B flat major, K 281
  - ▲ 1st *and* 2nd movements *or* 2nd *and* 3rd movements
- ▶ Sonata in E flat major, K 282 (189g)
- Sonata in C major, K 309
  - ▲ 1st *and* 2nd movements *or* 2nd *and* 3rd movements
- Sonata in F major, K 332
  - ▲ 1st *and* 2nd movements *or* 2nd *and* 3rd movements
- Sonata in B flat major, K 570
  - ▲ 2nd *and* 3rd movements

List C

Romantic Repertoire

Brahms, Johannes
- Ballade in D minor, op. 10, no. 1
- Ballade in B major, op. 10, no. 4
- Intermezzo in A major, op. 76, no. 6
- Intermezzo in E major, op. 116, no. 6
- Intermezzo in E flat major, op. 117, no. 1
- Intermezzo in B flat minor, op. 117, no. 2
- Intermezzo in C sharp minor, op. 117, no. 3
- Intermezzo in F minor, op. 118, no. 4
- Intermezzo in B minor, op. 119, no. 1
- ▶ Intermezzo in E minor, op. 119, no. 2
- Intermezzo in C major, op. 119, no. 3
- Romance in F major, op. 118, no. 5

Chopin, Frédéric
- Mazurka in B flat minor, op. 24, no. 4
- Mazurka in C major, op. 33, no. 3 *and* Mazurka in B minor, op. 33, no. 4
- Mazurka in B major, op. 63, no. 1
- Nocturne in B flat minor, op. 9, no. 1
- Nocturne in F major, op. 15, no. 1
- ▶ Nocturne in F sharp major, op. 15, no. 2
- Nocturne in A flat major, op. 32, no. 2
- Nocturne in E minor, op. 72, no. 1

Chopin, Frédéric (continued)
- ▶ Polonaise in C sharp minor, op. 26, no. 1
- Polonaise in A major, op. 40, no. 1
- Polonaise in G sharp minor, op. posth. KK IVa, No. 3
- Prelude in A flat major, op. 28, no. 17
- Prelude in C sharp minor, op. 45
- Waltz in A flat major, op. 34, no. 1
- Waltz in E minor, op. posth., B 56

Trois Écossaises, op. 72, no. 3, CT 13
- no. 1 in D major, no. 2 in G major, *and* no. 3 in D flat major

Grieg, Edvard
Lyric Pieces, op. 57
- Vanished Days (no. 1)
Lyric Pieces, op. 65
- Wedding Day at Troldhaugen (no. 6)
Pictures from Life in the Country, op. 19
- Norwegian Bridal Procession (no. 2)

Liszt, Franz
- Liebestraum no. 1
- ▶ Liebestraum no. 3
Années de pèlerinage, 2 DUR
- Canzonetta del Salvator Rosa
Trois valses oubliées, op. 1
- Valse oubliée no. 1
Vier kleine Klavierstücke
- Klavierstücke no. 2

Mendelssohn, Felix
- Lied ohne Worte, op. 53, no. 1
- Lied ohne Worte, op. 67, no. 4 ("Spinning Song")
- Albumblatt in E minor, op. 117

Schubert, Franz
Vier Impromptus für Klavier, op. 90, D 899
- Impromptu in E flat major (no. 2)
- Impromptu in A flat major (no. 4)
Vier Impromptus für Klavier, op. 142, D 935
- Impromptu in B flat major (no. 3)
- Impromptu in F minor (no. 4)
Six moments musicaux, op. 94, D 780
- ▶ no. 2 in A flat major
- no. 4 in C sharp minor

Schumann, Clara
Quatre pièces fugitives, op. 15 BRE
- Andante espressivo (no. 3)

Schumann, Robert
- Arabesque, op. 18
- Intermezzo, op. 4, no. 5
Faschingsschwank aus Wien, op. 26
- Intermezzo (no. 4)
Novelletten, op. 21
- no. 1 *or* no. 7
Fantasiestücke, op. 12
- Aufschwung (no. 2)
Waldszenen, op. 82
- Vogels als Prophet (no. 7)

List D
Post-Romantic and Early 20th-century Repertoire

Albéniz, Isaac
- ▶ Córdoba, op. 232, no. 4

Beach, Amy
- A Hermit Thrush at Eve, op. 92, no. 1 (*Piano Music: Amy Beach DOV*)
Trois morceaux caractéristiques, op. 28
- Barcarolle (no. 1) (*Piano Music: Amy Beach DOV*)

Debussy, Claude
Deux arabesques
- ▶ no. 1
- no. 2
Children's Corner Suite
- Doctor Gradus ad Parnassum
- La plus que lente
- Serenade for the Doll
- The Snow is Dancing
Préludes, 1
- Danseuses de Delphes (no. 1)
- Des pas sur la neige (no. 6)
- La sérénade interrompue (no. 9)
- Minstrels (no. 12)
Préludes, 2
- Brouillards (no. 1)
- Feuilles mortes (no. 2)
- Bruyères (no. 5)
- General Lavine–eccentric (no. 6)
- Hommage à S. Pickwick, Esq. (no. 9)
Suite bergamasque
- Prélude
- Menuet
- Clair de lune
- Passepied
Pour le piano
- Sarabande

Falla, Manuel de
- ▶ Danse du meunier (from *El sombrero de tres picos*) CHS
- Ritual Fire Dance (*from El amor brujo*) CHS

Fauré, Gabriel
- ▶ Barcarolle no. 4 in A flat major, op. 44 INT; LED; PET

Gershwin, George
- Rialto Ripples ALF

Griffes, Charles T.
Roman Sketches, op. 7 SCH
- The Fountain of the Acqua Paola (no. 3)
- Clouds (no. 4)

Hofmann, Josef
- ▶ Berceuse, op. 20, no. 5

Ibert, Jacques
- Le vent dans les ruines LED

Janáček, Leoš
V *mlhách* (In the Mist), JW VIII/22 MAS; BAR
- any *two*

Palmgren, Selim
- The Sea CHS

Poulenc, Francis
- Pastourelle (L'éventail de Jeanne) HEU
- Trois mouvements perpétuels CHS
Cinq impromptus CHS; MAS
- *two* impromptus
Trois novelettes CHS
- no. 1

Rachmaninoff, Sergei
10 Préludes, op. 23
- no. 8
- no. 10
13 Préludes, op. 32
- no. 11
Morceaux de fantasie, op. 3
- ▶ Élégie (no. 1)
- Prélude (no. 2)
- Mélodie (no. 3)
- Sérénade (no. 5)

Ravel, Maurice
Le tombeau de Couperin ALF; DUR; PET
- Prélude

Scott, Cyril
- Danse nègre, op. 58, no. 5 ALF; NOV
- Lotus Land, op. 47, no. 1 MAS; OTT

Scriabin, Alexander
24 Preludes, op. 11
- Prelude no. 2 *and* Prelude no. 14
- Prelude no. 4 *and* Prelude no. 6

Szymanowski, Karol
Mazurkas, op. 50 UNI
- no. 1
- no. 2
- no. 3

List E

20th- and 21st-century Repertoire

Archer, Violet
Six Preludes WAT
- Prelude no. 1
- Prelude no. 6

Barber, Samuel
Souvenirs, op. 28 SCH
- Waltz (no. 1)
- ▶ Pas de deux (no. 3)
- Galop (no. 6)

Bartók, Béla
- Roumanian Folk Dances UNI
Fourteen Bagatelles, op. 6 EMB
- no. 12
Fifteen Hungarian Peasant Songs UNI
- nos. 1–5

Bartók, Béla (continued)
Mikrokosmos, 6 B&H
- Six Dances in Bulgarian Rhythm
  - ▲ *two* of nos. 148–153
Three Rondos on Slovak Folk Tunes, op. 84
- ▶ Rondo (no. 1)

Behrens, Jack
- Hommage à Chopin CMC
- Léger (1996) CMC

Bissell, Keith
- Variations on a Folk Song WAT

Bolcom, William
- Graceful Ghost Rag EMB

Chatman, Stephen
Preludes for Piano, 3 FHM
- Spring Celebration

Copland, Aaron
- The Cat and the Mouse (Scherzo humoristique)
  ALF; B&H; MAS

Dela, Maurice
- Hommage BER
La vieille capitale BER
- Prélude (Veille sous la porte Saint-Jean)

Deshevov, Vladimir Mikhaylovich
- ▶ The Rails, op. 16

Duncan, Martha Hill
The Sunken Garden CMC
- The Japanese Tea Garden
- The River
- The Theatre

Eckhardt-Gramatté, Sophie-Carmen
From My Childhood, 1: Alphabet Pieces WAT
- "V" Valse chromatique

Gallant, Pierre
- ▶ Six Variations on "Land of the Silver Birch"

Gardiner, Mary
- ▶ Synergy CMC

Ginastera, Alberto
- ▶ Rondo sobre temas infantiles argentinos, op. 19
  B&H

Hovhaness, Alan
- Macedonian Mountain Dance, op. 144, no. 1 PET

Kabalevsky, Dmitri
- Sonatina in C major, op. 13, no. 1
  - ▲ 2nd *and* 3rd movements
- ▶ Variations in A minor, op. 40, no. 2
24 Preludes, op. 38 SCH
- Prelude no. 3
- Prelude no. 5 *and* Prelude no. 9
- Prelude no. 6 *and* Prelude no. 20

Liu Zhuang
- Variations TIM

McDonald, Boyd
Three Preludes for Piano CMC
- no. 1 (Maestoso) *and* no. 2 (Moderato)
- no. 2 (Moderato) *and* no. 3 (Vivo)

McInytre, David L.
- Toccata ALK

Messiaen, Olivier
Huit préludes pour piano DUR
- Plainte calme (no. 7)

Morel, François
Deux études de sonorité BER
- no. 1

Muczynski, Robert
Six Preludes, op. 6 (Muczynski: Collected Piano Pieces SCH)
- ▶ Prelude no. 1 *and* Prelude no. 6

Nancarrow, Conlon
Three Two-Part Studies for Piano PET; SON
- no. 1 (Presto)
- no. 2 (Andantino) *and* no. 3 (Allegro)

Papineau-Couture, Jean
- Ideé... DOM

Pentland, Barbara
- Shadows / Ombres AVO

Pépin, Clermont
- ▶ Trois pièces pour la légende dorée CMC

Peterson, Oscar
Canadiana Suite HAL
- Hogtown Blues
- Land of the Misty Giants

Prokofiev, Sergei
- March from *The Love for Three Oranges*, op. 33 B&H
- Sonatina, op. 54, no. 2 B&H
  - ▲ 1st *or* 3rd movement

Prokofiev, Sergei (continued)
Episodes: Ten Pieces, op. 12 MCA; SCH
- March (no. 1)
- Prelude (Harp) (no. 7)

Schoenberg, Arnold
- Six Little Piano Pieces, op. 19 BEL

Shostakovich, Dmitri
- Three Fantastic Dances, op. 5
24 Preludes, op. 34
- *two* of nos. 5, 9, 11, 12, 18, 20

Somers, Harry
- ▶ Strangeness of Heart BER

Southam, Ann
Four Bagatelles BER
- no. 2 *and* no. 4
Rivers (second set) CMC
- any *one*

Takács, Jenő
- ▶ Toccata, op. 54 DOB

Tsitsaros, Christos
Nine Tales FHM
- ▶ Snow Games

Substitutions

Candidates may substitute *one* repertoire selection and/or *one* study / etude selection with a musical work *not found* in the Repertoire Lists for Grade 10. See p. 130 for more information on substitutions.

Total Substitutions Permitted	Requires Prior Approval (Submit an Examination Substitute Piece Request)		Does Not Require Prior Approval		
	Repertoire Substitution		**Repertoire Substitution**		**Study / Etude Substitution**
one Repertoire selection *and/or* *one* Study / Etude	One repertoire selection from piano literature comparable in style and difficulty to the corresponding List A, B, or C of Grade 10 (including *two* movements of a Sonata from List B of the ARCT in Piano Performance)	*or*	One selection from the corresponding List of the ARCT in Piano Performance including a complete Sonata from List B of the ARCT in Piano Performance (Discretion must be shown with regards to the length of the work in relation to the length of the examination.) *or* One Own Choice selection may replace a piece from List D or E	*and/ or*	One selection from the Concert Etudes List of the ARCT in Piano Performance

2 Technical Requirements

Studies / Etudes

Candidates must prepare *two contrasting* selections from the following list of studies / etudes. Memorization is *not* required and will not be rewarded with extra marks.

Bullets used to denote selections for examination purposes:
▶ selection is found in *Celebration Series Perspectives*®: *Piano Studies / Etudes* 10 FHM

Alkan, Charles-Valentin
Cinquième recueil de chants, op. 70
▶ La voix de l'instrument (no. 4)

Bartók, Béla
Fourteen Bagatelles, op. 6 EMB
▶ Bagatelle no. 5

Concone, Giuseppe
20 Études chantantes, op. 30
▶ Study in A flat major (no. 19)

Czerny, Carl
▶ Study in A minor, op. 740, no. 41

Chopin, Frédéric
Trois nouvelles études
▶ Étude in A flat major

Haberbier, Ernst
Études-Poésies, op. 53
▶ Serenade (no. 5)

Heller, Stephen
24 Preludes, op. 81
▶ Prelude in C sharp minor (no. 10)

Hofmann, Heinrich
Nachklänge, op. 37
▶ By the Mountain Torrent (no. 2)

Loeschhorn, Carl Albert
Etuden für Geübtere, op. 67
▶ Etude in E minor (no. 5)

Lyadov, Anatoli Konstantinovich
Trifles, op. 2
▶ no. 12

Moszkowski, Moritz
Sechs Fantasiestücke, op. 52
▶ Zwiegesang (no. 3)

Rachmaninoff, Serge
Étude-tableaux, op. 33
▶ no. 8

Takács, Jenő
Wenn der Frosch auf Reisen geht DOB
▶ When the Frog Goes Wandering

Tsitaros, Christos
Nine Tales FHM
▶ Gallop

Technical Tests

Candidates must play all Technical Tests from memory, ascending and descending, with good tone and logical fingering, at a steady tempo. Metronome markings indicate minimum speeds. All scales are to be played *legato* unless otherwise indicated.

See "Technical Patterns" on p. 19 for examples.

Keys for Grade 10:   all major keys; all minor keys

Scales	Keys	Played	Tempo	Note values
Parallel Motion	all major keys all minor keys (harmonic and melodic)	HT 4 octaves	♩ = 120	(four sixteenth notes)
Staccato	B♭, A♭, G♭ major F♯, C♯, E♭ minor (harmonic and melodic)	HT 3 octaves	♩ = 120	(two eighth notes staccato)
Separated by a 3rd	C, D♭ D, E♭, major	HT 4 octaves	♩ = 104	(four sixteenth notes)
Separated by a 6th	E, F, G♭ G major	HT 4 octaves	♩ = 104	(four sixteenth notes)
Separated by a 10th	A♭, A, B♭, B major	HT 4 octaves	♩ = 104	(four sixteenth notes)
Formula Pattern	B♭, A♭, G♭ major F♯, C♯, E♭ minor (harmonic)	HT 4 octaves	♩ = 112	(four sixteenth notes)
Chromatic	beginning on any note	HT 4 octaves	♩ = 120	(four sixteenth notes)
Scales in Octaves solid (blocked) *staccato*	B♭, A♭, G♭ major F♯, C♯, E♭ minor (harmonic and melodic)	HT 2 octaves	♩ = 80	(four sixteenth notes)
Chromatic Scales in Octaves solid (blocked) *staccato*	beginning on any note	HT 2 octaves	♩ = 80	(four sixteenth notes)

Chords	Keys	Played	Tempo	Note values
Tonic Four-note Chords broken	all keys	HT 2 octaves (root position and inversions ending with I–IV–I$_4^6$–V^7–I chord progression)	♩ = 120	(four sixteenth notes)
solid (blocked)			♩ = 120	(two half notes)
broken alternate-note pattern			♩ = 96	(four sixteenth notes)
Dominant 7th broken	all keys	HT 2 octaves (root position and inversions)	♩ = 120	(four sixteenth notes)
solid (blocked)			♩ = 120	(two half notes)
broken alternate-note pattern			♩ = 96	(four sixteenth notes)
Diminished 7th broken	all minor keys	HT 2 octaves (root position and inversions)	♩ = 120	(four sixteenth notes)
solid (blocked)			♩ = 120	(two half notes)
broken alternate-note pattern			♩ = 96	(four sixteenth notes)

Arpeggios	Keys	Played	Tempo	Note values
Tonic	all keys	HT 4 octaves	♩ = 92	(four sixteenth notes)
Dominant 7th		(root position and inversions, either individually or in sequence beginning in root position or in any inversion)		
Diminished 7th	all minor keys			

Exercises	Keys	Played	Tempo	Note values
Candidates must prepare one exercise from the following list:				
Triplet Repeated-Note Pattern Scales (3–2–1 fingering)	D, A♭, G♭ major D, F♯ minor (harmonic and melodic)	HT 2 octaves	♩ = 100	(triplet eighth notes)
Double 3rd Scales, *legato*	C, B, B♭ major	HT 2 octaves	♩ = 60	(two eighth notes)
Scales in Octaves with Alternating Hands (solid *staccato*)	any major key	HT LH leads 2 octaves	♩ = 84	(four sixteenth notes)
Cross-Rhythm Scales (2 against 3) parallel or contrary motion – candidate's choice	D, A♭, G♭ major D, F♯ minor (harmonic)	HT LH 2 octaves RH 3 octaves	♩ = 100	LH (two eighth notes) RH (triplet eighth notes)
Chromatic Scales Separated by a Minor 3rd	LH beginning on any note	HT 4 octaves	♩ = 100	(four sixteenth notes)

Examples of Exercises

Triplet Repeated-note Pattern Scales (3–2–1 fingering) (to be played two octaves)

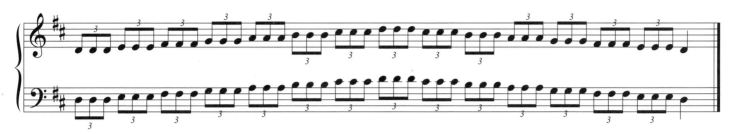

Double 3rd Scales, *legato*

Scales in Octaves with Alternating Hands, solid (blocked) *staccato* (to be played two octaves)

Cross-Rhythm Scales (parallel motion)

Chromatic Scales Separated by a Minor 3rd (to be played four octaves)

Grade 10

3 Ear Tests

Intervals

Candidates will be asked to identify the following intervals. The examiner will play each interval *once* in broken form.

or

Candidates may choose to sing or hum the following intervals. The examiner will play the first note of each interval *once*.

Above a given note	Below a given note
any interval within the octave	any interval within the octave

Chords

Candidates will be asked to identify any of the following chords and their inversion or position after the examiner has played the chord *once* in solid (blocked) form, close position.

Chords	Position
major and minor four-note chords	root position, 1st inversion, 2nd inversion
dominant 7th	root position
diminished 7th	root position

Cadences

Candidates will be asked to identify by name or symbols the following cadences played within a single phrase. The phrase may be in a major or a minor key and may contain up to three cadences. The examiner will play the tonic chord *once*, then play the phrase *twice*.

Name of Cadence	Symbols
perfect or authentic	V$^{(7)}$–I
plagal	IV–I
imperfect	I–V
deceptive	V$^{(7)}$–VI

Example only

V^7 VI
Deceptive (Interrupted)

iv i   V i
Plagal   Perfect (Authentic)

Playback

Candidates will be asked to play back the lower voice of a two-voice phrase. The examiner will name the key, play the tonic chord *once*, and play the phrase *twice*.

Approximate length	Keys
two to four measures	C, F, D major

Example only

4 Sight Reading

Playing

Candidates will be asked to play a short composition at sight.

Difficulty	Time signature	Keys
Grade 7 repertoire	any time signature	any major or minor key up to seven sharps or seven flats

Clapping

Candidates will be asked to clap or tap the rhythm of a melody. A steady pace and rhythmic accentuation are expected.

Time signature	Approximate length
$\frac{2}{4}$ $\frac{3}{4}$ $\frac{4}{4}$ $\frac{6}{8}$	six measures

Example only

The Senior Musicianship examination can be substituted for the Ear Tests and Sight Reading sections of the Grade 10 piano examination (see p. 123).

Supplemental Examinations

Improve a Grade 10 Piano examination mark

Supplemental Examinations are available for the Technical Requirements, Ear Tests, and Sight Reading sections of the Grade 10 practical examination. Please note that supplemental examinations are *not* available for the Repertoire section of the examination.

- Candidates must achieve a minimum mark of 65 percent overall and 70 percent in the Repertoire section to be eligible for a Supplemental Examination.
- Candidates may take a maximum of two Supplemental Examinations per complete examination
- Supplemental Examinations must be taken within two years of the original examination, during a regularly scheduled examination period.

ARCT *in Piano Performance*

The ARCT in Piano Performance examination is evaluated as a concert performance. Candidates are expected to perform with confidence, to communicate the essence of the music, to demonstrate keyboard command, and to show an understanding of the stylistic and structural elements of each repertoire selection. The ARCT in Piano Performance examination may be attempted when the candidate has met the following conditions:

- The candidate has completed the Grade 10 Piano examination with a total mark of 75 or a minimum of 70 percent in each section of the examination, at least one session prior.
- The candidate has completed the theory co-requisite examinations for Grade 10 with a total mark of at least 60 for each examination, at least one session prior.

Two years of examination preparation following Grade 10 is recommended for the ARCT examination.

The examiner will stop the performance if the time exceeds 60 minutes.

	ARCT in Piano Performance Requirements	Marks
1	**Repertoire**	**100**
	one selection from List A: Works of J.S. Bach	20
	one selection from List B: Sonatas	25
	one selection from List C: Romantic Repertoire	15
	one selection from List D: Post-Romantic and Early 20th-century Repertoire	15
	one selection from List E: 20th- and 21st-century Repertoire	15
	one Concert Etude	10
	Theory Co-requisites	
	Counterpoint [Grade 4 Counterpoint] Advanced Harmony *or* Advanced Keyboard Harmony [Grade 5 Harmony *or* Grade 5 Keyboard Harmony] History 3: 19th Century to Present [Grade 5 History] Analysis [Grade 5 Analysis]	
	Theory Prerequisites	
	Advanced Rudiments [Grade 2 Rudiments] History 1: An Overview [Grade 3 History] History 2: Middle Ages to Classical [Grade 4 History] Intermediate Harmony *or* Intermediate Keyboard Harmony [Grade 4 Harmony *or* Grade 4 Keyboard Harmony]	
	Total possible marks (pass = 70)	**100**

Classification of Marks

First Class Honors *with Distinction* 90–100
First Class Honors 80–89
Honors 70–79
Pass 70

Criteria for Pass and Failure

A continuous, convincing performance is a fundamental requirement for a passing mark in the ARCT in Piano Performance examination. A failing mark may be given for one or more of the following reasons:

- lack of stylistic awareness
- repeated interruptions in continuity
- substantial omissions
- textual inaccuracies
- complete breakdown of performance

Memorization is compulsory. A mark of zero will be given for any selection played from the score. Consultation of the score is not permitted.

1 Repertoire

Candidates must prepare *six* contrasting selections from memory: *one* from each of List A, List, B, List C, List D, List E, and Concert Etudes. A single selection is indicated by a bullet (●).

List A
Works of J.S. Bach

Please note: In order to graduate with an ARCT in Piano Performance, candidates must include a Prelude and Fugue by J.S. Bach on their examination program for their Grade 9, Grade 10, or ARCT examinations.

Bach, Johann Sebastian
- Chromatic Fantasia and Fugue, BWV 903
- English Suite no. 1 in A major, BWV 806
  - Prelude, Sarabande, *and* Gigue
- English Suite no. 2 in A minor, BWV 807
  - Prelude, Sarabande, *and* Gigue
- English Suite no. 3 in G minor, BWV 808
  - Prelude, Sarabande, *and* Gigue
- English Suite no. 5 in E minor, BWV 810
  - Prelude, Sarabande, *and* Gigue
- English Suite no. 6 in D minor, BWV 811
  - Prelude, Sarabande, *and* Gigue
- Fantasia and Fugue in A minor, BWV 904
- Italian Concerto, BWV 971
- Partita no. 1 in B flat major, BWV 825
  - Praeludium, Sarabande *and* Gigue
- Partita no. 2 in C minor, BWV 826
  - Sinfonia, *or*
  - Allemande, Sarabande, *and* Capriccio
- Partita no. 3 in A minor, BWV 827
  - Fantasia, Sarabande, *and* Gigue
- Partita no. 4 in D major, BWV 828
  - Overture *and* one additional movement

Bach, Johann Sebastian (continued)
- Partita no. 5 in G major, BWV 829
  - ▲ Praeambulum, Sarabande, *and* Gigue
- Suite in A minor, BWV 818
- Toccata in F sharp minor, BWV 910
- Toccata in C minor, BWV 911
- Toccata in D major, BWV 912
- Toccata in D minor, BWV 913
- Toccata in E minor, BWV 914
- Toccata in G minor, BWV 915

Das wohltemperierte Klavier, 1
- Prelude and Fugue in C major, BWV 846
- Prelude and Fugue in C sharp major, BWV 848
- Prelude and Fugue in C sharp minor, BWV 849
- Prelude and Fugue in E flat major, BWV 852
- Prelude and Fugue in D sharp minor, BWV 853
- Prelude and Fugue in F minor, BWV 857
- Prelude and Fugue in G major, BWV 860
- Prelude and Fugue in A major, BWV 864
- Prelude and Fugue in A minor, BWV 865
- Prelude and Fugue in B flat minor, BWV 867
- Prelude and Fugue in B minor, BWV 869

Das wohltemperierte Klavier, 2
- Prelude and Fugue in C sharp minor, BWV 873
- Prelude and Fugue in D major, BWV 874
- Prelude and Fugue in F major, BWV 880
- Prelude and Fugue in F sharp major, BWV 882
- Prelude and Fugue in F sharp minor, BWV 883
- Prelude and Fugue in G minor, BWV 885
- Prelude and Fugue in A flat major, BWV 886
- Prelude and Fugue in G sharp minor, BWV 887
- Prelude and Fugue in B flat major, BWV 890
- Prelude and Fugue in B flat minor, BWV 891
- Prelude and Fugue in B major, BWV 892

List B

Sonatas

Beethoven, Ludwig van
- Sonata in A major, op. 2, no. 2
- Sonata in C major, op. 2, no. 3
- Sonata in E flat major, op. 7
- Sonata in D major, op. 10, no. 3
- Sonata in C minor, op. 13
- Sonata in B flat major, op. 22
- Sonata in A flat major, op. 26
- Sonata in C sharp minor, op. 27, no. 2
- Sonata in G major, op. 31, no. 1
- Sonata in D minor, op. 31, no. 2
- Sonata in E flat major, op. 31, no. 3
- Sonata in C major, op. 53
- Sonata in F major, op. 54
- Sonata in F minor, op. 57
- Sonata in F sharp major, op. 78
- Sonata in E flat major, op. 81a
- Sonata in E minor, op. 90
- Sonata in A major, op. 101
- Sonata in E major, op. 109
- Sonata in A flat major, op. 110
- Sonata in C minor, op. 111

Clementi, Muzio
- Sonata in B minor, op. 40, no. 2

Haydn, Franz Joseph
- Sonata in C minor, Hob. XVI:20
- Sonata in A flat major, Hob. XVI:46
- Sonata in E flat major, Hob. XVI:49
- Sonata in C major ("English"), Hob. XVI:50
- Sonata in E flat major, Hob. XVI:52

Mozart, Wolfgang Amadeus
- Sonata in D major, K 284
- Sonata in A minor, K 310
- Sonata in D major, K 311
- Sonata in A major, K 331
- Sonata in B flat major, K 333
- Sonata in C minor, K 457
- Sonata in F major, K 533

Schubert, Franz
- Sonata in A minor, op. 42, D 845
- Sonata in G major, op. 78, D 894
- Sonata in A major, op. 120, D 664
- Sonata in A minor, op. 143, D 784
- Sonata in A minor, op. 164, D 537
- Sonata in B flat major, op. posth., D 960

List C

Romantic Repertoire

Brahms, Johannes
- Ballade in D major, op. 10, no. 2
- Ballade in G minor, op. 118, no. 3
- Capriccio in F sharp minor, op. 76, no. 1 *and* Capriccio in B minor, op. 76, no. 2
- Capriccio in C sharp minor, op. 76, no. 5
- Intermezzo in A minor, op. 118, no. 1 *and* Intermezzo in A major, op. 118, no. 2
- Intermezzo in E flat minor, op. 118, no. 6
- Rhapsody in B minor, op. 79, no. 1
- Rhapsody in G minor, op. 79, no. 2
- Rhapsody in E flat major, op. 119, no. 4
- Scherzo in E flat major, op. 4

Chopin, Frédéric
- Ballade in G minor, op. 23
- Ballade in F major, op. 38
- Ballade in A flat major, op. 47
- Ballade in F minor, op. 52
- Barcarolle in F sharp major, op. 60
- Berceuse, op. 57
- Fantaisie in F minor, op. 49
- Fantaisie-Impromptu in C sharp minor, op. 66
- Impromptu in F sharp major, op. 36
- Nocturne in C sharp minor, op. 27, no. 1
- Nocturne in D flat major, op. 27, no. 2
- Nocturne in G major, op. 37, no. 2
- Nocturne in C minor, op. 48, no. 1
- Nocturne in E flat major, op. 55, no. 2
- Nocturne in B major, op. 62, no. 1
- Polonaise in F sharp minor, op. 44
- Polonaise in A flat major, op. 53
- Scherzo in B minor, op. 20
- Scherzo in B flat minor, op. 31
- Scherzo in C sharp minor, op. 39
- Scherzo in E major, op. 54
- Waltz in E flat major, op. 18

Chopin, Frédéric (continued)
Préludes, op. 28
- *four* of nos. 1, 2, 3, 5, 8, 10, 11, 12, 14, 16, 18, 19, 21, 22, 23, 24

Franck, César
- Prélude, chorale, et fugue

Grieg, Edvard
- Sonata in E minor, op. 7

Liszt, Franz
- Ballade no. 2 in B minor
- Mephisto Waltz no. 1 (Episode from Lenau's poem "Faust")
- Polonaise no. 2 in E major
Années de pèlerinage, 1
- Au bord d'une source
Années de pèlerinage, 2
- Sonetto 47 del Petrarca
- Sonetto 104 del Petrarca
- Sonetto 123 del Petrarca
- Sposalizio
Hungarian Rhapsodies
- *one* rhapsody (excluding nos. 3, 17, and 18) *Légendes*
- St François d'Assise: La prédication aux oiseaux
- St François de Paule marchant sur les flots

Mendelssohn, Felix
- Andante and Rondo capriccioso, op. 14
- Andante con variazioni, op. 82
- Prelude and Fugue in E minor, op. 35, no. 1
- Scherzo in E minor, op. 16, no. 2
- Variations sérieuses, op. 54

Schubert, Franz
Drei Klavierstücke, D 946
- no. 1 *or* no. 3
Vier Impromptus für Klavier, op. 90, D 899
- Impromptu in C minor (no. 1)
Vier Impromptus für Klavier, op. 142, D 935
- Impromptu in F minor (no. 1)

Schumann, Robert
- Abegg Variations, op. 1
- Papillons, op. 2
- Fantasiestücke, op. 111
Fantasiestücke, op. 12
- In der Nacht (no. 5)
- Traumes-Wirren (no. 7)
Novelletten, op. 21
- no. 2 *or* no. 8

List D

Post-Romantic and Early 20th-century Repertoire

Albéniz, Isaac
Asturias INT
- Leyenda
Cantos de España HEN; INT
- Seguidillas
Iberia Suite, 1 HEN; INT
- El Puerto

Albéniz, Isaac (continued)
Iberia Suite, 2 HEN; INT
- Triana
Iberia Suite, 3 INT
- El Albaicin

Beach, Amy
- Ballad, op. 6 (*Piano Music: Amy Beach* DOV)

Debussy, Claude
- Ballade
Estampes
- Jardins sous la pluie
- La soirée dans Grenade
- Pagodes
Images, 1
- Hommage à Rameau
- Mouvement
- Reflets dans l'eau
Images, 2
- Cloches à travers les feuilles
- Et la lune descend sur le temple qui fut
- L'isle joyeuse
- Poissons d'or
Préludes, 1
- Le vent dans la plaine (no. 3)
- Les collines d'Anacapri (no. 5)
- Ce qu'a vu le vent d'ouest (no. 7)
- La cathédrale engloutie (no. 10)
- La danse de Puck (no. 11)
Préludes, 2
- La puerta del Vino (no. 3)
- Les fées sont d'exquises danseuses (no. 4)
- La terrasse des audiences du clair de lune (no. 7)
- Feux d'artifice (no. 12)
Suite pour le piano
- Prélude
- Toccata

Dohnányi, Ernö
Four Pieces, op. 2 B&H; DOB
- Capriccio in B minor (no. 4)
Four Rhapsodies, op. 11 DOB; KAL
- Rhapsody in F sharp minor (no. 2)
- Rhapsody in C major (no. 3)
- Rhapsody in E flat minor (no. 4)

Fauré, Gabriel
- Barcarolle no. 5 in F sharp minor, op. 66
- Barcarolle no. 6 in E flat major, op. 70
- Barcarolle no. 8 in D flat major, op. 96
- Impromptu no. 2 in F minor, op. 31
- Impromptu no. 3 in A flat major, op. 34
- Nocturne no. 1 in E flat minor, op. 33
- Nocturne no. 4 in E flat major, op. 36
- Nocturne no. 5 in B flat major, op. 37
- Nocturne no. 6 in D flat major, op. 63

Gershwin, George
- Three Preludes ALF

Granados, Enrique
Escenas romanticas SAL; SCH
- no. 3 (Lento) *or* no. 5 (Allegro appassionato)
Goyescas (Los majos enamorados) KAL; SCH
- El fandango de candil (no. 3)
- La maja y el ruiseñor (no. 4)

Griffes, Charles T.
Fantasy Pieces, op. 6 MAS
- Barcarolle (no. 1)
- Notturno (no. 2)
- Scherzo (no. 3)
Roman Sketches, op. 7 SCH
- The White Peacock

Ireland, John
Decorations S&B
- Island Spell (no. 1)

MacDowell, Edward
- Witches' Dance, op. 17, no. 2

Medtner, Nikolai Karlovich
- Fairy Tale, op. 20, no. 1 B&H

Poulenc, Francis
- Intermezzo in A flat major ESC
Improvisations SAL
- any *four*
Trois pièces HEU
- Toccata (no. 3)

Rachmaninoff, Sergei
Morceaux de fantasie, op. 3
- Polichinelle (no. 4)
10 Préludes, op. 23
- *one* of nos. 2, 4, 5, 6, 7
13 Préludes, op. 32
- *one* of nos. 3, 5, 9, 10, 12

Ravel, Maurice
- Jeux d'eau DUR; PET
- Sonatine DUR; PET
- Valses nobles et sentimentales
Gaspard de la nuit DUR
- Ondine
Miroirs DUR; PET
- Alborada del gracioso
- Une barque sur l'océan
- Noctuelles
- Oiseaux tristes
- La vallée des cloches
Le tombeau de Couperin DUR; PET
- Toccata

List E

20th- and 21st-century Repertoire

Anhalt, István
- Fantasia BER

Barber, Samuel
- Ballade, op. 46 SCH
- Nocturne (Homage to John Field), op. 33 SCH
Excursions, op. 20 SCH
- any *two*

Bartók, Béla
- Allegro barbaro ALF; MAS; UNI
- Sonatina ALF; EMB
Suite, op. 14 UNI
- *three* movements

Bartók, Béla (continued)
Szabadban (Out of Doors Suite) UNI
- *two* movements
Two Roumanian Dances, op. 8a B&H
- no. 1 *or* no. 2
Two Elegies, op. 8b EMB
- no. 1 *or* no. 2
Three Burlesques, op. 8c EMB
- *two* burlesques
Mikrokosmos, 6 B&H
- *two* of nos. 142, 144, 146

Behrens, Jack
- DiBella Variations CMC
- Feast of Life CMC

Bell, Allan Gordon
- Old Coyote's Saturday Night ALK

Berg, Alban
- Sonata, op. 1 HEN; UNI

Bolcom, William
Nine Bagatelles (1996) MAR
- five consecutive movements

Buczynski, Walter
- Amorphous CMC
- Aria and Toccata CMC

Camilleri, Charles
- Sonatina no. 1 CRA

Champagne, Claude
- Quadrilha brasileira BER

Copland, Aaron
- Passacaglia MAS; SAL

Coulthard, Jean
- Image astrale (1981) AVO; CMC *musiccentre.ca*
- Image terrestre (1991) AVO; CMC

Crumb, George
- Processional PET (memory not required)

Finney, Ross Lee
- Sonata no. 1 in D minor (1933) PRE
- Variations on a Theme by Alban Berg PET

Gardiner, Mary
- Polarities CMC

Ginastera, Alberto
- Danzas argentinas, op. 2 DUR
- Malambo, op. 7 RIC
- Suite de danzas criollas, op. 15 B&H

Hétu, Jacques
- Ballade, op. 30 DOB
- Variations pour piano, op. 8 BER

Hindemith, Paul
- Sonata no. 2 OTT

Ho, Vincent
- Three Scenes of Childhood ALK

Honegger, Arthur
Trois pièces SAL
- Hommage à Ravel (no. 2) *and* Danse (no. 3)

Jaque, Rhené
- Deuxième suite BER

Joachim, Otto
- L'eclosion BER

Kabalevsky, Dmitri
- Sonata no. 3 in F major, op. 46

24 Preludes, op. 38
- *two* of nos. 10, 14, 16, 22, 24

Kenins, Talivaldis
- Sonata no. 1 (1961) CMC

Kennan, Kent
- Three Preludes SCH

Kuzmenko, Larysa
- In Memoriam to Victims of Chornobyl PLA

Kymlicka, Milan
- Five Preludes for Piano CAN

Lambro, Phillip
- Toccata for Piano TRG; WIM

Night Pieces for Piano TRG; WIM
- *two* of nos. 1, 2, 3, 4

Liebermann, Lowell
Gargoyles, op. 29 PRE
- any *two*

Louie, Alexina
- I leap through the sky with stars GVT

Scenes from a Jade Terrace (1996) CMC
- Southern Sky
- Warrior

Martin, Frank
Eight Preludes for Piano UNI
- *three* preludes

McIntyre, David
- Butterflies and Bobcats ALK

Messiaen, Olivier
Huit préludes pour piano DUR
- Chant d'extase dans un paysage triste (no. 2)
- Le nombre léger (no. 3)
- Un reflet dans le vent (no. 8)

Vingt regards sur l'enfant-Jésus DUR
- Regard de la vierge (no. 4)
- Regard du fils sur le fils (no. 5)
- Regard des hauteurs (no. 8)
- Première communion de la Vierge (no. 11)
- Regard des Anges (no. 14)
- Regard du silence (no. 17)
- Je dors, mais mon coeur veille (no. 19)

Morawetz, Oskar
- Fantasy, Elegy, and Toccata JAY [OP]
  - ▲ Toccata
- Scherzo B&H

Mozetich, Marjan
- Three Pieces for Piano Solo (1989) CMC

Muczynski, Robert
- Desperate Measures (Paganini Variations), op. 48 PRE
- Maverick Pieces, op. 37 PRE [OP]
  - ▲ *five consecutive* movements
- Toccata, op. 15 SCH

Nancarrow, Conlon
- Prelude and Blues PRE; SON

Papineau-Couture, Jean
- Suite pour piano BER
  - ▲ 5th movement: Rondo

Paulus, Stephen
Preludes, 1 OTT
- Rollicking (no. 5)

Peeters, Flor
- Toccata, op. 51a PET

Pentland, Barbara
- Studies in Line BER
- Toccata BER

Pépin, Clermont
- Suite pour piano CMC
  - ▲ *one* movement

Persichetti, Vincent
Poems for Piano, vol. 2, op. 5 ELK
- And warm winds spilled fragrance into her solitudes (no. 7)
- To whose more clear than crystal voice the frost had joined a crystal spell (no. 8)
- Make me drunken with deep red torrents of joy (no. 11)

Prokofiev, Sergei
- Sonata no. 3, op. 28 B&H
- Toccata, op. 11 MAS

Four Pieces, op. 4 MAS
- Diabolical Suggestion
- *two* of Elan, Despair, Reminiscences

Episodes: Ten Pieces, op. 12 MCA; SCH
- Scherzo (no. 10)

Sarcasms, op. 17 MAS
- *two consecutive* movements

Visions fugitives, op. 22 B&H; MAS
- *five* movements

Rapoport, Alexander
- Sonata for Pianoforte no. 2 (1997) PLA

Rawsthorne, Alan
- Bagatelles (*Rawsthorne: Selected Piano Pieces* OUP)

Rochberg, George
- Nach Bach PRE

Rorem, Ned
- Barcarolles (1949) PET
- Toccata (4th movement of Piano Sonata no. 1, 1948) PET

104

Rudnyts'kyi, Antin
- Variations on a Simple Theme, op. 38 WIM; TRI

Sancan, Pierre
- Toccata DUR

Shchedrin, Rodion Konstantovich
Polyphonisches Spielheft SIK
- Basso Ostinato (no. 16)

Shostakovich, Dmitri
24 Preludes and Fugues, op. 87 PET
- *one* prelude and fugue (excluding nos. 1, 5, 7)

Skarecky, Jana
- Tekarra CMC

Somers, Harry
- Sonata no. 1: "Testament of Youth" BER [OP]; CMC
- Three Sonnets BER [OP]

Tajcevic, Marko
- Balkantanze OTT
  - ▲ *five* movements

Webern, Anton
- Variations, op. 27 UNI

Concert Etudes

Bartók, Béla
Three Etudes, op. 18 B&H
- any *one*

Beach, Amy
- Fireflies, op. 15, no. 4 (*Amy Beach: Piano Music* DOV)

Chopin, Frédéric
Études, op. 10
- any *one*
Études, op. 25
- any *one* (except no. 2)

Coulthard, Jean
Four Etudes for Piano BER
- any *one*

Debussy, Claude
Douze études DUR
- any *one*

Dohnányi, Ernö
Six Concert Etudes, op. 28 EMB
- no. 5 *or* no. 6

Dubois, Pierre Max
Études de concert LED
- any *one*

Eckhardt-Gramatté, Sophie-Carmen
From My Childhood, 2 WAT
- Étude de concert

Kapustin, Nikolai
Eight Concert Etudes, op. 40 ARM
- any *one*

Lavallée, Calixa
- Le papillon / The Butterfly WIL

Ligeti, György
Études for Piano, 1 OTT
- any *one* *Book 1 no 5 arc-en-ciel*

Liszt, Franz
- Gnomenreigen
- Waldesrauschen
Études d'exécution transcendante
- any *one*
Études d'exécution transcendante d'après Paganini
- any *one* (excluding La chasse)
Trois études de concert
- any *one* *un sospiro*

MacDowell, Edward
- Étude de concert, op. 36
Zwölf virtuosen-étuden, op. 46
- any one (except no. 4)

Mendelssohn, Felix
- Étude in F minor
- Perpetuum mobile, op. 119
Three Preludes, op. 104a
- any *one*

Morel, François
Deux études de sonorité BER
- Etude no. 2

Moscheles, Ignaz
12 charakteristiche Studien, op. 95
- any *one*
Three Concert Études (Allegri di bravura), op. 51 PET; MAS
- any *one*

Moszkowski, Moritz
15 Virtuoso Etudes, op. 72 ("Per aspera") ALF; SCH
- any *one* (excluding no. 4 or no. 10)
École des doubles-notes (third part), op. 64 ENO
- any *one*
Three Concert Studies, op. 24
- any *one*

Poulenc, Francis
- Presto en si-bémol SAL

Prokofiev, Sergei
Four Etudes, op. 2
- any *one*

Rachmaninoff, Sergei
Études-tableaux, op. 33 B&H
- any *one* (except no. 8)
Études-tableaux, op. 39 B&H
- any *one*

Saint-Saëns, Camille
Six études, op. 52
- *one* of nos. 1, 2, 3, 5, 6
Six études, op. 111
- any *one*

Schumann, Robert
Six Etudes on the Caprices of Paganini, op. 10
- any *one*

Scriabin, Alexander
Douze études, op. 8
- any *one*
Four Pieces, op. 56
- Étude (no. 4)
Huit études, op. 42
- *one* of nos. 1, 5, 6, 7, 8
Three Pieces, op. 49
- Étude (no. 1)
Trois études, op. 65
- any *one*

Stravinsky, Igor
Four Etudes, op. 7 (*Stravinsky: Short Piano Pieces* B&H)
- any *one*

Szymanowski, Karol
Four Etudes, op. 4 MAS
- *one* of nos. 1, 2, 3

Weber, Carl Maria von
- Momento capriccioso in B flat major, op. 12
- Piano Sonata no. 1 in C major, op. 24
- Perpetuum mobile (Rondo)

Substitutions

Candidates may substitute *one* repertoire selection with a musical work *not found* in the ARCT Repertoire Lists. See p. 130 for more information on substitutions.

Total Substitutions Permitted	Requires Prior Approval (Submit an Examination Substitute Piece Request)		Does Not Require Prior Approval
	Repertoire Substitution		Repertoire Substitution
one Repertoire selection	One repertoire selection from piano literature comparable in style and difficulty to the corresponding List A, B, or C of the ARCT in Piano Performance	*or*	One Own Choice selection may replace a piece from List D or E

ARCT *in Piano Pedagogy*

Fostering Excellence in Teaching

The Piano Pedagogy Certificate Program is designed to strengthen the qualifications and teaching techniques of private studio teachers. Pedagogical ability and accomplishment are assessed through a three-level examination and certificate program.

Elementary Piano Pedagogy: Pedagogy for teaching beginners through to Grade 2 piano students

Intermediate Piano Pedagogy: Pedagogy for teaching Grades 3 to 6 piano students

Advanced Piano Pedagogy: Pedagogy for teaching Grades 7 to 10 piano students

Certificates will be awarded upon the successful completion of each of the Elementary and Intermediate Piano Pedagogy requirements.

Advantages of the Piano

Pedagogy Certificate Program

- Candidates can begin pedagogy training while completing requirements for the Grade 9 Piano Certificate.
- Candidates build knowledge and develop skills gradually over a period of several years.
- Candidates receive an ARCT in Piano Pedagogy Diploma upon successful completion of the requirements of all three Piano Pedagogy levels.

Elementary Piano Pedagogy

Elementary Piano Pedagogy—the first stage of the ARCT in Piano Pedagogy—addresses pedagogical issues at Preparatory, Grade 1, and Grade 2.

- Candidates are advised to complete all the requirements for the Grade 8 Piano Certificate before attempting the Elementary Piano Pedagogy examination.
- The Elementary Piano Pedagogy Certificate is awarded upon completion of three parts: a Grade 9 Piano Certificate, a *Viva Voce* (oral) Examination, and a Written Examination.
- The three parts may be completed in any order, at one or more examination sessions. There is no time limit for completion.

Resources for Examination Preparation

See "Resources" on p. 135 for suggested reading.

Part 1   Grade 9 Piano Certificate

Candidates must complete performance and theoretical requirements for the Grade 9 Piano Certificate. See p. 83 for detailed examination requirements.

	Elementary Piano Pedagogy Requirements	Marks
Part 1	**Grade 9 Piano Certificate** (Please see p. 83 for detailed requirements)	
Part 2	**Viva Voce Examination (45 minutes)**	100 (pass = 70)
	• Discussion of general pedagogical topics, the beginning student, and the professional studio	25
	• Teaching rhythm, technique, musicianship, and other essential skills	25
	• Performance of selections from the Teaching Repertoire Sample	25
	• Detailed pedagogical discussion of selections from the Teaching Repertoire Sample	25
Part 3	**Written Examination (3 hours)** Discussion of general pedagogy, the professional studio, beginner methods, the beginning student, technique, artistry, other essential skills, and the Teaching Repertoire Sample	100 (pass = 70)

Classification of Marks

First Class Honors *with Distinction* 90–100
First Class Honors 80–89
Honors 70–79
Pass 70

Part 2   *Viva Voce* Examination

Teaching Repertoire Sample

Candidates must prepare a balanced program of *fourteen* contrasting selections as outlined in the chart below. *One* selection must be memorized. Candidates may choose selections from the following sources:

- a well-known beginner method (chosen from the following: *The ABC of Piano Playing*; *Alfred's Premier Piano Course*; *Alfred's Basic Piano Library*; *Bastien Piano Basics*; *Celebrate Piano!*®; *Hal Leonard Student Piano Library*; *The Music Tree*; or *Piano Adventures*®)
- repertoire and studies / etudes listed in the *Syllabus* for Preparatory, Grade 1, and Grade 2

Candidates should be prepared to:
- Perform selections chosen by the examiner from the Teaching Repertoire Sample.
- Discuss teaching approaches for the chosen selections.
- Discuss materials for technical exercises, sight reading, and ear training suitable for elementary levels.
- Describe the chosen beginner method series and compare it with two other methods.

Level	Repertoire	Studies / Etudes
Beginner	*four* selections from one of the beginner methods listed above (showing level of study at the *end* of the first and second years of study) *two* repertoire selections from *Celebration Series: Perspectives*®: *Preparatory Piano Repertoire*	
Grade 1	*three* contrasting selections: one from each List	*one* study / etude
Grade 2	*three* contrasting selections: one from each List	*one* study / etude

Elementary Piano Pedagogy Examination Topics

Candidates should be prepared to discuss the following topics with reference to their chosen Teaching Repertoire Sample.

General Pedagogy

- plans for and structure of lessons in the early years (including practicing and setting goals)
- nurturing creativity through imagery and analogy
- developing critical listening
- basic performance preparation (recitals, festivals)
- evaluating student progress
- practice strategies and effective practicing

The Professional Studio

- resource materials including dictionaries, history books, flashcards, Internet
- basics of studio management
- communication with parents

The Beginning Student

- initial meeting with a prospective student and parents and the first lesson
- introducing basic theoretical concepts and relating them to repertoire
- introducing note reading, sight reading, and ear training including recognition of rhythmic patterns, interval relationships, pitch memory, and rote playing of familiar tunes

Technique

- developing healthy technique and physiology, including posture, hand position, thumb movement, and finger movement
- developing basic motor skills, technical control, finger strength, and hand independence
- basic touch: *legato* and *staccato*
- fingering strategies
- approaches to tone production

Rhythm and Tempo

- developing an internal sense of rhythm
- introducing counting, time signatures, and the difference between meter and rhythm

Artistry

- developing imagination and expression
- developing dynamic range, tone color, and variety of touch
- articulation, slurs, phrasing, and detached notes
- introducing the damper pedal

Repertoire

- suitable teaching materials including sight reading and ear training, repertoire collections, and duets
- beginner piano methods (comparison of three methods)
- elementary-level popular styles and materials

Part 3   Written Examination

In this written examination, candidates should be prepared to discuss the "Elementary Piano Pedagogy Examination Topics" listed in Part 2. The Teaching Repertoire Sample must be chosen from *Celebration Series Perspectives*® and the beginner methods listed in Part 2. Please note that this is a closed-book examination.

Candidates will also be asked to discuss and edit a given sample selection, adding:
- fingering
- phrasing
- dynamics
- pedaling
- expression marks
- realization of ornamentation

Intermediate Piano Pedagogy

Intermediate Piano Pedagogy—the second stage of the ARCT in Piano Pedagogy—addresses pedagogical issues at Grades 3, 4, 5, and 6, but familiarity with earlier levels and some teaching experience is expected.

- Candidates must have completed the Elementary Piano Pedagogy Certificate at least one session prior to attempting the Intermediate Piano Pedagogy *Viva Voce* and Written Examinations.
- The Intermediate Piano Pedagogy Certificate is awarded upon completion of three parts: a Grade 10 Piano Certificate, a *Viva Voce* (oral) Examination, and a Written Examination.
- The three parts may be completed in any order, at one or more examination sessions. There is no time limit for completion.

	Intermediate Piano Pedagogy Requirements	Marks
Part 1	**Grade 10 Piano Certificate** (Please see p. 90 for detailed requirements)	
Part 2	**Viva Voce Examination (45 minutes)**	**100** (pass = 70)
	• Discussion of general pedagogical topics and the professional studio	25
	• Teaching rhythm, technique, musicianship, and other essential skills	25
	• Performance of selections from the Teaching Repertoire Sample	25
	• Detailed pedagogical discussion of selections from the Teaching Repertoire Sample	25
Part 3	**Written Examination (3 hours)** Discussion of general pedagogy, the professional studio, technique, artistry, and the candidate's Teaching Repertoire Sample	**100** (pass = 70)

Classification of Marks

First Class Honors *with Distinction* 90–100
First Class Honors 80–89
Honors 70–79
Pass 70

Resources for Examination Preparation

See "Resources" on p. 135 for suggested reading.

Part 1 Grade 10 Piano Certificate

Candidates must complete all required performance and theoretical requirements for the Grade 10 Piano Certificate. See p. 90 for detailed examination requirements.

Part 2 *Viva Voce* Examination

Teaching Repertoire Sample

Candidates must prepare a balanced program of sixteen contrasting selections as outlined in the chart below. Memorization of *one* selection is required. Studies / etudes should demonstrate specific technical issues at the intermediate level.

Candidates may choose selections from repertoire and studies / etudes for Grades 3, 4, 5, and 6 listed in the *Syllabus*. One study / etude selection must be chosen from the *Popular Selection List*.

Candidates should be prepared to:
- Perform selections chosen by the examiner from the Teaching Repertoire Sample.
- Discuss teaching methods for the chosen selections.
- Discuss technical exercises, sight-reading, and ear-training materials suitable for Grades 3, 4, 5, and 6.

Level	Repertoire	Studies / Etudes*
Grade 3	*three* contrasting selections: one from each List	*one* study / etude
Grade 4	*three* contrasting selections: one from each List	*one* study / etude
Grade 5	*three* contrasting selections: one from each List	*one* study / etude
Grade 6	*three* contrasting selections: one from each List	*one* study / etude

*Please note that one study / etude *must* be chosen from the *Popular Selection List*.

Intermediate Piano Pedagogy Examination Topics

Candidates should be prepared to discuss the following topics with reference to the Teaching Repertoire Sample:

General Pedagogy
- planning and structure as applied to lessons, practicing, and long-term objectives
- development of diagnostic skills and strategies for addressing common learning and performance challenges
- teaching practice techniques and time management
- motivating students
- fostering critical listening

- memorization techniques and strategies
- characteristics of different musical genres (for example, Baroque dances, sonatinas)
- stylistic characteristics of the significant composers and style periods taught in the intermediate grades

The Professional Studio

- teaching materials for students in the intermediate grades (including repertoire, ensemble works, studies / etudes, and technical exercises) with an emphasis on the major style periods of keyboard music (Baroque, Classical, Romantic, Post-Romantic, and 20th and 21st centuries)
- knowledge of the basic physiology for promoting a healthy technique and preventing injury
- role of complementary teaching technologies in the studio, including software, Internet resources and digital keyboards
- basics of studio management
- opportunities for professional development

Rhythm and Tempo

- teaching the difference between meter, counting, and rhythm
- intermediate level rhythmic patterns (dotted rhythms, triplets)
- achieving consistency of tempo

Technique

- developing coordination between the hands, finger strength, and independence
- development of fluency, facility, and agility
- practice strategies for solving technical problems
- intermediate level scales, chords, and arpeggios
- approaches to tone production

Artistry

- development of musical imagination through imagery and analogy
- stylistic awareness: teaching phrasing, articulation, and *rubato* specific to each style period
- introducing ornamentation
- developing dynamic range, voicing, and balance
- developing performance communication
- developing pedaling technique

Part 3   Written Examination

In this written examination, candidates should be prepared to discuss the "Intermediate Piano Pedagogy Examination Topics" listed in Part 2. The Teaching Repertoire Sample must be chosen from *Celebration Series Perspectives*®. Please note that this is a closed-book examination.

Candidates will also be asked to discuss and edit a given sample selection, adding:
- fingering
- phrasing
- dynamics
- pedaling
- expression marks
- realization of ornamentation

Advanced Piano Pedagogy

Advanced Piano Pedagogy is the final step towards the ARCT in Piano Pedagogy. It addresses pedagogical issues at Grades 7, 8, 9, and 10. Candidates should have teaching experience and be familiar with pedagogical issues concerning all levels of instruction.

- Candidates must have completed the Intermediate Piano Pedagogy Certificate at least one session prior to attempting any of Parts 1, 2, or 3 of the Advanced Piano Pedagogy level.
- Candidates must have completed the Grade 10 Piano examination with a total mark of 75 or minimum of 70 percent in each section, at least one session prior to attempting any of Parts, 1, 2, or 3 of the Advanced Piano Pedagogy level.
- Candidates must have fulfilled all the Grade 10 theory co-requisites with a total mark of at least 60 for each examination, at least one session prior to attempting any of Parts 1, 2, or 3 of the Advanced Piano Pedagogy level.

Successful candidates will be awarded the ARCT in Piano Pedagogy Diploma if they meet the following criteria:

- Candidates must be at least 18 years old.
- Candidates must have completed all three levels of the Piano Pedagogy Certificate Program (Elementary, Intermediate, and Advanced).
- Candidates must have completed all the ARCT theory co-requisites.

The Advanced Piano Pedagogy level comprises three parts: a practical examination, a *Viva Voce* (oral) Examination, and a Written Examination.

- The three parts may be completed in any order, in one or more sessions. There is no time limit for completion.
- Candidates who have passed the ARCT in Piano Performance may choose to be exempted from the Repertoire section of the practical examination. The remaining sections of Part 1 must be taken during the same session as the Part 2: *Viva Voce* Examination and within five years of the date of the ARCT in Piano Performance examination.

Classification of Marks
First Class Honors *with Distinction* 90–100
First Class Honors 80–89
Honors 70–79
Pass 70

Resources for Examination Preparation
See "Resources" on p. 135 for suggested reading.

	Advanced Piano Pedagogy Requirements	Marks
Part 1	**Practical Examination**	**100**
1	**Repertoire** *one* Prelude and Fugue by J.S. Bach chosen from List A of the Grade 10 or ARCT in Piano Performance repertoire list *one* selection from the Grade 9 Repertoire Lists *one* selection from the Grade 10 Repertoire Lists *two* selections from the ARCT in Piano Performance Repertoire Lists	**50** (pass = 35)
2	**Technical Requirements** Technical Tests 　Major keys: all 　Minor keys: all 　– parallel motion scales　　　　　– chromatic scales in octaves 　– *staccato* scales　　　　　　　– tonic four-note chords 　– scales separated by 3rds, 6ths, and 10ths　– dominant 7th and diminished 7th chords 　– formula pattern scales　　　　– tonic arpeggios 　– chromatic scales　　　　　　– dominant 7th and diminished 7th arpeggios 　– scales in octaves　　　　　　– *one* exercise of candidate's choice, see p. 113	**20** (pass = 14)
3	**Ear Tests** Meter Intervals Chords Playback	**15** (pass = 10.5) 2 5 4 4
4	**Sight Reading** Playing Clapping	**15** (pass = 10.5) 4 + 4 + 4 3
Part 2	**Viva Voce Examination (45 minutes)**	**100** (pass = 70)
	• Discussion of general pedagogical topics and the professional studio • Teaching rhythm, technique, musicianship, and other essential skills • Performance of selections from the Teaching Repertoire Sample • Detailed pedagogical discussion of selections from the Teaching Repertoire Sample	25 25 25 25
Part 3	**Written Examination (3 hours)**	**100** (pass = 70)
	Discussion of general pedagogy, the professional studio, technique, artistry, and other essential skills. The Teaching Repertoire Sample for this level must be chosen from the *Piano Syllabus, 2008 Edition*.	
	Theory Co-requisites and Prerequisites	
	Theory Co-requisites Counterpoint [Grade 4 Counterpoint] Advanced Harmony *or* Advanced Keyboard Harmony [Grade 5 Harmony *or* Grade 5 Keyboard Harmony] History 3: 19th Century to Present [Grade 5 History] Analysis [Grade 5 Analysis]	
	Theory Prerequisites Advanced Rudiments [Grade 2 Rudiments] History 1: An Overview [Grade 3 History] Intermediate Harmony *or* Intermediate Keyboard Harmony [Grade 4 Harmony *or* Grade 4 Keyboard Harmony] History 2: Middle Ages to Classical [Grade 4 History]	

Part 1　Practical Examination
1 Repertoire

Candidates must prepare *five* contrasting selections from the following list of sources. Memorization is encouraged but not required. The candidate's examination program should include selections from each of Lists A, B, C, D, and E. One total mark will be awarded for the performance of the Repertoire section.
- *one* Prelude and Fugue by J.S. Bach from List A of Grade 9, Grade 10, or ARCT in Piano Performance
- *one* selection from Grade 9 repertoire
- *one* selection from Grade 10 repertoire
- *two* selections from the ARCT in Piano Performance repertoire

2 Technical Requirements
Technical Tests

Candidates must play all Technical Tests from memory, ascending and descending, with good tone and logical fingering, at a steady tempo. Metronome markings indicate minimum speeds. All scales are to be played *legato* unless otherwise indicated.

See "Technical Patterns" on p. 19 for examples.

112

Keys for Advanced Piano Pedagogy: all major keys; all minor keys

Scales	Keys	Played	Tempo	Note values
Parallel Motion	all major keys all minor keys (harmonic and melodic)	HT 4 octaves	♩ = 120	♬♬
Staccato	B♭, E♭, A♭, D♭, G♭ major B♭, E♭, G♯, C♯, F♯, F, B minor (harmonic and melodic)	HT 3 octaves	♩ = 120	♬ (triplet)
Separated by a 3rd	A♭, A, B♭, B, major	HT 4 octaves	♩ = 104	♬♬
Separated by a 6th	C, D♭, D, E♭, major	HT 4 octaves	♩ = 104	♬♬
Separated by a 10th	E, F, G♭, G major	HT 4 octaves	♩ = 104	♬♬
Formula Pattern	B♭, E♭, A♭, D♭, G♭ major B♭, E♭, G♯, C♯, F♯, F, B minor (harmonic)	HT 4 octaves	♩ = 120	♬♬
Chromatic	beginning on any note	HT 4 octaves	♩ = 120	♬♬
Scales in Octaves solid (blocked) *staccato*	B♭, E♭, A♭, D♭, G♭ major B♭, E♭, G♯, C♯, F♯, F, B (harmonic and melodic)	HT 2 octaves	♩ = 84	♬♬
Chromatic Scales in Octaves solid (blocked) *staccato*	beginning on any note	HT 2 octaves	♩ = 104	♬♬

Chords	Keys	Played	Tempo	Note values
Tonic Four-Note Chords broken	all keys	HT 2 octaves (root position and inversion) (ending with I–vi–ii$^6_5$–I$^6_4$–V^7–I chord progression)	♩ = 120	♬♬
solid (blocked)			♩ = 120	♩♩
broken alternate-note pattern			♩ = 104	♬♬
Dominant 7th broken	all keys	HT 2 octaves (root position and inversion)	♩ = 120	♬♬
solid (blocked)			♩ = 120	♩♩
broken alternate-note pattern			♩ = 104	♬♬
Diminished 7th broken	all minor keys	HT 2 octaves (root position and inversion)	♩ = 120	♬♬
solid (blocked)			♩ = 120	♩♩
broken alternate-note pattern			♩ = 104	♬♬

Arpeggios	Keys	Played	Tempo	Note values
Tonic	all keys	HT 4 octaves root position and inversions, either individually or in sequence beginning in root position or in any inversion	♩ = 92	♬♬
Dominant 7th				
Diminished 7th	all minor keys			

Exercises	Keys	Played	Tempo	Note values
Candidates must prepare one exercise from the following list.				

Modal Scales
  Supertonic (Dorian)
  Mediant (Phrygian)
  Subdominant (Lydian)
  Dominant (Mixolydian)
	beginning on different scale degrees of A, D♭, E♭ major	HT
		4 octaves
			♩ = 100	♬♬

Double 3rd Scales, *legato*	D, A♭ major A, D minor (harmonic)	HT 2 octaves	♩ = 60	♫
Tonic Arpeggios Beginning at the 6th or 10th	C, D, A♭ major C, D, G♯ minor	6th: RH begins tonic, LH begins mediant 10th: RH begins mediant, LH begins tonic 4 octaves	♩ = 80	♬♬
Arpeggio Sequence I–i–♭VI^6–vi^6–IV$^6_4$–iv$^6_4$–I	beginning and ending on C or F	HT 4 octaves	♩ = 80	♬♬
Chromatic Scales in Octaves, solid (blocked) *legato*	beginning on any note	HT 2 octaves	♩ = 72	♫

ARCT in Piano Pedagogy

Examples of Exercises

Scale beginnning on the Supertonic (of A major)—Dorian Mode (beginning on B) (to be played four octaves)

Scale beginning on the Mediant (of A major)—Phrygian Mode (beginning on C♯) (to be played four octaves)

Scale beginning on the Subdominant (of A major)—Lydian Mode (beginning on D) (to be played four octaves)

Scale beginning on the Dominant (of A major)—Mixolydian Mode (beginning on B) (to be played four octaves)

Double 3rd Scales, *legato*

Tonic Arpeggios Beginning at the 6th

Tonic Arpeggios Beginning at the 10th

Arpeggio Sequence (beginning and ending on C, two octaves shown; when playing the four-octave version, ascend four octaves in each key before descending)

Chromatic Scales in Octaves, solid (blocked) *legato*

3 Ear Tests

Meter

Candidates will be asked to identify the time signature of a four-measure passage. The examiner will play each passage *once*.

Time Signatures $\frac{2}{4}$ $\frac{3}{4}$ $\frac{6}{8}$ $\frac{9}{8}$

Intervals

Candidates will be asked to identify the following intervals. The examiner will play each interval *once* in broken form.
or
Candidates may choose to sing or hum the following intervals. The examiner will play the first note *once*.

Above a given note	Below a given note
any interval within a major 9th	any interval within the octave

Chords

Candidates will be asked to identify the chords used in a four-measure phrase. The examiner will play the tonic chord *once* and the phrase *twice* at a slow to moderate tempo. During the second playing, the candidate will name each chord after it is played.

- The phrase will be in a major key and will begin with a tonic chord.
- The phrase may include chords built on the first, second, fourth, fifth, and sixth degrees of the scale.
- The final cadence may contain a cadential six-four chord and / or a dominant 7th chord.

Example only

Playback

Candidates will be asked to play back a two-part phrase of approximately three measures in a major key. The examiner will name the key, play the tonic chord *once*, and play the two-part phrase *three times*.

Example only

4 Sight Reading

Playing

Candidates will be asked to play *three* passages at sight:

- Two passages will be approximately equal in difficulty to Grade 8 repertoire.
- One passage will be a piece of simulated Grade 3 teaching repertoire. Candidates are expected to demonstrate musical features through articulate playing meant to inspire a Grade 3 student to learn this piece.

Clapping

Candidates will be asked to clap or tap the rhythm of a melody. A steady pace and rhythmic accentuation are expected.

Example only

The Senior Musicianship examination can be substituted for the Ear Tests and Sight Reading sections of the Advanced Piano Pedagogy examination (see p. 123).

Supplemental Examinations

Improve an Advanced Piano Pedagogy Part 1 examination mark

In order to improve an overall mark, candidates may take *one* Supplemental Examination in Part 1. Please note that Supplemental Examinations are *not* available for the Repertoire section of the examination or for Part 2 or Part 3. Supplemental Examinations are available for Technical Requirements, Ear Tests, and Sight Reading sections of the Advanced Piano Pedagogy practical examination only:

- Candidates must achieve a minimum of 70 percent in the Repertoire section to be eligible for a supplemental examination.
- Supplemental examinations must take place within two years of the original examination, during the regularly scheduled examination period.

Part 2   *Viva Voce* Examination

Teaching Repertoire Sample

Candidates must prepare a balanced program of thirteen contrasting selections as outlined in the chart below. *One repertoire selection* must be memorized. Studies / etudes should demonstrate specific technical issues at the advanced level.

Candidates may choose selections from Repertoire and Studies / Etudes for Grades 7, 8, 9, and 10 listed in the *Piano Syllabus, 2008 edition*. One of the study / etude selections *may* be chosen from the *Popular Selection List*.

Candidates should be prepared to:
- Perform selections chosen by the examiner from the Teaching Repertoire Sample.
- Discuss teaching approaches for the chosen selections.
- Bring samples of technical exercises, sight-reading, and ear-training materials suitable for Grades 7, 8, 9, and 10.

Level	Repertoire	Studies / Etudes*
Grade 7**	*two* contrasting selections	*one* study / etude
Grade 8**	*two* contrasting selections	*one* study / etude
Grade 9**	*two* contrasting selections	*one* study / etude
Grade 10**	*three* contrasting selections including a Prelude and Fugue by J.S. Bach and a List E piece. (Candidates may substitute the Grade 10 Prelude and Fugue with an ARCT Prelude and Fugue.)	*one* study / etude

*Please note that one study / etude *may* be chosen from the *Popular Selection List*.

** All List designations (List A, B, etc.) must be represented including two movements from a sonata (at Grade 9 or 10 level) one movement of which must be in sonata form.

Advanced Piano Pedagogy Examination Topics

Candidates should be prepared to discuss the following topics with reference to their chosen Teaching Repertoire Sample. An understanding of elementary- and intermediate-level pedagogy is also required.

General Pedagogy
- development of diagnostic skills and strategies for addressing common learning and performance challenges
- fostering critical listening skills
- characteristics of different musical genres (for example, fugues, sonatas) in training students
- integrating advanced ear, sight, and theory into the learning process
- memorization techniques for advanced repertoire
- suitable teaching materials and their editions, including popular styles and ensembles, pieces

The Professional Studio
- teaching materials for students in the advanced grades (including repertoire, ensemble works, concerti, studies / etudes, and technical exercises) with an emphasis on major style periods of keyboard music—Baroque, Classical, Romantic, Post-Romantic, and 20th and 21st centuries
- role of complementary teaching technologies in the studio, including software, Internet resources, and digital keyboards
- studio management considerations
- opportunities for professional development

Technique
- knowledge of basic physiology as applied to piano performance, to develop a healthy technique and to prevent injury
- refinement of technical skills
- teaching scales, chords, arpeggios, and octaves, appropriate to this level
- development of coordination, agility, and speed
- extension of the hand position: four-note chords and octaves
- relevant physical approaches to tone production, in both level and quality
- practice strategies for solving technical problems

Artistry
- awareness of historical performance practice including ornamentation, articulation, tone, and dynamics
- use of *rubato* and artistic pedaling
- interpreting 20th- and 21st-century notational symbols
- relationship of form and harmony to interpretation
- use of imagery and analogy to develop musical imagination
- developing performance artistry

Part 3   Written Examination

In this written examination candidates should be prepared to discuss the Advanced Piano Pedagogy Examination Topics listed in Part 2. Reference to specific repertoire found in the Teaching Repertoire Sample and in *Celebration Series Perspectives*® is expected. Please note that this is a closed-book examination.

Candidates maybe asked to write and explain relevant technical exercises at any level.

Candidates will also be asked to discuss and edit a given sample selection, adding:
- fingering
- phrasing
- dynamics
- pedaling
- expressions marks
- realization of ornamentation

Register for an Examination

Check the "Getting Started" section on p. 6.

Examination Sessions and Registration Deadlines

Exact dates and deadlines can be found online. Register early to avoid disappointment: late registrations are subject to an additional fee and may be denied.

Canada

Winter Session—register by early November
- practical examinations take place in January
- theory examinations take place in December

Spring Session—register by early March
- practical examinations take place in June
- theory examinations take place in May

Summer Session—register by early June
- practical examinations take place in August
- theory examinations take place in August

USA

Check the website, www.nationalmusiccertificate.org, for information on examination dates and deadlines.

Online Registration

All registrations should be submitted using the online registration process.

To register online, click on "Register for an Examination," and follow the instructions provided. Be prepared to enter:
- the candidate's RCME Number/Candidate ID Number and birth date
- the teacher's phone number or Teacher Number
- the examination center
- payment information—Visa or MasterCard accepted

Teachers may register their students by logging into "Teacher Services" and using the "Studio Registration" feature.

Make sure the correct RCME Number/Candidate ID Number is entered upon registration. This number ensures that candidates receive all the certificates for which they are eligible.

Once a registration has been submitted, it may not be withdrawn.

Need an RCME Number/Candidate ID Number? New candidates will receive an RCME Number/ Candidate ID Number when they register. The full name must be entered as it should appear on certificates, along with your birth date, address, telephone numbers, and email address.

Examination Fees

Examination fees must be paid at registration using Visa or MasterCard. Fees for the current academic year are listed online under "Examination Information."

Examination Centers

Examinations are conducted in more than 300 communities across North America. Each examination center has a local Examination Center Representative who ensures that students and teachers have a successful examination experience.

Teachers may verify their students' examination schedules by logging into "Teacher Services."

To find the nearest examination center, look online under "Examination Information."

Examination Scheduling

Once they have registered, piano examination candidates may schedule the exact date and time of their examination through "Online Services" using "Examination Scheduling." This service helps candidates to manage their schedules and avoid examination conflicts. Candidates who choose not to use "Examination Scheduling" at the time of registration will be assigned an examination date and time.

All candidates must verify their examination schedules online two weeks before the first day of the examination session by visiting "Examination Scheduling." Examination schedules will *not* be mailed.

Candidates must print out the Examination Program Form" using the "Examination Scheduling" feature. Candidates should fill out the form and bring it on the examination day.

Candidates who, for any reason, are unable to attend an examination should contact the Center Representative listed on their Examination Schedule immediately.

Examination Regulations

Examination Procedures

Candidates must be ready to perform at least fifteen minutes before their scheduled time. *Please note that candidate examination times cannot be exchanged.*

admitted to the examination room.

- Page turners and other assistants are not permitted in the examination room. Waiting areas are provided for parents, teachers, and assistants.
- Warm-up rooms are not provided for piano candidates.
- Photo ID may be requested before candidates are admitted to the examination room.
- Candidates should list all repertoire and studies / etudes to be performed on the Examination Program Form and bring it to the examination.
- Candidates should bring all music to be performed to the examination, whether or not selections are memorized. *Please note that photocopied music is not permitted in the examination room unless the candidate has a letter of permission from the publisher.* (Please see "Copyright and Photocopying" on p. 129.)
- Recording devices are strictly prohibited in the examination room.

The candidate's performance may be interrupted at the examiner's discretion when an assessment has been reached.

Credits and Refunds for Missed Examinations

Credits (formerly called "fee extensions") and refunds are only granted under two specific conditions. Candidates who are unable to attend an examination for medical reasons or because of a direct time conflict with a school examination are eligible to request either an examination credit for the full amount of the examination fee or a 50 percent refund of the examination fee.

Requests for examination credits or refunds must be made to RCM Examinations *in writing* and accompanied by the following documentation:

- for medical reasons—a physician's letter and the candidate's examination schedule
- for direct time conflicts with school examinations— a letter from a school official on school letterhead and the candidate's Examination Schedule

All requests must be submitted by mail or by fax within two weeks following the examination.

Candidates who, for any reason, are unable to attend an examination should contact the Center Representative listed on their Examination Schedule immediately.

Examination Credit

An examination credit (formerly called a "fee extension") may be applied to the fee of a future examination. Examination credits are valid for *one year* from the date of the original scheduled examination.

Examination credits can be redeemed when the candidate registers for their next examination. The credit will be automatically applied during the online registration process.

Fee Refund

Candidates who cannot redeem an examination credit within a year may apply instead for a 50 percent refund of the examination fee.

Requests for examination refunds or credits must be made to RCM Examinations in writing and accompanied by the necessary documentation (see above). *All requests must be submitted within two weeks following the examination by mail or by fax.*

Candidates with Special Needs

Candidates with special needs should submit a Special Needs Request Form—by mail or fax to the RCM Examinations or NMCP Office—as soon as possible before the application deadline. Each case will be assessed individually.

Candidates may receive help in and out of the examination room if required. Please note that helpers must remain in the waiting area during the actual examination.

> The Special Needs Request Form is available online under "Online Forms."

Examination Results

Candidates and teachers can access examination results online within six weeks of the examination:

1) Go to www.rcmexaminations.org *or* www.nationalmusiccertificate.org

2) Click on "Examination Results"

3) Click on the appropriate Examination Session you wish to view

4) Enter the candidate's RCME/Candidate ID Number and date of birth

5) Click on the mark to download and view the examiner's comments

6) Click on the candidate's name to view an unofficial transcript

---

Please note that results will not be mailed or given by telephone.

Teachers may access their student's examination results by logging into "Teacher Services."

Official transcripts are available upon written request to the RCM Examinations or NMCP office and payment of the requisite fee. (Download the official transcript request form from the "Online Forms" section of the website.)

Interpreting Examination Results

All candidates may access their official results (including examiners' comments) online four to six weeks after the examination. The examiner's report explains in general terms how the final mark was calculated. It is intended to assist candidates in their future musical development. Please note that the mark reflects the examiner's evaluation of the candidate's performance during the examination. Examination results do not reflect a candidate's previously demonstrated abilities or potential for future development. *Appeals on practical examinations will not be considered.*

Classification of Marks

First Class Honors with Distinction 90–100
First Class Honors 80–89
Honors 70–79
Pass (Grades 1 to 10) 60
Pass (ARCT in Piano Performance) 70
Pass (ARCT in Piano Pedagogy) 70 percent in each section

Marking Criteria

First Class Honors with Distinction: 90–100

Only truly exceptional candidates achieve this standing. Candidates must demonstrate complete technical command and perform with a confident, masterful style. These candidates clearly demonstrate an authentic personal performance spark.

First Class Honors: 85–89

Candidates present a truly engaging and intelligent performance, displaying technical polish and finesse, definite and apt characterization, and a sense of spontaneity.

First Class Honors: 80–84

Candidates are technically solid and demonstrate sensitivity, intelligence, and talent. They are well prepared and able to execute the examination requirements thoughtfully and confidently.

Honors: 70–79

Candidates exhibit thorough and careful preparation and demonstrate some interpretive skills. Repertoire is presented with overall command and accuracy. There is awareness and general security in technical elements.

Access examination results online at "Examination Results."

Table of Marks

	Preparatory A–B	Grade 1	Grades 2–5	Grades 6–7	Grades 8–9	Grade 10	ARCT in Piano Performance	ARCT in Piano Pedagogy Elementary	Intermediate	Advanced
Repertoire	60	50	50	50	56	56 (70% = 39)	100	Grade 9 — Certificate	Grade 10 — Certificate	50
List A	20 (2)	18	18	18	16 (1.5)	12 (1.5)	20			50 (pass = 35)
List B	20 (2)	18	18	18	16 (1.5)	14 (1.5)	25			
List C	20 (2)	14	14	14	12 (1)	10 (1)	15			
List D	-	-	-	-	12 (1)	10 (1)	15			
List E	-	-	-	-	-	10 (1)	15			
Concert Etudes	-	-	-	-	-	-	10			-
Memory	-	6	6	6	-	-	-			20
Technical Requirements	20	24	24	24	24	24 (70% = 17)	-			20 (pass = 14)
Studies / Etudes	-	6 + 6	6 + 6	6 + 6	6 + 6	6 + 6	-			-
Technical Tests	20	12	12	12	12	12	-			20
Ear Tests	10	10	10	10	10	10 (70% = 7)	-			15 (pass = 10.5)
Meter	-	-	-	-	-	-	-			2
Rhythm	5	5	3	2	-	-	-			-
Intervals	-	-	3	3	3	2	-			5
Chords	-	-	-	2	2	2	-			4
Cadences	-	-	-	-	2	3	-			-
Playback	5	5	4	3	3	3	-			4
Sight Reading	10	10	10	10	10	10 (70% = 7)	-			15 (pass = 10.5)
Melody	7	7	7	7	7	7	-			4 + 4 + 4
Rhythm	3	3	3	3	3	3	-			3
Totals	100	100	100	100	100	100	100 (pass = 70)			100 (pass = 70)

Viva Voce								Elementary	Intermediate	Advanced
General Topics	-	-	-	-	-	-	-	25	25	25
Essential Skills								25	25	25
Performance								25	25	25
Discussion								25	25	25
Totals								100 (pass = 70)	100 (pass = 70)	100 (pass = 70)

| **Written** | - | - | - | - | - | - | - | 100 (pass = 70) | 100 (pass = 70) | 100 (pass = 70) |

Note: Figures in regular parentheses indicate marks awarded for memory.

Supplemental Examinations

Improve an examination mark

Candidates seeking to improve their overall mark at the Grade 10 or Advanced Piano Pedagogy levels may take a Supplemental Examination.

- Supplemental Examinations must occur within *two* years of the original examination.
- Supplemental Examinations are given during regular examination sessions.
- Candidates in Grade 10 may repeat *any two sections* of a practical examination, *except repertoire.*
- To be eligible for a Supplemental Examination in Grade 10, candidates must achieve a minimum mark of 65 overall and 70 percent in the Repertoire section.
- Candidates in Advanced Piano Pedagogy may repeat *any one section* of Part 1, *except repertoire.*
- To be eligible for a Supplemental Examination in Part 1 of Advanced Piano Pedagogy, candidates must achieve at least 70 percent in the Repertoire section.

Candidates in Grade 10 must complete the Grade 10 theory co-requisites within five years of the *original practical examination*, not any subsequent supplemental examinations.

Musicianship Examinations

A musicianship examination may replace the Ear Tests and Sight Reading sections of a Grade 8, 9, 10, or Advanced Piano Pedagogy examination. Please consult the current *Theory Syllabus* for examination requirements. The musicianship examination must be taken at least one session *before* the practical examination.

Musicianship Level	Practical Examination Level
Junior Musicianship	Grade 8
Intermediate Musicianship	Grade 9
Senior Musicianship	Grade 10 and Advanced Piano Pedagogy

Candidates who have completed a musicianship examination should submit the following documentation when registering for the corresponding practical examination:
- a photocopy of the musicianship examination results
- a letter requesting exemption from the Ear Tests and Sight Reading sections of the upcoming practical examination

Practical Examination Certificates

Certificates are awarded to candidates who successfully complete the requirements for their grade.

Beginning in Grade 5, certificates are awarded *after* the theory co-requisites for that grade have been successfully completed. Theory co-requisites must be completed within *five* years of the original practical examination.

Please note that ARCT diplomas are awarded to candidates at the annual Convocation ceremony. Candidates may not use the designation "ARCT" before Convocation.

School Credits

RCM Examinations results can sometimes be used as a credit toward high school graduation or toward university entrance. In Canada, the policies of provincial education ministries can be found online under "Academic Information, High School Accreditation." Candidates are advised to discuss the eligibility of their examination results with their school principal or guidance counselor.

Medals

Each academic year (September to August) medals are awarded to the candidates who achieve exceptional examination results. No application is required.

Silver Medals (Canada only)

Silver medals are awarded by province or region to the candidates in Preparatory A, Preparatory B, and Grades 1 to 10 who receive the highest marks for the respective practical examinations. To be eligible, a candidate must receive a minimum mark of 80 percent in the practical examination, and have completed all the theory co-requisites for the respective grade.

Silver medals are also awarded by province or region to the candidates in Elementary and Intermediate Piano Pedagogy who receive the highest average for Parts 2 and 3 (*Viva Voce* and Written Examination) of the respective Piano Pedagogy level. To be eligible a candidate must:

- receive a minimum of 80 percent in each of the Part 2 and 3 examinations
- have completed the Grade 9 Piano Certificate (for the Elementary Piano Pedagogy level) or Grade 10 Piano Certificate (for the Intermediate Piano Pedagogy level)

Gold Medals (Canada and USA)

A gold medal is awarded to the graduating ARCT in Piano Performance candidate who receives the highest mark for the practical examination. To be eligible, a candidate must receive:

- a minimum of 85 percent in the practical examination
- a minimum of 70 percent in each theory co-requisite examination

A gold medal is awarded to the graduating ARCT in Piano Pedagogy candidate who receives the highest average for Advanced Piano Pedagogy Parts 1, 2, and 3 (Practical, *Viva Voce*, and Written Examinations). To be eligible, a candidate must receive:

- a minimum overall average of 85 percent for the Advanced Piano Pedagogy Parts 1, 2, and 3 examinations
- a minimum of 70 percent in each theory co-requisite examination

A gold medal for excellence in theory is also awarded to the graduating ARCT candidate who completes the theory examinations listed below with the highest average mark. To be eligible, a candidate must receive a minimum overall average of 80 percent for the eight examinations.

Basic Harmony *or* Basic Keyboard Harmony
Intermediate Harmony *or* Intermediate Keyboard Harmony
Advanced Harmony *or* Advanced Keyboard Harmony
Counterpoint
Analysis
History 1: An Overview
History 2: Middle Ages to Classical
History 3: 19th Century to Present

Certificates of Excellence (USA only)

Each academic year (September to August) Certificates of Excellence are awarded to candidates who achieve exceptional examination results. No application is required.

Center Certificates of Excellence

Center Certificates of Excellence are awarded in each center to the candidates in Preparatory A, Preparatory B, and Grades 1 to 10 who receive the highest marks for the respective practical examinations. To be eligible, a candidate must receive a minimum of 80 percent in the practical examination and have completed the theory co-requisite examinations for the respective grade.

State Certificates of Excellence

State Certificates of Excellence are awarded by state to the candidates in Preparatory A, Preparatory B, and Grades 1 to 10 who receive the highest marks for the respective practical examinations. To be eligible, a candidate must receive a minimum of 80 percent in the practical examination and have completed the theory co-requisite examinations for the respective grade.

State Certificates of Excellence are also awarded by state to the candidates in Elementary and Intermediate Piano Pedagogy who receive the highest average for Parts 2 and 3 (*Viva Voce* and Written Examinations) of the respective Pedagogy level. To be eligible, a candidate must:

- receive a minimum of 80 percent in each of the Part 2 and 3 examinations
- have completed the Grade 9 Piano Certificate (for the Elementary Piano Pedagogy level) or Grade 10 Piano Certificate (for the Intermediate Piano Pedagogy level)

RESPs (Canada only)

Use of Education Funds for music studies

Candidates who have a Registered Education Savings Plan (RESP) may be eligible to use these funds to support private studies in music at the Grade 9, Grade 10, Piano Pedagogy, and ARCT levels. Candidates should consult their RESP providers for more information.

Examination Repertoire

The *Syllabus* lists the repertoire eligible for examinations. Information given for each item includes:

- the composer
- the larger work of which the selection is a part (where applicable)
- the title of the selection
- collections or anthologies in which the selection can be found (where applicable)
- performance directions (where applicable) indicating the section(s) or movement(s) of a work to be prepared
- the publisher of a suggested edition (where applicable)

Names of publishers are indicated by an assigned abbreviation. Please see p. 132 for a list of publishers and their respective abbreviations.

Da Capo Signs and Repeats

- When performing repertoire at an examination, *da capo* signs should be observed.
- Repeat signs should ordinarily be ignored. However, repeats in repertoire from *Celebration Series Persepctives*® should be observed if indicated in a footnote below the music.

Memory

- In Preparatory A and Preparatory B, marks for memorization are included in the repertoire marks. Two marks will be awarded for each repertoire selection that is played from memory.
- In Grades 1 to 7, memorization of repertoire is marked separately. Up to two marks will be awarded for each repertoire selection that is played from memory.
- In Grades 8 to 10, marks for memorization are included in the repertoire marks: 1.5 marks are awarded for memory for each piece in Lists A and B; 1 mark is awarded for memory for each piece in Lists C, D, and E.
- For the ARCT in Piano Performance examination, memorization is compulsory. Candidates not playing from memory will receive comments only. Any selection played with the music will receive a mark of zero.
- In all grades, studies / etudes need not be memorized, and no extra marks will be awarded for memory.
- In all grades, technical tests must be played from memory.

Fingering

Any appropriate fingering will be accepted for repertoire, studies / etudes, and technical tests.

Syllabus Repertoire Lists

The Repertoire for each grade (except Preparatory A and B) is divided into several lists, according to stylistic period.

Syllabus Repertoire Lists

Grade	List A	List B	List C	List D	List E	List F
Grades 1 and 2	Baroque and Classical Repertoire	Romantic, 20th-, and 21st-century Repertoire	Inventions			
Grades 3–7	Baroque Repertoire	Classical and Classical-style Repertoire	Romantic, 20th-, and 21st-century Repertoire			
Grade 8	Baroque Repertoire	Classical and Classical-style Repertoire	Romantic Repertoire	Post-Romantic, 20th-, and 21st-century Repertoire		
Grade 9	Baroque Repertoire	Classical Repertoire	Romantic Repertoire	Post-Romantic, 20th-, and 21st-century Repertoire		
Grade 10	Works of J.S. Bach	Classical Repertoire	Romantic Repertoire	Post-Romantic and Early 20th-century Repertoire	20th- and 21st-century Repertoire	
ARCT	Works of J.S. Bach	Sonatas	Romantic Repertoire	Post-Romantic and Early 20th-century Repertoire	20th- and 21st-century Repertoire	Concert Etudes

Editions

For many repertoire items, the *Syllabus* listing includes a suggested edition (indicated by an assigned publisher abbreviation). These editions have been chosen for their quality or for their availability in North America. When no publisher is indicated, students are encouraged to use the best edition available—the edition that most accurately reflects the composer's intentions.

Editorial markings vary from one edition to another. Examination marks will not be deducted for altering these editorial suggestions as long as the resulting change is musically and stylistically acceptable.

Availability

RCM Examinations has made every effort to ensure that most of the materials listed in this *Syllabus* are in print and easily available at leading music retailers throughout North America. If you experience difficulty in obtaining piano music in your community, then you may contact:

Long and McQuade (RCM Music and Book Store)
273 Bloor Street West
Toronto, ON Canada M5S 1W2
telephone: 416-585-2225
toll-free: 1-866-585-2225
fax: 416-585-7801

Canadian Music Centre
www.musiccentre.ca
20 St. Joseph Street
Toronto, ON Canada M4Y 1J9
telephone: 416-961-6601
fax: 416-961-7198

128

However, please note that the publishing industry changes rapidly. Works go out of print, and copyrights move from one firm to another. In addition, the repertoire lists contain a few works or anthologies that are no longer in print but that teachers or candidates may have in their personal collections. Out-of-print titles are indicated in the lists as "[OP]." Candidates may use an out-of-print work for examination purposes provided they can obtain the published work or written permission to use a photocopy. (Please see "Copyright and Photocopying" on p. 129.)

Anthologies and Collections

If a repertoire selection is published in a collection of a composer's music or in an anthology containing music by a number of composers, the title of the collection or anthology is usually included in the *Syllabus* listing. Individual selections may also be found in other sources. In order to save space, the words "volume" and "book" have usually been omitted; a number following a title indicates the number of the volume, book, or set number in which a selection can be found (for example, *Music of Our Time*, 2).

Celebration Series Perspectives®

In order to ensure the ready availability of high-quality examination materials, The Frederick Harris Music Co., Limited has published *Celebration Series Perspectives®*. This series includes eleven *Piano Repertoire* books (Preparatory to Level 10), ten *Piano Studies / Etudes* books (Levels 1 to 10), nine *Student Workbooks* (Preparatory to Level 8), the *Answer Book for Student Workbooks*, *Compact Discs* for each level (Preparatory to Level 10), nine volumes of *Technical Requirements for Piano* (Preparatory to Level 8), and the *Handbook for Teachers*, a resource book designed for use with the series.

Piano Repertoire

The eleven *Celebration Series Perspectives®* *Repertoire* books serve as repertoire selections for Preparatory B to Grade 10. The *Piano Repertoire* books present an extensive sampling of styles and composers covering a broad spectrum of piano music from four centuries, and are suitable for examinations, recitals, competitions, and for enjoyment. The pieces in Levels 1 to 10 are organized according to the style periods listed in the *Syllabus*.

Piano Studies / Etudes

The examination requirements for Grades 1 to 10 include studies / etudes. These studies / etudes may be selected from *Celebration Series Perspectives®*: *Piano Studies / Etudes*. The ten *Piano Studies / Etudes* books can be used effectively as technique builders, for recitals or competitions, and for enjoyment.

Student Workbooks

The nine *Student Workbooks* from *Celebration Series Perspectives®* are companion volumes to the *Piano Repertoire* books for the Preparatory level to Level 8. The *Student Workbooks* are written for the student, using language and music terminology appropriate for students at each level. Each *Workbook* contains a detailed discussion of each selection in the *Piano Repertoire* album for that level and a glossary of terms.

Answer Book for Student Workbooks

The *Answer Book for Student Workbooks* is a comprehensive answer book for *Celebration Series Perspectives®*: *Student Workbooks* (Preparatory to Level 8). Teachers and parents will find the *Answer Book* a useful and convenient resource.

Handbook for Teachers

The *Celebration Series Perspectives®*: *Handbook for Teachers* by Cathy Albergo, Reid Alexander, and Marvin Blickenstaff is a comprehensive teaching aid that organizes the material in the *Piano Repertoire* and *Piano Studies / Etudes* books for optimum use in the teaching studio. In addition to a detailed discussion of each selection in the *Piano Repertoire* and *Piano Studies / Etudes* books, the *Handbook for Teachers* also includes suggestions for presenting and teaching *Celebration Series Perspectives®* from start to finish, as well as a complete composer and works index for the series.

Recordings

Celebration Series Perspectives® includes compact disc recordings of the complete works from the *Piano Repertoire* and *Piano Studies / Etudes* books (Preparatory to Level 10). The recordings may be used by students as a reliable reference and inspiration for a polished performance, and teachers will find them an invaluable resource for style period performance practice.

Technical Requirements for Piano

The nine *Technical Requirements for Piano* books reflect the revised technical requirements outlined in the *Piano Syllabus, 2008 Edition* for the Preparatory level to Level 8. Summary charts provide a helpful overview of the scales, chords, arpeggios, tempos, and note values for the required keys for each level.

Popular Selection List

The *Popular Selection List* is an addendum to the *Piano Syllabus*. The *Popular Selection List* is a compilation of non-classical pieces, carefully selected to suit each level of study for Grades 3 to 9. Candidates in Grades 3 to 9 may choose a work from the *Popular Selection List* for a study / etude selection as outlined under "Substitutions." Please note that candidates are advised to use the edition of the chosen piece specified in the *Popular Selection List*—other editions may not be accepted as appropriate. The *Popular Selection List* is also available online at www.rcmexaminations.org and www.nationalmusiccertificate.org.

Copyright and Photocopying

Federal and international copyright laws prohibit the use of photocopies without the permission of the publisher. The use of unauthorized photocopies for examination purposes constitutes copyright infringement as outlined in the *Copyright Act* of Canada, and in Title 17 of the *United States Code*. Additional information about federal copyright law is available online through the Copyright Board of Canada at www.cb-cda.gc.ca and U.S. Copyright Office at www.copyright.gov.

Please note that photocopied music will not be permitted in the examination room. Candidates who bring unauthorized photocopies to the examination will not be examined.

Candidates should bring all music to be performed to the examination. Candidates who wish to photocopy one page of a selection for the purpose of facilitating a page turn must do so with permission from the publisher.

With this notice, The Frederick Harris Music Co., Limited grants permission to festival, recital, and examination participants to photocopy single pages from their publications to facilitate a page turn.

Substitutions

As outlined in the chart below, candidates may make substitute selections for their examination. If approval is required, candidates must submit an *Examination Substitute Piece Request* (available online) by the Examination Registration deadline. Candidates are advised to prepare an alternate work in case the request is denied.

Teacher's Choice

A selection of the teacher's choice (Teacher's Choice) may be substituted for a study / etude at Grades 1 to 8. The Teacher's Choice selection must be of equal difficulty and musical quality to the required works in that grade. The Teacher's Choice selection should not exceed the normal time allotted for a study / etude, according to the level. (For example, at the earliest levels, the Teacher's Choice selection should be shorter than one minute.) Judgement shown in choosing an appropriate Teacher's Choice selection will be considered in the marking.

Candidates should clearly indicate "Teacher's Choice" on the Examination Program Form.

Own Choice

For Grades 9 to ARCT, the substitute repertoire selection must be of equal difficulty, length, and musical quality to works in the appropriate *Syllabus* list for that grade, and it must be from the same historical style period. The mark for the performance of this selection will include an assessment of the appropriateness of the choice. For this reason, RCM Examinations will not answer questions or give advice regarding Own Choice substitutions.

Candidates should clearly indicate "Own Choice" on the Examination Program Form.

Substitutions

Total Substitutions Permitted	*Requires* Prior Approval		*Does Not Require* Prior Approval		
	Repertoire Substitution		Repertoire Substitution		Study / Etude Substitution
Grades 1–2: *one* Repertoire selection *or* *one* Study / Etude	One repertoire selection from piano literature comparable in style and difficulty to the corresponding List A or B	*or*	One selection from the corresponding List of the next highest grade (Except Grade 2 List C)	*or*	One study / etude from next highest grade *or* One Teacher's Choice selection
Grades 3–8: *one* Repertoire selection *or* *one* Study / Etude	**Grades 3–7:** One repertoire selection from piano literature comparable in style and difficulty to the corresponding List A, B, or C **Grade 8:** One repertoire selection from piano literature comparable in style and difficulty to the corresponding List A, B, C, or D	*or*	One selection from the corresponding List of the next highest grade	*or*	One study / etude from next highest grade *or* One Teacher's Choice selection *or* One selection from the *Popular Selection List*
Grade 9: *one* Repertoire selection *or* *one* Study / Etude	One repertoire selection from piano literature comparable in style and difficulty to the corresponding List A, B, or C	*or*	One selection from the corresponding List of Grade 10 *or* One Own Choice selection may replace a piece from List D	*or*	One study / etude from Grade 10 *or* One selection from the *Popular Selection List*
Grade 10: *one* Repertoire selection *and/or* *one* Study / Etude	One repertoire selection from piano literature comparable in style and difficulty to the corresponding List A, B, or C (including *two* movements of a Sonata from List B of the ARCT in Piano Performance)	*or*	One selection from the corresponding List of the ARCT in Piano Performance (including a complete Sonata from List B of the ARCT in Piano Performance) *or* One Own Choice selection may replace a piece from List D or E	*and/ or*	One selection from the Concert Etudes List of the ARCT in Piano Performance
ARCT in Piano Performance: *one* Repertoire selection	One repertoire selection from piano literature comparable in style and difficulty to the corresponding List A, B, or C	*or*	One Own Choice selection may replace a piece from List D or E		

Abbreviations

Names of Publishers

The following abbreviations identify publishers listed throughout the *Syllabus*. When no publisher or edition is indicated for a specific piece, the work is available in several standard editions. For more information, please see "Examination Repertoire" on p. 126.

ABR	Associated Board of the Royal Schools of Music
ALF	Alfred Publishing Co., Inc.
ALK	Alberta Keys Music Publishing (Calgary)
ANE	Anerca
ARM	A-Ram Moscow
AVO	Avondale
B&H	Boosey & Hawkes (London, New York)
BAR	Bärenreiter
BEL	Belwin-Mills (Alfred Publishing Co., Inc.)
BER	Berandol Music
BOS	Bosworth
CAN	Cantus
CFP	Clifford Ford Publications
CHC	Chanteclair Music
CHS	J. & W. Chester Music
CMC	available from the Canadian Music Centre
COM	Éditions Combe
CRA	Cramer Music
DIA	Diapason
DOB	Doblinger
DOM	Doberman
DOV	Dover Publications
DUR	Durand et Cie (Paris)
ECS	ECS Publishing
EDW	Edward Marks
ELK	Elkin and Co.
EMB	Editio Musica Budapest
ENO	Enoch
ESC	Max Eshig
FAI	Fairbank Music
FHM	The Frederick Harris Music Co., Limited
FIS	Carl Fischer (New York)
FJH	FJH Music Company
FOE	Foetisch (Lausanne)
FOR	Forsythe
GEN	General Music Publishing
GVT	Gordon V. Thompson (Alfred Publishing Co., Inc.)
HAL	Hal Leonard Corporation
HEN	Henle
HEU	Heugel et Cie (Paris)
HIL	Hildegard
HMP	Heritage Music Press
HOM	Homeland Press
HSN	Hansen
INT	International Music
JAY	Jaymar
JCC	John Church Company
KAL	Kalmus
KAW	Kawai
KJO	Neil A. Kjos Music Company
KON	Könemenn Music (Budapest)
LAG	Lagos
LED	Alphonse Leduc
LEE	Leeds Music (Canada)

LEG	Lengnick
LEM	Lemoine
MAN	Manduca
MAS	Masters Music Publications
MAY	Mayfair
MCA	MCA Canada
MMB	MMB Music
MYC	Music for Young Children
MYK	Myklass Press
NSM	New School for Music Study Press
NOV	Novello
OCE	Oceanna Music
OTT	B. Schotts Söhne (Mainz)
OUP	Oxford University Press
PER	Peer International
PET	Edition Peters (Frankfurt)
PLA	Plangere Editions
PRE	Theodore Presser
PWM	Polskie Wydawnictwo Muzyczne Edition (Krakow)
RIC	G. Ricordi (Milan)
S&B	Stainer &Bell
SAL	Éditions Salabert
SCH	G. Schirmer (New York)
SHA	Shawnee
SIK	Sikorski
SIM	Simrock
SON	Sonic Art
STU	Studea Musica
SUM	Summy-Birchard (Alfred Publishing Co., Inc.)
SWA	Swan House
TIM	Time Art
TRG	Trigram Music
UNI	Universal Edition
WAR	Warner Bros. Publications
WAT	Waterloo Music Co.
WIE	Wiener Urtext
WIL	Willis Music
WIM	Wimbleton Music
YOR	Yorktown Music Press

Other Abbreviations and Symbols

8ve	octave
arr.	arrangement/arranged by
attr.	attributed to
bk	book
ed.	edition/edited by
HS	hands separately
HT	hands together
no.	number
[OP]	out of print
op.	opus
p.	page
rev.	revised
trans.	translated by
vol.	volume

● represents one selection for examination purposes

▲ parts or sections of works to be performed at examinations

▶ selection is found in *Celebration Series Perspectives*®

▲ part or section of a larger work is found in *Celebration Series Perspectives*®

Thematic Catalogs

Opus Numbers and Catalog Numbers

"Opus" (op.) is a term used with a number to designate the position of a given work in the chronological sequence of works by the composer. However, these numbers are often an unreliable guide, and may have been assigned by a publisher rather than the composer. Sometimes a single work will have conflicting opus numbers. Certain genres, such as operas and other vocal works, were not always assigned opus numbers. For these reasons, individual works by a number of composers are identified by numbers assigned in scholarly thematic catalogs. A number of the more important thematic catalogs are listed below.

Carl Philipp Emanuel Bach

Works by C.P.E. Bach are often identified by "Wq" and/or "H" (Helm) numbers (for example, *Morceaux divers pour clavecin*, Wq 117/39, H 98). Alfred Wotquenne (1867–1939) was a Belgian music bibliographer and author of *Thematisches Verzeichnis der Werke von Carl Philipp Emanuel Bach* (Leipzig, 1905, revised 1964). Eugene Helm is an American musicologist and author of A *Thematic Catalogue of the Works of* C.P.E. Bach (New Haven: Yale University Press, 1989).

Johann Sebastian Bach

Works by J.S. Bach are identified by "BWV" numbers (for example, Allemande in G Minor, BWV 836). "BWV" is the abbreviation for B*ach-Werke-Verzeichnis*, the short title of the *Thematisch-systematisches Verzeichnis der musikalischen Werke von Johann Sebastian Bach* (Leipzig, 1950), a thematic catalog of Bach's complete works originally compiled by the German music librarian Wolfgang Schmieder.

Ludwig van Beethoven

Works published during Beethoven's lifetime were given opus numbers. In the thematic catalog of Beethoven's works, *Das Werk Beethovens* (Munich and Duisburg, 1955, completed by H. Halm), compiled by German musicologist Georg Ludwig Kinsky (1882–1951), works which were published posthumously were designated "WoO" (see below).

George Frideric Handel

Works by George Frideric Handel are identified by "HWV" numbers (for example, Gavotte in G Major, HWV 491). "HWV" is an abbreviation for H*andel Werke Verzeichnis*. The full title for this thematic catalog, compiled by Margaret and Walter Eisen, is *Händel-Handbuch, gleichzeitig Suppl. zu Hallische Händel-Ausgabe* (Kassel: Bärenreiter, 1978–1986).

Franz Joseph Haydn

Works by Haydn are identified by Hoboken numbers (for example, Sonata in D Major, Hob. XVI:37). Anthony van Hoboken was a Dutch musicologist. His thematic catalog, *Joseph Haydn: Thematisch-bibliographisches Werkverzeichnis* (Mainz, B. Schott, 1957–1971) divides Haydn's works into a number of categories that are indicated by Roman numerals.

Wolfgang Amadeus Mozart

Works by Mozart are identified by "K" numbers (for example, Sonata in C Major, K 545). "K" stands for *Köchel Verzeichnis*, first published in 1862. Ludwig Ritter von Köchel (1800–1877) was an Austrian professor of botany who devoted his retirement years to collecting all the known works by Mozart. He created a chronological catalog in which these works are listed and numbered.

Henry Purcell

Works by Henry Purcell are identified by "Z" numbers (for example, Minuet in G major, Z 651). These numbers were assigned by Franklin B. Zimmerman in his thematic catalog of Purcell's works, *Henry Purcell: An Analytical Catalogue of his Music* (London: MacMillan, 1963).

Domenico Scarlatti

Works by Scarlatti are usually identified by two numbers, one beginning with "L" and one beginning with "K". The L numbers are from Opere complete per cavicembalo (Milan: Ricordi, 1906–1908), compiled by Alessandro Longo. K stands for Ralph Kirkpatrick, and American harpsichordist and scholar who provided a revised and more exact chronology and a new numbering system for the sonatas in his book Domenico Scarlatti (Princeton:Princeton University press, 1953, rev. 1968).

Franz Schubert

Works by Schubert are identified by "Deutsch" numbers (for example, Waltz in A Flat, op. 9, no. 12, D 365). These numbers were assigned by Otto Erich Deutsch (1883–1967) in his thematic catalog of Schubert's works, *Thematisches Verzeichnis seiner Werke in chronologischer Folge* (*Neue Schubert Ausgabe* Serie VIII, Bd. 4, Kassell, 1978).

Georg Philipp Telemann

Works by Telemann are identified by "TWV" numbers (for example, Fantasia in D Minor, TWV 33:2). "TWV" is an abbreviation for *Telemann Werkverzeichnis*. This thematic catalog— *Thematischer-Systematisches Verzeichnis seiner Werke: Telemann Werkverzeichnis* (Kassel: Bärenreiter, 1984)—was compiled by Martin Runke.

Anhang

Some catalog numbers include the prefix "Anh." (for example, BWV Anh. 121). "Anh." is an abbreviation for *Anhang*, a German word meaning appendix or supplement.

WoO

Some catalog numbers include the prefix "WoO" (for example, WoO 63). "WoO" is an abbreviation for *Werk ohne Opuszahl* (work without opus number). These numbers are used to designate works for which the composer did not assign an opus number.

Resources

The following texts are useful for reference, teaching, and examination preparation. No single text is necessarily complete for examination purposes, but these recommended reading and resource lists are an indispensable source of:

- teaching techniques for ages and abilities
- tips for interpretation of repertoire
- tools for better sight reading
- advice on fostering talent in young people

General Resources

Celebration Series Perspectives®

Celebration Series Perspectives®: *Compact Discs*. 15 compact discs (Preparatory–Level 10). Mississauga, ON: The Frederick Harris Music Co., Limited, 2008.

Celebration Series Perspectives®: *Handbook for Teachers*. Mississauga, ON: The Frederick Harris Music Co., Limited, 2008.

Celebration Series Perspectives®: *Piano Studies / Etudes*. 10 vols. (Levels 1–10). Mississauga, ON: The Frederick Harris Music Co., Limited, 2008.

Celebration Series Perspectives®: *Piano Repertoire*. 11 vols. (Preparatory–Level 10). Mississauga, ON: The Frederick Harris Music Co., Limited, 2008.

Celebration Series Perspectives®: *Student Workbooks*. 9 vols. (Preparatory–Level 8). Mississauga, ON: The Frederick Harris Music Co., Limited, 2008.

Popular Selection List

Popular Selection List. Mississauga, ON: The Frederick Harris Music Co., Limited, published bi-annually.

Also available online at www.rcmexaminations.org and www.nationalmusiccertificate.org.

Ear Training and Sight Reading

Bennett, Elsie, and Hilda Capp. *Complete Series of Sight Reading and Ear Tests*. 10 vols. Mississauga, ON: Frederick Harris Music, 1968–1970.

Berlin, Boris, and Andrew Markow. *Ear Training for Practical Examinations: Melody Playback/ Singback*. 4 vols. (Levels 1–ARCT). Mississauga, ON: The Frederick Harris Music Co., Limited, 1986–1988.

Berlin, Boris, and Andrew Markow. *Ear Training for Practical Examinations: Rhythm Clapback/ Singback*. 3 vols. (Levels 1–7). Mississauga, ON: The Frederick Harris Music Co., Limited, 1989–1991.

Berlin, Boris, and Andrew Markow. *Four Star Sight Reading and Ear Tests*. Ed. Scott McBride Smith. 11 vols. (Introductory–Level 10). Mississauga, ON: The Frederick Harris Music Co., Limited, 2002.

Berlin, Boris, and Warren Mould. *Rhythmic Tests for Sight Reading* (Level 8–ARCT). Miami, FL: Warner Bros. First published Toronto: Gordon V. Thompson, 1969.

Berlin, Boris, and Warren Mould. *Basics of Ear Training* (Level 8–ARCT). Miami, FL: Warner Bros. First published Toronto: Gordon V. Thompson, 1968.

Braaten, Brenda, and Crystal Wiksyk. *Sound Advice: Theory and Ear Training* (Levels 1–8) (online audio tracks at www.soundadvicedirect.com). Mississauga, ON: The Frederick Harris Music Co., Limited, 2005–2006.

Finn, Cheryl and Eamonn Morris. *Perfection Ear: Ear Training Practice Sets*. 11 compact discs (Introductory–Level 10). Mississauga, ON: The Frederick Harris Music., Limited, 1997.

Schlosar, Carol. *Comprehensive Ear Training, Professional Series: Exercises Based on the Examination Requirements of The Royal Conservatory of Music and National Music Certificate Program.* 10 vols. (Levels 1–ARCT) (book with CD or MIDI). Mississauga, ON: The Frederick Harris Music Co., Limited. First published Sicamous, BC: Keystroke Publishing, 1993.

Schlosar, Carol. *Comprehensive Ear Training: Student Series.* 11 compact discs (Levels 1–ARCT). Mississauga, ON: The Frederick Harris Music Co., Limited. First published Sicamous, BC: Keystroke Publishing, 1998.

Official Examination Papers

RCM *Examinations Official Examination Papers.* 15 vols. Mississauga, ON: The Frederick Harris Music Co., Limited, published annually.

Basic Rudiments [Preliminary Rudiments]
Intermediate Rudiments [Grade 1 Rudiments]
Advanced Rudiments [Grade 2 Rudiments]
Introductory Harmony
Basic Harmony [Grade 3 Harmony]
  Basic Keyboard Harmony [Grade 3 Keyboard Harmony]
History 1: An Overview [Grade 3 History]
Intermediate Harmony [Grade 4 Harmony]
Intermediate Keyboard Harmony [Grade 4 Keyboard Harmony]
History 2: Middle Ages to Classical [Grade 4 History]
Counterpoint [Grade 4 Counterpoint]
Advanced Harmony [Grade 5 Harmony and Counterpoint]
Advanced Keyboard Harmony [Grade 5 Keyboard Harmony]
History 3: 19th Century to Present [Grade 5 History]
Analysis [Grade 5 Analysis]
Piano Pedgogy Written (Elementary, Intermediate, Advanced)

General Reference Works

Burkolder, J. Peter, Donald J. Grout, and Claude V. Palisca. A *History of Western Music.* 7th ed. New York, NY: Norton, 2005.

Donnington, Robert. *The Interpretation of Early Music.* Rev. ed. London: Faber, 1989.

Kallmann, Helmut, Gilles Potvin, and Kenneth Winters, eds. *Encyclopedia of Music in Canada.* 2nd ed. Toronto, ON: University of Toronto Press, 1992; available online at www. thecanadianencyclopedia.com

Kamien, Roger. *Music: An Appreciation.* 9th ed. New York, NY: McGraw-Hill, 2008.

Latham, Alison, ed. *The Oxford Companion to Music.* Oxford: Oxford University Press, 2002.

Machlis, Joseph and Kristine Forney. *The Enjoyment of Music.* 10th ed. New York, NY: Norton, 2007.

Randel, Don Michael, ed. *The Harvard Biographical Dictionary of Music.* Cambridge, MA: Harvard University Press, 1996.

Randel, Don Michael, ed. *The Harvard Dictionary of Music.* 4th ed. Cambridge, MA: Belknap Press of Harvard University Press, 2003.

Sadie, Stanley, ed. *The New Grove Dictionary of Music and Musicians.* 2nd ed. 29 vols. London: Macmillan, 2001. Also available online.

Slonimsky, Nicolas, editor emeritus. *Baker's Biographical Dictionary of Music and Musicians.* Centennial ed. 6 vols. New York, NY: Schirmer, 2001.

Stolba, K. Marie. *The Development of Western Music: A History.* 3rd ed. New York, NY: McGraw-Hill, 1997.

Keyboard Resources

Reference Books

Bach, Carl Philipp Emanuel. *Essay on the True Art of Playing Keyboard Instruments.* Trans. William J. Mitchell. New York, NY: Norton, 1949.

Ferguson, Howard. *Keyboard Interpretation from the 14th to the 19th century: An Introduction.* New York, NY: Oxford University Press, 1975.

Gillespie, John. *Five Centuries of Keyboard Music: An Historical Survey of Music for Harpsichord and Piano.* New York, NY: Dover, 1972.

Gordon, Stewart. *A History of Keyboard Literature: Music for the Piano and Its Forerunners.* New York, NY: Schirmer, 1996.

Hinson, Maurice. *Guide to the Pianist's Repertoire.* 3rd ed. Bloomington, IN: Indiana University Press, 2001.

Hinson, Maurice. *The Pianist's Dictionary.* Bloomington, IN: Indiana University Press, 2004.

Iliffe, Francis. *Bach's 48 Preludes and Fugues Analysed for Students.* 2 vols. London: Novello, [n.d.].

Lloyd-Watts, Valery, Carole L. Bigler, and Willard A. Palmer. *Ornamentation: A Question and Answer Manual.* Van Nuys, CA: Alfred Publishing Co., Inc., 1995.

Magrath, Dorothy Jane. *The Pianist's Guide to Standard Teaching and Performance Literature.* Van Nuys, CA: Alfred Publishing Co., Inc., 1995.

Rosenblum, Sandra P. *Performance Practices in Classic Piano Music: Their Principles and Applications.* Bloomington, IN: Indiana University Press, 1988.

Tovey, Donald Francis. *A Companion to the Beethoven Pianoforte Sonatas.* New York, NY: AMS Press, 1976. First published London: Associated Board of the Royal Schools of Music, 1931.

Technique

Bastien, James. *Magic Finger Technique.* 3 vols. San Diego, CA: Neil A. Kjos Music Company. First published Park Ridge, IL: General Words and Music, 1966.

Berlin, Boris. *Essential Daily Exercises for Piano.* Miami, FL: Warner Bros. First published Toronto: Gordon V. Thompson, 1949.

Burnam, Edna Mae. *Dozen a Day.* Cincinnati, OH: Willis Music, 2003. First published 1950.

Czerny, Carl. *Selected Piano Studies Arranged in Systematic Order.* Ed. Heinrich Germer. 2 vols. Boston, MA: Boston Music, 1944.

Dohnányi, Ernö. *Essential Finger Exercises for Obtaining a Sure Piano Technique.* Budapest: Editio Musica Budapest, 1929.

Hanon, Charles-Louis. *The New Hanon / Le nouveau Hanon.* Ed. Boris Berlin. Rev. ed. Mississauga, ON: The Frederick Harris Music Co., Limited, 1995.

Hanon, Charles-Louis. *The Virtuoso Pianist / Le pianiste virtuose.* Ed. Healey Willan. Mississauga, ON: The Frederick Harris Music Co., Limited, 1970.

Hutcheson, Ernest. *The Elements of Piano Technique.* Cincinnati, OH: Willis Music, 1967.

Last, Joan. *Freedom Technique: Three Books of Exercises and Studies for Piano.* Oxford: Oxford University Press, 1971.

Loth, John Ferris. *Beginners Scales and Chords for Piano.* Waterloo, ON. Waterloo Music, 1946.

The Royal Conservatory of Music Piano Technique Book, 2008 Edition. Mississauga, ON: The Frederick Harris Music Co., Limited, 2008.

Scales, Chords, and Arpeggios for Piano: "The Brown Scale Book." Mississauga, ON: The Frederick Harris Music Co., Limited, 2002. First published 1948.

Schmitt, Aloys. *Five Finger Exercises / Exercices pour les cinq doigts,* op. 16. Ed. Healey Willan. Mississauga, ON: The Frederick Harris Music Co., Limited, 1946.

Technical Requirements for Piano. 9 vols. (Preparatory–Level 8). Mississauga, ON: The Frederick Harris Music Co., Limited, 2008.

Performance

Banowetz, Joseph. *The Pianist's Guide to Pedaling*. Bloomington, IN: Indiana University Press, 1985.

Bernstein, Seymour. *Twenty Lessons in Keyboard Choreography: The Basics of Physical Movements at the Piano*. New York, NY: Seymour Bernstein Music, 1991.

Bowen, York. *Pedalling the Modern Pianoforte*. London: Oxford University Press, 1936.

Faricy, Katherine. *Artistic Pedal Technique: Lessons for Intermediate and Advanced Pianists*. Mississauga, ON: The Frederick Harris Music Co., Limited, 2004.

Fink, Seymour. *Mastering Piano Technique: A Guide for Students, Teachers and Performers*. Portland, OR: Amadeus, 1992.

Lampl, Hans. *Turning Notes into Music: An Introduction to Musical Interpretation*. Lanham, MD: Scarecrow Press, 1996.

Leimer, Karl, and Walter Gieseking. *Piano Technique*. New York, NY: Dover, 1972.

Rosenblum, Sandra P. *Performance Practices in Classic Piano Music*. Bloomington, IL: Indiana University Press, 1988.

Sandor, Gyorgy. *On Piano Playing: Motion, Sound and Expression*. New York, NY: Schirmer; London: Collier Macmillan, 1981.

Schnabel, Karl Ulrich. *Modern Technique of the Pedal*. Milan: Edizioni Curci, 1954.

Siki, Béla. *Piano Repertoire: A Guide to Interpretation and Performance*. New York, NY: Schirmer, 1990.

Taylor, Kendall. *Principles of Piano Technique and Interpretation*. Kent, England: Novello, 1981.

Whiteside, Abby. *Indispensables of Piano Playing*. 2nd ed. New York, NY: Coleman-Ross, 1961.

Pedagogy

Agay, Denes, and Hazel Ghazarian Skaggs, eds. *Teaching Piano: A Comprehensive Guide and Reference Book for the Instructor*. New York, NY: Yorktown Music, 1981.

Albergo, Cathy, and Reid Alexander. *Intermediate Piano Repertoire: A Guide for Teaching*. 4th ed. Mississauga, ON: The Frederick Harris Music Co., Limited, 2000.

Albergo, Cathy, Reid Alexander, and Marvin Blickenstaff. *Celebration Series Perspectives®: Handbook for Teachers*. Mississauga, ON: The Frederick Harris Music Co., Limited, 2008.

Baker-Jordan, Martha. *Practical Piano Pedagogy: The Definitive Text for Piano Teachers and Pedagogy Students*. Miami, FL: Warner Bros., 2003.

Bastien, James W., and E. Gregory Nagode. *How to Teach Piano Successfully*. 3rd ed. San Diego, CA: Neil A. Kjos Music Company, 1988.

Bernstein, Seymour. *With Your Own Two Hands: Self-Discovery through Music*. London: Collier Macmillan; New York, NY: Schirmer, 1981.

Bloom, Benjamin S., ed. *Developing Talent in Young People*. New York, NY: Ballantine, 1985.

Bruser, Madeline. *The Art of Practicing: A Guide to Making Music from the Heart*. New York, NY: Bell Tower, 1997.

Byman, Isabelle Yalkovsky. *The Piano Teacher's Art: Guidelines for Successful Teaching*. New York, NY: Kenyon Publications; Schirmer, 1979.

Camp, Max W. *Teaching Piano: The Synthesis of Mind, Ear and Body*. Van Nuys, CA: Alfred Publishing Co., Inc., 1992.

Camp, Max W. *Developing Piano Performance: A Teaching Philosophy*. Chapel Hill, NC: Hinshaw Music Inc., 1981.

Chronister, Richard. *A Piano Teacher's Legacy: Selected Writings by Richard Chronister*. Ed. Edward Darling. Kingston, NJ: The Frances Clark Center for Keyboard Pedagogy, 2005.

Clark, Frances. *Questions and Answers: Practical Solutions and Suggestions Given to Questions Commonly Asked by Piano Teachers*. Northfield, IL: Instrumentalist Publishing, 1992.

Frisken, James, and Irwin Freundlich. *Music for the Piano: A Handbook of Teaching and Concert Material from 1580 to 1952*. New York, NY: Dover, 1973. First published 1954.

Golay, Keith. *Learning Patterns and Temperament Styles*. Newport Beach, CA: Manas-Systems, 1982.

Jacobsen, Jeanine Mae. *Professional Piano Teaching: A Comprehensive Piano Pedagogy Textbook for Teaching Elementary-Level Sudents*. Ed. E.L. Lancaster. Van Nuys, CA: Alfred Publishing Co., Inc., 2006.

Kropff, Kris, ed. *A Symposium for Pianists and Teachers: Strategies to Develop the Mind and Body for Optimal Performance*. Dayton, OH: Heritage Music Press, 2002.

Last, Joan. *The Young Pianist: A New Approach for Teachers and Students*. 2nd ed. London: Oxford University Press, 1972.

Lyke, James, Yvonne Enoch, and Geoffrey Haydon. *Creative Piano Teaching*. 3rd ed. Champaign, IL: Stipes, 1996.

Moss, Earle. *More than Teaching: A Manual of Piano Pedagogy*. Miami, FL: Warner Bros. First published Toronto: Gordon V. Thompson Music, 1989.

Ortmann, Otto. *The Physiological Mechanics of Piano Technique*. New York, NY: Da Capo, 1981. Reprint of 1929 edition.

Rubinstein, Beryl. *Outline of Piano Pedagogy*. New York, NY: Carl Fischer, 1929.

Rubinstein, Beryl. *The Pianist's Approach to Sight Reading and Memorizing*. New York, NY: Carl Fischer, 1950.

Seroff, Victor. *Common Sense in Piano Study*. New York, NY: Crescendo, 1977.

Shockley, Rebecca Payne. *Mapping Music for Faster Learning and Secure Memory: A Guide for Piano Teachers and Students*. Madison, WI: A-R Editions, 1997.

Uszler, Marienne. *Play It Again, Sam: What, Why and When to Repeat*. Fort Lauderdale, FL: FJH Music, 2003.

Uszler, Marienne. *That's a Good Question: How to Teach by Asking Questions*. Fort Lauderdale, FL: FJH Music, 2003.

Uszler, Marienne. *Time Flies: How to Make the Best Use of Teaching Time*. Fort Lauderdale, FL: FJH Music, 2004.

Uszler, Marienne, Stewart Gordon, and Scott McBride Smith. *The Well-Tempered Keyboard Teacher*. 2nd ed. New York, NY: Schirmer, 2000.

Waterman, Fanny. *On Piano Teaching and Performing*. London: Faber, 1983.

Methods

Albergo, Cathy, J. Mitzi Kolar, and Mark Mrozinski. *Celebrate Piano!®: A Comprehensive Piano Method*. Mississauga, ON: The Frederick Harris Music Co., Limited, 2003–2004.

Alexander, Dennis, Gayle Kowalchyk, E.L. Lancaster, Victoria McArthur, and Martha Mier. *Alfred's Premier Piano Course*. Van Nuys, CA: Alfred Publishing Co., Inc., 2005.

Balodis, Frances. *Music for Young Children®*. Kanata, ON: Music for Young Children, 2002–2005.

Bastien, James. *Bastien Piano Basics*. San Diego, CA: Neil A. Kjos Music Company, 1985.

Bates, Leon and Janet Vogt. *Piano Discoveries: Discovering the World of Music at the Keyboard*. Dayton, OH: Heritage Music Press, 2001.

Berlin, Boris. *The ABC of Piano Playing*. Rev. ed. Mississauga, ON: The Frederick Harris Music Co., Limited, 1985.

Bianchi, Louise, Marvin Blickenstaff, and Lynn Freeman Olson. *Music Pathways*. New York, NY: Carl Fischer, 1974, 1983.

Clark, Frances, Louise Goss, and Sam Holland. *The Music Tree: A Plan for Musical Growth at the Piano*. Miami, FL: Summy-Birchard Music, 2000. First published 1973.

Faber, Nancy and Randall Faber. *Piano Adventures®: A Basic Piano Method*. Fort Lauderdale, FL: The FJH Music Company Inc., 1993.

Kaplan, Leigh. *Teaching Little Fingers to Play More*. Florence, KY: Willis Music, 1997.

Kreader, Barbara, Fred Kern, and Phillip Keveren. *Hal Leonard Student Piano Library*. Milwaukee, WI: Hal Leonard Corporation, 1996.

Lethco, Amanda Vick, Morton Manus, and Willard A. Palmer. *Alfred's Basic Piano Library*. Van Nuys, CA: Alfred Publishing Co., Inc., 1999–2000.

Suzuki, Shinichi. *Suzuki Piano School*. Rev. ed. Miami, FL: Summy-Birchard Music, 2000.

Frequently Asked Questions

Practical Examinations

What is a practical examination?

A practical examination is the test of repertoire, studies / etudes, technique, ear training, and sight reading for instruments, voice, or speech arts and drama.

Why are out-of-print selections included in the *Syllabus*?

Many teachers have out-of-print music in their personal libraries. A number of out-of-print selections have been retained in the *Syllabus* both as a courtesy to these teachers, and because the pieces are excellent repertoire choices.

How can I obtain permission to photocopy an out-of-print selection that I find in a library or receive from a teacher?

Contact the publisher to request permission to make an authorized photocopy. Contact information for most publishers can be found online or obtained from a music retailer. Some music retailers can obtain authorized photocopies through a special online service.

Can I photocopy a page of music to facilitate a page turn?

You may photocopy a single page once you have obtained permission from the publisher. With this notice, The Frederick Harris Music Co., Limited grants permission to festival, recital, and examination participants to photocopy single pages from their publications to facilitate a page turn.

How do I choose the best edition for a piece?

The best editions have minimal editorial markings. These editions, often called Urtext, are available from most music retailers. If you are unsure about the best edition, ask your music retailer for suggestions.

Should candidates follow repeat signs? *Da capo* markings?

Candidates should observe *da capo* markings at an examination performance. Repeat signs should usually be ignored. However, repeat signs in the *Celebration Series Perspectives*® repertoire books should be observed if indicated in a footnote below the music.

Why are teachers and parents not allowed in the room during practical examinations?

Practical examinations provide a unique opportunity for candidates to perform in a highly focused, one-on-one environment, without distraction.

What is the *Popular Selection List*?

The *Popular Selection List* includes selections by popular artists and from current films. The list is revised every two years to ensure that selections remain current and readily available. The *Popular Selection List* is also available online at www.rcmexaminations.org and www.nationalmusiccertificate.org.

Where can I find recordings of examination repertoire?

Celebration Series Perspectives® includes compact discs containing the repertoire and studies / etudes for each level from Preparatory to Grade 10, performed by artists from The Royal Conservatory of Music. These CDs are available at music retailers.

What do I do if I have an emergency situation on the day of my examination and I need to cancel?

Contact your Examination Center Representative listed on your Examination Schedule by phone *as soon as possible.*

Theory Co-requisites

What is a theory co-requisite?

A theory co-requisite is an examination that must be completed before or within five years of the practical examination if the candidate wishes to receive a certificate for the practical examination. Candidates are encouraged to begin theory studies as early as possible.

Do I have to take theory examinations if I don't need a piano examination certificate?

You may to take a piano examination without fulfilling theory requirements. If you later decide that you would like to receive a certificate, you have five years from the date of the piano examination to fulfill the theory requirements.

Where can I find sample theory examination papers?

Official Examination Papers are published annually by The Frederick Harris Music Co., Limited to aid with examination preparation. Each book includes three examinations from the previous December, May, and August examination sessions plus an additional examination created for extra practice. Editions for three academic years are available at any given time and may be purchased from your local music retailer.

Practical Examination Day Checklist for Candidates

Before you Leave Home

____ Plan to arrive 15 minutes early.

____ Complete your Examination Program Form.

____ Bring original copies of all the music being performed in the examination.

____ Mark the pieces being performed with a paper clip or a "sticky note."

____ Wear proper shoes (pedaling, for example, can be difficult with some types of shoes).

Points to Remember

• Bags and coats must be left in the waiting room.

• There are no warm-up rooms for piano candidates.

• Parents, other family members, friends, and teachers must wait in the designated waiting area.

• Standing and listening outside the examination room door is prohibited.

• Recording devices are strictly prohibited in the examination room.

• Photocopied music is prohibited (unless authorized by the publisher).

• The performance of repertoire may be interrupted by the examiner. An interrupted performance does *not* indicate a poor performance.

What to Expect from a Piano Examination

• A friendly yet professional atmosphere

• The undivided attention of an examiner

• An objective assessment of your performance of repertoire, studies / etudes, technique, ear training, and sight reading

• The examiner's written evaluation online within six weeks of the examination

After the Examination

Access your practical examination marks and examiner comments through the "Examination Results" link on the RCM Examinations website (www.rcmexaminations.org) or the NMCP website (www.nationalmusiccertificate.org) approximately 4–6 weeks after the examination.